Eric Voegelin and the Politics of
Spiritual Revolt

# Eric Voegelin and the Politics of Spiritual Revolt

## The Roots of Modern Ideology

Michael Franz

Louisiana State University Press
Baton Rouge and London

Copyright © 1992 by Louisiana State University Press
All rights reserved
Manufactured in the United States of America
First printing

01  00  99  98  97  96  95  94  93  92     5  4  3  2  1

Designer: Amanda McDonald Key
Typeface: Palatino
Typesetter: G&S Typesetters, Inc.
Printer and binder: Thomson–Shore, Inc.

Library of Congress Cataloging-in-Publication Data
Franz, Michael, 1957–
    Eric Voegelin and the politics of spiritual revolt : the roots of
modern ideology / Michael Franz.
        p.   cm.
    Includes bibliographical references and index.
    ISBN 0-8071-1740-4 (alk. paper)
    1. Voegelin, Eric, 1901–   .  2. Ideology—History—20th century.
3. Consciousness—History—20th century.  I. Title.
B3354.V884F73   1992
140—dc20                                                        91-48081
                                                                    CIP

The paper in this book meets the guidelines for permanence and durability of the
Committee on Production Guidelines for Book Longevity of the Council on
Library Resources. ∞

*For Margaret and George Franz*

# Contents

# Preface

This book is devoted to an examination of Eric Voegelin's analysis of the spiritual and historical roots of modern ideological politics. Like many other European scholars who came of age in the 1930s, Voegelin's encounters with ideological mass movements were prominent events in his personal and intellectual development. He was one of the most gifted and accomplished of a remarkable generation of philosophers, historians, and theologians who emigrated to the United States and gravitated toward political questions in response to the rising tide of ideological fanaticism. Yet the war of the various "isms" was more than a point of physical and theoretical departure for Voegelin. His early experiences of spiritual disorder in the form of ideological activism motivated a lifelong effort to understand the forms of politically relevant disorientation that are described in this book. Voegelin's brilliant work as a philosopher of order in history is inextricably linked to a theory of spiritual disorder that is, in its own right, among the most important achievements in political science in the twentieth century.

Although Voegelin's critique of ideological movements as "gnostic" attempts at world transformation was widely noted in the 1950s and 1960s, the full importance of his analysis of spiritual disorder has yet to be recognized—partly because his writings are very demanding, even for professional philosophers and political theorists, and partly because his analysis was never given a full and final expression in any single work. Voegelin held that "the search for truth concerning the order of being cannot be conducted without diagnosing the modes of existence in untruth," and, accordingly, his analyses of spiritual disorder are woven into the sixteen books and more than one hundred articles in which his analysis of personal and political order was set forth.[1] Further difficulties arise because these writings reflect several important shifts in Voegelin's terminology and methodology between the 1930s and 1980s. One who is not well versed in the entire corpus simply cannot know whether a particular passage or article embodies a discarded approach or a perennial theme. Because a conscientious scholar who wishes to understand Voegelin's work on spiritual disorder is thus confronted with what might amount to a year's worth of reading, it is not surprising that this theory is not more generally known. Although a secondary treatment can hardly capture the rich and intricate character of a theory that was molded and remolded by a great thinker for sixty years, there is clearly a need for a synthetic, critical introduction to Voegelin's analysis of disorder.

In the hope of making Voegelin's work on ideology and gnosticism more accessible and useful to those new to his writings, I have provided unusually extensive notes that direct the reader to Voegelin's publications. In many cases I have cited four or five works in which he discussed a single topic or figure. Readers should thus be able to examine the nuances and development of Voegelin's analyses and also to determine whether I have succeeded in sifting the perennial from the discarded. One cost imposed by my emphasis on references to primary sources is that I could not provide an optimal guide to the secondary literature on Voegelin without overburdening the text. Although a number of outstanding books and articles on Voegelin are available, virtually every discussion of ideology and gnosticism was intended to introduce Voegelin's distinctive approach to the uninitiated. As such, the secondary articles cover much the same ground as this book but in a less concerted and sustained manner. Nevertheless, because this is the first full-length monograph on Voegelin's response to ideology, I have tried to provide direction to some of the best secondary works, especially those that are critical in nature. I hope that the bibliography (which is the most inclusive yet to appear in print) will prove helpful for those in search of other commentaries.

This book is truly the product of many hands and minds, and it is a great pleasure to acknowledge the contributions of those who have helped me. I wish first to thank my parents, Margaret and

1. Eric Voegelin, Preface to *Israel and Revelation* (Baton Rouge, 1956), xiv, Vol. I of Voegelin, *Order and History*.

George Franz, who have been unfailingly supportive of my efforts. The Arthur J. Schmitt Foundation funded a year of uninterrupted research that formed the basis for this study, and Dean David F. Roswell of Loyola College in Maryland helped to bring it to completion by underwriting two trips to the Hoover Institution Archives at Stanford University. William Kitchin of Loyola College provided important assistance as department chair at a crucial stage of the writing, and I thank my colleagues in the Department of Political Science for providing a stimulating and convivial environment. My friend Traci M. Dayhoff indexed the book with characteristic precision. Margaret Fisher Dalrymple and her staff at Louisiana State University Press were helpful at every turn, and it is an honor to have this study brought out by Voegelin's primary publisher.

My thinking on the questions explored herein was deeply influenced by James L. Wiser, to whom I am grateful for insightful commentary on the entire manuscript. John A. Gueguen offered innumerable suggestions, and Ellis Sandoz and Gerhart Niemeyer provided a wealth of helpful criticism as reviewers for the Press. Charles Bobertz, Thomas S. Engeman, Richard S. Hartigan, Hans Mair, Peter C. Myers, Russell Nieli, and James M. Rhodes generously commented on early versions of the manuscript. The traditional acceptance of responsibility for errors is especially important in the case of this book, for each of the aforementioned readers has objected to at least one aspect of my interpretation. Finally, special thanks are owed to my wife, Christina Franz, the love and joy of my life, for unrelenting insistence on greater clarity through countless readings.

Eric Voegelin and the Politics of
Spiritual Revolt

# 1

## The Spiritual Sources of Ideological Rebellion

The rise of political mass movements based upon comprehensive intellectual systems has been widely recognized as one of the most prominent features of nineteenth- and twentieth-century political history. The impact of such movements, along with their apparent novelty, has in fact led certain scholars to characterize the years since the mid-nineteenth century as the "Age of Ideology."[1] Although the impact of ideological movements has indeed been great, and though the ideologies of the nineteenth and twentieth centuries are certainly novel in important respects, the suspicion has persisted among many analysts that these movements cannot be understood simply as products of the political conditions or climate of opinion of the late modern period. Because ideologies such as Hegelianism, Marxism, fascism, progressivism, and positivism continue to attract adherents long after the passing of the political conditions present during the period of their development (and, some would argue, long after these ideologies have been decisively refuted), it is difficult to see how the generation and expansion of ideology can be explained in terms of events surrounding the advent of capitalism, for example, or the French Revolution or the breakup of feudal society. As a broader background seems to be needed to account for the diversity and persistence of ideological phenomena, much attention has been devoted to the "modern project" in general or to the various "waves" of modernity.

Yet, in works such as Norman Cohn's *The Pursuit of the Millen-*

1. *E.g.*, Henry David Aiken, *The Age of Ideology: The Nineteenth Century Philosophers* (Boston, 1957); Karl Dietrich Bracher, *The Age of Ideologies: A History of Political Thought in the Twentieth Century* (New York, 1985); Isaac Kraminick and Frederick M. Watkins, eds., *The Age of Ideology: Political Thought 1750 to the Present* (Englewood Cliffs, N.J., 1979). See also Voegelin, *Anamnesis* (Notre Dame, 1978), 146.

*nium* one can find reason to question whether the patterns of thought and activity typical of ideological movements can be contained even within the modern period as a whole. Cohn's analysis of the similarities between medieval millenarianism and modern ideological movements suggests that the movements of our age are not products of that age but, rather, manifestations of a pattern of psychic disorientation that may arise in widely varying cultural and political contexts. This line of thinking has been supported to some extent by sociological, anthropological, and historical research but finds its fullest and most competent theoretical expression in the work of Eric Voegelin.[2] In Voegelin's last writings the origins of ideological types of activism are traced not to modernity but to antiquity and are explained as reactions not to particular circumstances but to the human condition itself.

Voegelin's widely noticed but infrequently analyzed attempt to uncover the historical and intellectual roots of ideological activism was initiated by his early realization that "the academic institutions of the Western world, the various schools of philosophy, the rich manifold of methodologies, did not offer the intellectual instruments that would make the political movements . . . of Communism, Fascism, National Socialism, and racism, of constitutionalism, liberalism and authoritarianism . . . intelligible."[3] A distinct and continuous theme running throughout Voegelin's voluminous writings is the argument that the proliferation of ideological movements is symptomatic of a deeper civilizational crisis. Voegelin's important work as a philosopher of history and consciousness was paralleled by a lifelong effort in response to this crisis, an effort that was near the center of his theoretical activity in general. His response to the civilizational crisis of modernity can be described as a search for (1) the historical and experiential wellsprings of the crisis, (2) the analytical tools required to render it intelligible, and (3) sources for an appropriate therapy. Although Voegelin's writings were by no means confined to the modern period, and though he was ultimately to find neither the cause nor the cure for the crisis within modernity, he frequently noted that his theoretical project as a whole could be understood as a response to "the spiritual disorder of our time, the civilizational crisis of which everyone

2. See esp. Sylvia L. Thrupp, ed., *Millennial Dreams in Action: Essays in Comparative Study* (The Hague, 1962), *passim*.

3. Voegelin, *Anamnesis*, 3.

so readily speaks."[4] Given Voegelin's characterization of philosophy itself as "an act of resistance illuminated by conceptual understanding," it is clear that an evaluation of his analysis of ideological phenomena must be central to any assessment of his stature as a political philosopher.[5]

The nature of ideological consciousness as Voegelin understood it is somewhat easier to grasp when distinguished from ideological systems and from disordered consciousness in general. For the purposes of this discussion, ideological systems will be treated as constructs based on a seemingly comprehensive account of reality and the human's place within it and intended to provide a program for the transformation of society. For Voegelin they are relatively recent in origin. Ideological consciousness, in contrast, was understood by Voegelin as a modern variant of a broader, more inclusive type of spiritually disordered or "closed" consciousness that can be found throughout history. Indeed, Voegelin found examples of this generic form of consciousness, referred to here by the terms *pneumapathological consciousness*[6] or *disorientation*, in several of the earliest writings known to historians.[7] Voegelin's argument does not imply that premodern writings in which pneumapathological consciousness is expressed are "ideologies" or ideological systems, because he maintained that such systems were simply unknown prior to the eighteenth century.[8] Hence, it has been necessary to

4. Voegelin, *Science, Politics and Gnosticism* (Chicago, 1968), 22.

5. Voegelin, *Plato and Aristotle* (Baton Rouge, 1957), 68, Vol. III of Voegelin, *Order and History*.

6. Voegelin used the term *pneumapathological consciousness* in several works as a designation for disorders of the spirit. See, for example, *From Enlightenment to Revolution*, ed. John H. Hallowell (Durham, N.C., 1975), 117, 259; and "On Hegel: A Study in Sorcery," *Studium Generale*, XXIV (1971), 353. Voegelin attributes the term to Friedrich W.J. Schelling; see *Science, Politics and Gnosticism*, 101.

7. *E.g.*, Thorkild Jacobsen, *The Sumerian Kinglist*, Assyriological Studies, XI (Chicago, 1939), cited in Voegelin, *The Ecumenic Age* (Baton Rouge, 1974), 65–67, Vol. IV of Voegelin, *Order and History*; "Dispute of a Man, Who Contemplates Suicide, with His Soul" (Egypt, *ca.* 2000 B.C.), discussed in Voegelin, "Immortality: Experience and Symbol," *Harvard Theological Review*, LX (1967), 241–48. See also Voegelin, "Response to Professor Altizer's 'A New History and a New but Ancient God?'" in *Eric Voegelin's Thought: A Critical Appraisal*, ed. Ellis Sandoz (Durham, N.C., 1982), 190.

8. Voegelin, *Conversations with Eric Voegelin*, ed. R. Eric O'Connor (Montreal, 1980), 13–18, 147.

develop concepts (based on terms found in Voegelin's writings) that are capable of denoting pre-ideological forms of consciousness that are nonetheless included within the general category of pneumapathological consciousness. Voegelin's argument on the relationship of these forms ("metastatic faith," "prometheanism" and "parousiasm") to ideological consciousness represents the center around which the major questions of historical accuracy and explanatory power regarding his treatment of modernity revolve.

These concepts and the nature of the distinctions among them will be explored more fully below. At this juncture it is sufficient to note that our understanding of modern ideological movements would be greatly enhanced if it could be shown that the types of thought and activism characteristic of such movements are not simply the results of present circumstances or of the idiosyncrasies of influential individuals. For if these forms of thought and activism are rooted in a general pattern of consciousness that is a historical constant, as Voegelin argued, important implications would be suggested for an appropriate response to the political crisis of modernity. These implications will be discussed in the final chapter. On the other hand, the helpfulness of Voegelin's analysis must be called into question if ideological consciousness cannot persuasively be related to the other, older forms of pneumapathological disorientation. Should this turn out to be the case, Voegelin would appear (as William C. Havard, Jr., speculated he must appear to partisans of this or that ideology) as "a sort of intellectual anachronism trying to apply the outmoded internecine arguments of the Christian Middle Ages to a modern secular world in which they have no place."[9]

Voegelin's attempt to provide a broader theoretical context for the understanding of ideological phenomena was founded on a more formidable base than can be furnished by a history of ideas. Rather than simply tracing the development of specific ideas that eventually came to be expressed in ideological forms, Voegelin structured his analysis in the form of a philosophical anthropology informed by a theory of consciousness and a philosophy of history. As a result, it was possible for Voegelin to conceptualize the disordered or "pathologically closed" consciousness of the ideologue

9. William C. Havard, Jr., "Notes on Voegelin's Contributions to Political Theory," in *Eric Voegelin's Thought: A Critical Appraisal*, ed. Ellis Sandoz (Durham, N.C., 1982), 98.

by reference to well-ordered or "open" patterns of consciousness. Voegelin's analysis of the relationship between these most general patterns of (disordered or well-ordered) consciousness is, however, much more subtle than a comparison of "true" and "false" doctrines, since closed as well as open consciousness arise from fundamental experiences of the human condition that cannot, as such, be simply false:

> The conflict of Truth and Delusion, thus, is not a conflict between true and false propositions. In fact, the Delusion is quite as true as the Truth if by truth we mean an adequate and consistent articulation of an experience. Truth is the philosophy of the realissimum that we experience if we follow the way of immortalization in the soul; Delusion is the philosophy of the reality that we experience as men who live and die in a world that itself is distended in time with a beginning and an end. The characterization of this philosophy of reality as a Delusion derives its justification from the experience of a superior reality.[10]

Ideological thought, no less than philosophical or religious thought, is engendered by experiences of uncertainty and contingency, incompleteness and suffering in a world where all things pass away.[11] The Platonic symbolism of imprisonment in darkness also appears in ideological and proto-ideological symbolism. The parting of the ways of philosophy and ideology first becomes evident in characteristically different reactions to this condition.

For Voegelin, philosophical consciousness is exemplified by the Platonic *periagoge*, the turning-around of the soul in loving openness toward transcendent reality and the ground of being.[12] By contrast, ideological consciousness is typified by a turning-away from the transcendent ground in revolt against the tension of contingent existence. In the modern era this revolt has taken many forms, all of which are expressive of dissatisfaction with the degree of certainty afforded by faith, trust, and hope as sources of knowledge and existential orientation. According to Voegelin, the great ideologists sought to displace classical Greek philosophy and Judeo-Christian revelation by (mis)placing the transcendent ground within an immanent hierarchy of being, identifying the essence of human exis-

10. Voegelin, *The World of the Polis* (Baton Rouge, 1957), 216, Vol. II of Voegelin, *Order and History*.

11. *Cf.* Voegelin, "History and Gnosis," in *The Old Testament and Christian Faith*, ed. Bernard Anderson (New York, 1969), 82.

12. Voegelin, *Plato and Aristotle*, 115–17; *Anamnesis*, 183–85.

tence as, *e.g.*, productive relations, historical progress, racial composition, libidinous drives, scientific rationality, or the will to power. Within the intellectual systems constructed around these misplacements of the ground, humanity appears as an autonomous, self-created species capable of assuming control of its destiny through the self-conscious application of new forms of knowledge. Thus, on the level of individual experience, Voegelin regarded ideological consciousness as a form of existence in rebellion against human imperfection and the uncertainties of life in a world grounded in an ultimately mysterious order of being.[13] It is in this sense that Voegelin attributed the ideological impulse not to modern conditions but to the human condition as such. Viewed historically on the political level, ideological systems of thought represent a series of (counter) movements against the philosophical and revelatory traditions of the West, movements that seek to transform the nature of humanity and society beyond their divinely set parameters.

Yet pneumapathological disorientation cannot be limited to the modern form of ideological consciousness, because paths of escape from the tension of contingent existence are not limited to those taken by modern ideologists. Evidence of alienation, hubris, *libido dominandi*, closure, and other symptoms of ideological consciousness can be found long before the "Age of Ideology." The emergence of pneumapathological consciousness can be fixed in time because awareness of the tensions arising from existence between the transcendent and mundane poles of reality was itself an epoch-marking discovery in history.[14] This area within reality, symbolized by Plato as the *metaxy* or "In-Between," was unknown prior to what Voegelin called the "de-divinization" of the world.[15] Whereas mythological or "cosmological" accounts of reality could speak of human activity as occurring within a world "full of gods," the authors of the Old Testament and the philosophers of ancient Greece located the divine creative forces of the universe beyond the mun-

13. Voegelin's one (relatively early) definition of ideology runs as follows: "Ideology is existence in rebellion against God and man. It is the violation of the First and Tenth Commandments, if we want to use the language of Israelite order; it is the *nosos*, the disease of the spirit, if we want to use the language of Aeschylus and Plato." Voegelin, *Israel and Revelation*, xiv.

14. Voegelin, *The World of the Polis*, 1–16; *The Ecumenic Age*, 1–13.

15. Plato, *Symposium*, 202a–203, in *The Collected Dialogues of Plato*, ed. Edith Hamilton and Huntington Cairns (Princeton, 1961); Voegelin, *The Ecumenic Age*, 183–87; *Conversations with Eric Voegelin*, 44–45, 81.

dane realm of human activity in the world.[16] The tensions that lie behind pneumapathological disorientation first arise from the awareness that one exists in a de-divinized world that is incomplete and imperfect in essence; this condition becomes especially problematic when its recognition is accompanied by the experience or promise of participation in a transcendent realm of being.[17] As an example of the disorientation that may stem from this complex of experiences Voegelin frequently turned to Gnosticism, in which the world was regarded as a demonically created prison that restricts the divine spark within humanity. More generally, attempts to artificially relax the tensions associated with the de-divinization of the world tend to assume one or the other of two characteristic forms: disregard for the requirements of existence *in* the world or a turning-away from transcendent reality to live in *this* world alone.[18] This distinction is of great importance in Voegelin's work on disordered political consciousness. Both forms of "escapism" from the tensions of existence in the *metaxy* can be observed in all periods of history subsequent to the "leaps in being" identified by Voegelin in the ancient world.

As an example of the former type of disorientation, Voegelin noted a tendency toward chiliastic expectation of the "Kingdom of God" among those who gave credence to the promise of salvation but chafed impatiently under the corruption of life in worldly society. This variant of pneumapathological disorientation may be expressed in either a profound disregard for mundane necessities and an all-consuming desire for eternal perfection or a longing for an apocalyptic transformation of the worldly vale of tears. Voegelin found evidence of this general type of pneumapathological consciousness (which will be subdivided below into metastatic faith and parousiasm) in the apocalyptic strains of Old Testament prophecy and early Christianity, the Gospel of John, the Epistles of Paul, ancient Gnostic and Manichaean writings, the millennial "heresies" of the Middle Ages, and the tracts of militant Puritanism.

16. Voegelin, *Israel and Revelation*, 9–13; *Anamnesis*, 75, 159.

17. Voegelin, *The New Science of Politics: An Introduction*, (Chicago, 1952), 107–10.

18. Voegelin, *In Search of Order* (Baton Rouge, 1987), 37, Vol. V of Voegelin, *Order and History*. On this distinction, see also Gregor Sebba, "Order and Disorders of the Soul: Eric Voegelin's Philosophy of History," *Southern Review*, n.s., III (1967), 301–302; Eugene Webb, *Eric Voegelin: Philosopher of History* (Seattle, 1981), 201.

The other general path of escape from "existence-in-tension" is to eclipse the transcendent dimension of human experience by establishing man as the measure of all things. This type of pneumapathological consciousness (which will be subdivided below into prometheanism and ideological consciousness) may take the form of hatred of the gods or, among more ambitious moderns, of attempts to usher in an era of human autonomy through a redirection of humanity's energies toward a perfection of the "estate of man." Voegelin argued that the ideological form of this type of pneumapathological consciousness can be found, in varying degrees of prominence, in virtually every movement of note within modern political thought: [19]

| | |
|---|---|
| Anarchism | Liberalism |
| Behavioralism | Marxism |
| Biologism | Positivism |
| Constitutionalism | Progressivism |
| Existentialism | Psychologism |
| Fascism | Scientism |
| Hegelianism | Utilitarianism |

Common to all these movements, in one form or another, is what Voegelin identified as a hubristic revolt against the limitations of the creaturely nature of human beings.

Contrary to those who regard this revolt as a distinctly modern phenomenon, Voegelin argued that this form of consciousness and its pathological dimensions (although not its systematic, quasi-scientific trappings) were far from unknown to the ancients:

> In fact the Greek thinkers diagnosed it as a disease of the psyche from the time they had occasion to observe it in the embattled polis. Heraclitus and Aeschylus, and above all Plato, speak of the *nosos* or *nosema* of the psyche; and Thucydides speaks of the expansion of the disease into

19. Anarchism: *From Enlightenment to Revolution*, 195–239. Behavioralism: *Anamnesis*, 146. Biologism: *From Enlightenment to Revolution*, 69; *Israel and Revelation*, xii. Constitutionalism: *Anamnesis*, 3. Existentialism: "The Eclipse of Reality," in *Phenomenology and Social Research*, ed. Maurice Natanson (The Hague, 1970), *passim*. Fascism: *Anamnesis*, 3. Hegelianism: "On Hegel: A Study in Sorcery," *Studium Generale*, XXVI (1971), 335–68. Liberalism: "Liberalism and Its History," *Review of Politics*, XXXVII (1974), 502–20. Marxism: *From Enlightenment to Revolution*, 240–302. Positivism: *ibid.*, 136–94. Progressivism: *ibid.*, 110–35. Psychologism: *Israel and Revelation*, xii. Scientism: "The Origins of Scientism," *Social Research*, XXVI (1948), 462–64. Utilitarianism: *Israel and Revelation*, xii.

the disorders of the Peloponnesian War as a *kinesis*, as a feverish movement of society. . . . The Stoics, especially Chrysippos, were intrigued by the phenomenon, and Cicero, summarizing the findings of the preceding centuries, deals with the disease at length. . . . He calls it the *morbus animi*, the disease of the mind, and characterizes its nature as an *aspernatio rationis*, as a rejection of reason.[20]

Insofar as pneumapathological disorientation in general can be traced to an alienated dissatisfaction with the human condition as such, its origins appear not simply modern but universal and perennial. Moreover, since we have seen that this dissatisfaction becomes potentially radical only with the advent of doctrines that hold out the possibility of redemption in a transfigured reality beyond history, the necessary conditions for the expansion of pneumapathological disorientation arise within antiquity rather than within modernity. Among these traditions Christianity has proven to be the most powerful accelerant in the expansion process. Voegelin attributes the "popularization" of disordered consciousness in modern society not to a decline of the cultural influence of Christianity but rather to the spread of its influence during the late Middle Ages: "The more people are drawn into the Christian orbit, the greater will be the number among them who do not have the spiritual stamina for the heroic adventure of the soul that is Christianity."[21] Those who regard the excesses of the Age of Ideology as the logical consequence of a fall from Christianity will be no more pleased with Voegelin's argument than those who consider the age a triumph over the Christian past:

> Considering the history of Gnosticism, with the great bulk of its manifestations belonging to, or deriving from, the Christian orbit, I am inclined to recognize in the epiphany of Christ the great catalyst that made eschatological consciousness an historical force both in forming and deforming humanity.[22]

20. Voegelin, "Wisdom and the Magic of the Extreme: A Meditation," *Southern Review*, n.s., XVII (1981), 243.

21. Voegelin, *The New Science of Politics*, 123.

22. Voegelin, *The Ecumenic Age*, 20. Voegelin's use of the term *gnosticism*, which roughly parallels the generic usage of "pneumapathological consciousness" in these pages, will be discussed below. Voegelin's most extensive discussions of the concept (and the historical tradition) are in *Science, Politics and Gnosticism*, 3–12, 53–59, 83–103, and *The New Science of Politics*, 107–32. See also James L. Wiser, "From Cultural Analysis to Philosophical Anthropology: An Examination of Voegelin's Concept of Gnosticism," *Review of Politics*, XLII (1980), 92–104.

Although certain forms of pneumapathological consciousness pre-
cede the epiphany of Christ (such as the metastatic faith of Isaiah
and the disorders diagnosed by the ancient Greeks), Voegelin held
that "explicit persistence in the state of alienation [characteristic of
parousiasm and ideological consciousness] is possible only after
Christianity has differentiated the problem of existence—a relation
of man to the unknown God who is not intra-cosmic (as the poly-
theistic type is) but extra-cosmic."[23]

It is the epiphany of Christ, therefore, rather than the dawn of
the modern era, which signals the most important break in the
history of pneumapathological consciousness as understood by
Voegelin. If we incorporate his identification of this break in history
with the distinction he has drawn between the two characteristic
paths of escape from "existence-in-tension," it becomes possible to
construct a diagram (see chart) that will help to distinguish the
major forms of pneumapathological disorientation.

It should be emphasized that not every thinker in whom Voegelin discerned pneumapathological tendencies will fall neatly into
one or another of the cells in this diagram. Voegelin's distinction
along the vertical axis, and the diagram as a whole, should be
thought of as heuristic suggestions. The two characteristic patterns
of "imbalanced" consciousness—closure against transcendent experience and eclipse of worldly reality—are often observable in a
single writer. It could be argued, for example, that an ideologist

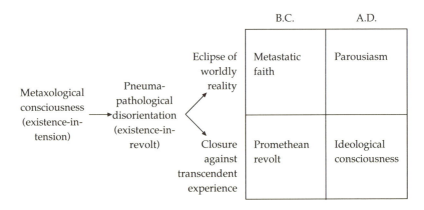

|  | B.C. | A.D. |
|---|---|---|
| Eclipse of worldly reality | Metastatic faith | Parousiasm |
| Closure against transcendent experience | Promethean revolt | Ideological consciousness |

Metaxological consciousness (existence-in-tension) ⟶ Pneuma-pathological disorientation (existence-in-revolt)

23. *Conversations with Eric Voegelin*, 80. On Isaiah, see Voegelin, *Israel and Revelation*, 476–501, and *The Ecumenic Age*, 25–27.

such as Marx has fallen into either or both patterns of imbalance. His manifest contempt for all speculation on transcendent realms of being would seem to place him in the lower-right cell, whereas a parousiastic disregard of worldly reality would seem to underlie his vision of a communistic future in which humanity will "succeed in ridding itself of all the muck of ages."[24] The horizontal axis will also not prove to be inflexible, except in a formal sense, since parousiastic writers borrowed heavily from the Jewish apocalyptic and messianic traditions, just as the symbol of a chosen people reappears in modern fascism and Marx makes Prometheus "the foremost saint and martyr in the philosopher's calendar."[25]

Because pneumapathological disorientation is a manifestation of "existence-in-revolt" against the spiritual demands of "existence-in-tension," it is perhaps not surprising that ideologists have turned, in their efforts to symbolize the revolt, to those symbols developed for the expression of that very tension. Voegelin argued that this is a virtual constant in ideological symbolism. For example, the Christian symbol of the "approaching Kingdom" is transposed and hypostatized into the Hegelian "end of history," the Marxism "realm of freedom," the National Socialist "Drittes Reich," or the Comtean "positivistic age of Mankind." Similarly, the "redemption of man" is transposed into a politically or scientifically altered human nature, and philosophical/theological searching for the order of being is transposed into a scientific knowledge of the laws of nature and history.

Of course, the identification of symbolic parallels does not lay to rest the question of whether Voegelin succeeded in establishing a relationship between modern ideological activism and the premodern forms of disordered consciousness. This question must be accorded a prominent place in any comprehensive evaluation of Voegelin's diagnostic analyses, and although a detailed examination must be reserved for Chapter 5, it may be helpful at this point to identify several of the central issues. It is likely that, as Voegelin's work becomes more widely known, criticism will revolve around

24. Karl Marx and Friedrich Engels, *The German Ideology* (Moscow, 1976), 60.

25. On the parousiasts, see Norman Cohn, *The Pursuit of the Millennium: Revolutionary Millenarians and Mystical Anarchists of the Middle Ages* (Rev. ed.; New York, 1970), 19–36. On Marxism, see Marx, Preface to doctoral thesis, "The Difference Between Democritus' and Epicurus' Philosophy of Nature," in *Karl Marx: Selected Writings*, ed. David McLellan (Oxford, 1977), 13.

the difficulties involved in his attempt to diagnose particular thinkers as spiritually diseased and the further difficulty of relating such
an analysis to ancient forms of disease. These lines of criticism
have already been suggested in the literature on Voegelin. For
example, to speak of thinkers of the stature of Hegel, Marx, and
Nietzsche as spiritually diseased, as sorcerers and magicians,[26] is a
step that even some of Voegelin's most sympathetic commentators
are unwilling to take.[27]

It may seem as though Voegelin fell into an enormous error by
applying age-old categories of analysis to distinctly modern phenomena. However, far from betraying uneasiness over the apparent antiquity of his basic thesis, Voegelin regarded this as the
surest form of corroboration. For the only significant test of philosophical propositions concerns not their originality but their truth,
and according to Voegelin "the test of truth, to put it pointedly,
will be the lack of originality in the propositions":

> The validating question will have to be: Do we have to ignore and
> eclipse a major part of the historical field, in order to maintain the truth
> of the propositions, as the fundamentalist adherents of this or that
> ideological doctrine must do; or are the propositions recognizably
> equivalent with the symbols created by our predecessors in the search
> of truth about human existence?[28]

If this, then, is the standard to which Voegelin's diagnosis of modernity should be held, it is nevertheless far from clear that a positive evaluation is assured simply because the test was of his own
making. The central issues can be framed in the terms of Voegelin's
test: Has he ignored and eclipsed the modern part of the historical
field by "de-modernizing" ideology? Are Voegelin's propositions
regarding modern ideologies in fact recognizably equivalent with
the symbols created by those he referred to as his predecessors? Is
modern ideological consciousness recognizably equivalent with
the phenomena described in their writings? Is this equivalence so
strong that "unoriginality" becomes a theoretical virtue, or has
Voegelin made a virtue of necessity?

26. Voegelin, "Wisdom and the Magic of the Extreme," 243–44; "On Hegel: A
Study in Sorcery," *passim.*
27. For example, Dante Germino, "Eric Voegelin's Framework for Political
Evaluation in His Recently Published Work," *American Political Science Review,* LXXII
(1978), 118 n. 29.
28. Voegelin, "Equivalences of Experience and Symbolization in History," *Eternità e Storia, I valori permanenti nel divenire storico* (Florence, 1970), 222.

The strength of this claimed equivalence must be measured by reference to the original sources, but in a manner that takes into account Voegelin's theory of experience and symbolization. According to Voegelin, writings expressive of spiritual disorientation tend, whether modern or premodern, to incorporate: (a) symbols engendered by distorted reactions to experiences of the world common to all mankind[29] and (b) deformations of symbols engendered by experiences of transcendent reality not shared by the deformers.[30] Voegelin argued that an equivalence can be detected among these symbols, the patterns of their deformation, and the experiences from which they are engendered. Yet it should not be expected that equivalence will take the form of strict doctrinal reproduction, because experiences and symbols of the world and of transcendent reality vary in terms of their "compactness" and "differentiation." For example, the Christian symbol of "God" is more differentiated than the intra-mundane "gods" of ancient Greece. Thus, the consciousness that hates the gods (*e.g.,* Aeschylus' Prometheus) and seeks to make man the measure of all things will express itself somewhat differently than the atheistic consciousness characteristic of modern ideology, which revolts against a more differentiated background. That a certain equivalence may be present nevertheless is suggested by Marx's praise of Prometheus:

> The proclamation of Prometheus—"in a word, I hate all the gods"—is [philosophy's] own profession, her own slogan against all the gods of heaven and earth who do not recognize man's self consciousness as the highest divinity. There shall be none other beside it.[31]

Voegelin persuasively maintains that Marx has transposed the Prometheus symbol of Aeschylus by failing to note the response of Hermes ("It strikes me as no small madness"[32]), and Marx clearly

---

29. Voegelin, *The New Science of Politics,* 167; *The World of the Polis,* 216; "History and Gnosis," 82.

30. Voegelin, *The New Science of Politics,* 64–65: "Theory as an explication of experiences is intelligible only to those in whom the explication will stir up parallel experiences as the empirical basis for testing the truth of the theory. Unless a theoretical exposition activates the corresponding experiences at least to a degree, it will create the impression of empty talk or will perhaps be rejected as an irrelevant expression of subjective opinions."

31. Marx, Preface to doctoral thesis, in *Karl Marx: Selected Writings,* 12–13.

32. Aeschylus, *Prometheus Bound,* line 977, in *Prometheus, with a Translation of Aeschylus' "Prometheus Bound,"* by E. A. Havelock (Seattle, 1968). See Voegelin, *The World of the Polis,* 253–64; *Conversations with Eric Voegelin,* 80–81.

felt a certain affinity with the Prometheus of his own making. Yet there remains the question of how Voegelin can demonstrate that disorders such as those known to Aeschylus are related to those he finds in the ideological activism of our own time. His attempt was premised upon the possibility of discovering the experiences (*e.g.*, alienation, hubris, *libido dominandi*, chiliasm) that lie "beneath" the symbols utilized for expression of a particular pattern of disordered consciousness. This is, at best, a difficult hermeneutical task, and neither the procedure nor the results can be vindicated apart from an extended presentation of Voegelin's theory of consciousness, his philosophical anthropology, and his perspective on the relation of history to theory. A section of Chapter 5 will be devoted to the problem, since Voegelin's diagnostic lexicon could be reduced to an untheoretical mash of invective if his exigetical procedure cannot be justified. While I am not of the opinion that so harsh a conclusion is warranted, there is a very real danger that less cautious polemicists will invoke Voegelin's categories without troubling themselves over the difficulties involved in establishing the presence of spiritual disease in the objects of their ridicule. Note Voegelin's awareness of these difficulties:

> I am speaking cautiously of a suspension of consciousness because it frequently is difficult, if not impossible, to determine in the case of an individual activist whether the suspension is an act of intellectual fraud or of persuasive self-deception, whether it is a case of plain illiteracy or of the more sophisticated illiteracy imposed by an educational system, whether it is caused by a degree of spiritual and intellectual insensitivity that comes under the head of stupidity, or whether it is due to various combinations of these and other factors such as the desire to attract public attention and make a career.[33]

The possibility of misuse of Voegelin's diagnostic categories is enhanced by their eminent suitability for polemical purposes. Since a detailed analysis of a thinker's work could be considered superfluous after pathological disorders are found lying behind his thought, reference to Voegelin's conclusions might easily be considered a convenient substitute for careful criticism. In light of the large investment of time required for careful criticism of figures such as Marx or Hegel, the attractiveness of such a shortcut for those not enamored of Marxism or Hegelianism is apparent. Voegelin's own approach may make this tack seem justifiable, for

33. Voegelin, "Wisdom and the Magic of the Extreme," 236.

he intentionally avoided point-by-point refutations of ideologists, largely because he viewed the errors that vitiate their work as *deliberate*:[34]

> If we were to accept the activist's counter-image as the "theory" it claims to be, as a theory to be verified or falsified on the positivistic level, we would play the activist's game, even if our evaluation of the details should turn out to be devastatingly negative. . . . [P]henomena of this class must certainly not be neglected in specialized studies of such counter-images. . . . Nevertheless, they are of symptomatic importance only and must not analytically obscure the intended analytical obscurity of the activist dreamer. Only if we disengage the dream story from the complicated counter-image can we bring the truly theoretical issue of reality and imaginative dreaming into focus.[35]

The inevitable result of this decision to disengage the consciousness of the dreamer from the particulars of the dream is that the seriousness of the charges occasionally seems incommensurate with the thoroughness of the analyses that support them. This problem is, in Voegelin's case, often more apparent than real. For example, only after a section of the manuscript of Voegelin's massive "History of Western Political Thought," written during the 1940s, was published in 1975 under the title *From Enlightenment to Revolution* did it become clear that the almost cryptic reflections on certain modern figures in *The New Science of Politics* and *Science, Politics and Gnosticism* were based upon a thorough familiarity with the period and writers in question. There are, nevertheless, certain points at which the problem is real, as when Voegelin referred in passing to "biologism" or "psychologism" as ideological inversions of human order.[36] Those who are versed in the Voegelinian corpus will probably know what is meant in such passages, but the unin-

---

34. Voegelin, *Science, Politics and Gnosticism*, 23–28; "The Eclipse of Reality," 188–89; "Remembrance of Things Past," in *Anamnesis*, 3–9; "Wisdom and the Magic of the Extreme," 235–39.

35. Voegelin, "Wisdom and the Magic of the Extreme," 239. The point is also made, less reservedly, in *Anamnesis*, 8–9: "A true scholar has better things to do than to engage in futile debate with men who are guilty of the *aspernatio rationis*. The revolt at large has not become vociferous enough, and perhaps never will, to match the paranoiac aggressiveness of the mental cases, but it has become extensive enough to leave no doubt that the restrictivist movements have maneuvered themselves out of the empirical advance of the historical and philosophical sciences." But *cf.* "On Debate and Existence," *Intercollegiate Review*, III (1967), 144, where Voegelin argues that debate is a philosophical obligation.

36. Voegelin, *Israel and Revelation*, xii; *From Enlightenment to Revolution*, 69.

itiated may be left wondering which thinkers Voegelin had in mind and how deeply ideological elements had, in his view, penetrated the disciplines of psychology and biology.

Although Voegelin's theoretical framework helps clarify the underlying similarities among the various and diverse ideologies of the age, there is reason to question whether the patterns of revolt and disorientation highlighted in his framework are of even remotely equivalent prominence in the movements listed above; there is some substance to Thomas J. J. Altizer's charge that "Professor Voegelin finds everything to be Gnostic."[37] The specifics of Voegelin's analyses, however, show that his approach should not be used to lump together and dismiss modern intellectual/political movements on grounds of their being all of one piece. Voegelin's intention was to bring into focus an experiential unity often obscured by the "dogmatomachy" of inter-ideological squabbles. It will be argued that Voegelin not only succeeded in clarifying this experiential unity but also, by basing his analysis of ideology on a theory of consciousness and human nature, made it possible to account for the motivations underlying the construction of such systems as well as the extremes to which the rank and file have gone in order to actualize them. Moreover, Voegelin's concept of pathologically closed consciousness can be persuasively applied to a remarkably wide range of phenomena across cultures, across time, and across differences such as those between ideological theoreticians, epigones, and functionaries.

Yet, just as Voegelin's diagnostic analyses may be prone to misuse, his conceptual innovations may give rise to confusion. From his first writings to his last, Voegelin complained of the lack of a developed terminology for dealing with the phenomena associated with pneumapathological consciousness.[38] Accordingly, he experimented with a wide variety of conceptual and descriptive terms, but somewhat distressingly, he never settled on a single terminological framework. As a result, implied theoretical distinctions are in certain important instances vague or unarticulated. For example,

37. Quoted by John William Corrington in *"Order and History:* The Breaking of the Program," *Denver Quarterly,* X (1975), 122.

38. Voegelin, *From Enlightenment to Revolution,* 263; review of *The Origins of Totalitarianism,* by Hannah Arendt (with a reply by Arendt and a concluding remark by Voegelin), *Review of Politics,* XV (1953), 68; "Wisdom and the Magic of the Extreme," 261.

when Voegelin refers to Isaiah and modern ideologues as "brothers under the skin," and of the latter as "descendants of the prophetic faith in a transfiguration of the world," the otherwise important distinction between pre- and post-Christian patterns of revolt becomes obscure.[39] Also obscured is the difference between the expectation of divine intervention in political events, on the one hand, and modern attempts to "murder God" and "immanentize the eschaton," on the other. An Isaiah and a Marx are "brothers under the skin" only in the sense that both seem to have lost the "balance of consciousness"; the direction and consequences of their respective imbalance are, however, vastly different. Finally, we might wish to know in what sense modern ideologues are "descendants" of the prophetic faith in a metastatic transfiguration of the world. Are they witting or unwitting descendants? If the latter is what Voegelin had in mind, as is presumably the case, but the sources and nature of their expected metastases are poles apart, is it not misleading to describe their relation in terms of kinship?

Although Voegelin's basic argument is relatively free of inconsistencies, his use of terms and analogies is often surprisingly indefinite. Concepts announced in one work fail to appear in the next,[40] distinctions drawn at one point are not developed or applied at others,[41] and terms that arise in differing contexts are often used interchangeably.[42] One is forced to wonder why Voegelin, who was a very careful writer, would not have been more rigorous in the specification of his conceptual tools—especially in light of his frequent references to the need for a diagnostic terminology. Not having an answer at hand, and at the risk of violating some hidden intention, I submit that both the strengths and weaknesses of Voegelin's argument will be easier to discern when treated within the conceptual scheme presented in diagram form above.

39. Voegelin, *Israel and Revelation*, xiii.

40. *E.g.*, "modern Prometheanism," from *The New Science of Politics*, 254; "social Satanism," from *From Enlightenment to Revolution*, 71, 195.

41. *E.g.*, those between teleological, axiological, and activist immanentization, and intellectual, emotional, and volitional gnosticism from *The New Science of Politics*, 124, 175, which do not, to my knowledge, reappear in any subsequent work.

42. For example, the following terms are among those utilized as apparent synonyms for *ideology* or *gnosticism* at various points in Voegelin's writings: pneumapathology, activist dreaming, egophantic revolt, metastatic faith, activist mysticism, demonic mendacity, Prometheanism, parousiasm, political religion, social Satanism, magic pneumatism, eristics.

The most serious terminological problem presents itself with Voegelin's use of the concept of *gnosticism*, which was usually employed in the same generic manner that I have used *pneuma-pathological consciousness*. Considerable confusion has resulted as to whether the adjective *gnostic* means that a thinker has been influenced by historical Gnosticism or merely thinks along analogous lines. Further complications have been introduced with the discovery of the Coptic Gnostic library at Nag Hammadi in Egypt, which suggested that the classical form of Gnosticism tended toward rejection, rather than transformation, of the world.[43] Voegelin had used *gnosticism* to denote both tendencies since 1952. To account for the world-transforming strand in modernity, he began speaking (in the early 1970s) of hermeticism, alchemy, and magic as being of importance comparable to gnosticism. Unfortunately, however, Voegelin had yet to make fully clear his views on the influence wielded by these elements at the time of his death in January, 1985. The works that Voegelin cited in this context (by Frances Yates and Mircea Eliade) do not themselves clarify why Voegelin would have thought hermeticism, alchemy, and magic so important for understanding ideological consciousness. Yates and Eliade do indeed suggest that these traditions may have been important in the development of the worldview characteristic of modern science, but this thesis is not without its informed detractors, and the connections between modern science and modern ideology are not explicitly drawn by Voegelin (or Yates or Eliade).[44] In any event, it is clear

43. English translation: Bentley Layton, trans. *The Gnostic Scriptures* (Garden City, 1987). See Stephen A. McKnight, "Understanding Modernity: A Reappraisal of the Gnostic Element," *Intercollegiate Review* XIV (1979), 107–109; Webb, *Eric Voegelin: Philosopher of History*, 201.

44. Mircea Eliade, *The Forge and the Crucible*, trans. Stephen Corrin (New York, 1962); Frances A. Yates, *Giordano Bruno and the Hermetic Tradition* (Chicago, 1964). Voegelin makes brief mention of these works in his "Response to Professor Altizer's 'A New History and a New but Ancient God?'" in *Eric Voegelin's Thought: A Critical Appraisal*, ed. Sandoz, 193, 194. Voegelin concludes his comments on the books of Eliade and Yates by stating "their obvious implication: the contemporary disorder will appear in a rather new light when we leave the 'climate of opinion' and, adopting the perspective of the historical sciences, acknowledge the problems of 'modernity' to be caused by the predominance of Gnostic, Hermetic and alchemistic conceits, as well as by the Magic of violence as the means for transforming reality." Cf., *e.g.*, Robert S. Westman, "Magical Reform and Astronomical Reform: The Yates Thesis Reconsidered," and J. E. McGuire, "Neoplatonism and Active Principles:

that none of these traditions can serve as a replacement for the overarching uses to which Voegelin once put the concept of gnosticism, *i.e.*, as including both rejection of the world and insistence upon its transformation.

Eugene Webb has proposed, as a way out of this problem, capitalizing the name of the ancient Gnostic movement while using the term *gnosticism* for "all movements based on claims to gnosis of any sort."[45] Leaving questions of (over) inclusiveness aside, along with the confusion this practice might occasion, Webb gives us reason to doubt the helpfulness of his distinction less than a page later when he argues for a link between Marx and Gnosticism. He points out that Marx was an admirer of Thomas Muntzer and that Muntzer was an admirer of Joachim of Fiore, who in turn is said to have been influenced by Gnostic texts.[46] So is Marx a gnostic or a historical Gnostic? Moreover, it would seem that a case such as that of the metastatic faith of Isaiah could be termed "gnostic" only by invoking a very liberal poetic license; there is something problematic about speaking of gnostic tendencies prior to the advent of historical Gnosticism, and even if the game of suggesting chains of literary influence can be made to work with Marx, it will certainly not work with Isaiah. Any attempt to patch up the concept of gnosticism as a generic term by dispensing with pre-Gnostic phenomena would not only have to ignore Voegelin's comments on the continuing significance of metastatic faith,[47] but would also run contrary to the basic thrust of Voegelin's argument, *viz.*, that disordered consciousness arises not from Gnosticism but from the tensions inherent in the human condition.

Because Voegelin mentioned late in life that he would probably not use the concept of gnosticism if he were starting over again,[48] I think it best to make a clean break with the term and use the concept of pneumapathological consciousness or disorientation, so as to incorporate the entire set of Voegelin's terms. While these are admittedly inelegant neologisms, they are nevertheless more faith-

---

Newton and the *Corpus Hermeticum*," both in *Hermeticism and the Scientific Revolution* (Los Angeles, 1977).

45. Webb, *Eric Voegelin: Philosopher of History*, 201.

46. *Ibid.*, 201–202.

47. Voegelin, *Israel and Revelation*, xiii, 454; *The Ecumenic Age*, 26–27.

48. Quoted in Webb, *Eric Voegelin: Philosopher of History*, 200.

ful to Voegelin's basic thesis than any alternative of which I am aware. *Psychopathological* would be somewhat easier on the contemporary ear, but that is precisely the problem, since *psyche* has come to mean something quite different in common parlance than it connoted to the ancient Greeks. And since psychoanalysis (Freudian or otherwise) was itself, for Voegelin, an ideologically charged symbol, *psychopathological* will clearly not suit our purposes.[49] *Pneuma*, or spirit, can replace psyche without bringing in its wake similar ideological baggage. *Consciousness* must be appended to avoid the misimpression that physiological or ontological states are in question, as well as to retain Voegelin's stress on experience as the source of both order and disorder in human existence. Since the term *consciousness* could appear to lack content if used repeatedly in this context, *disorientation* will also be employed to emphasize the departure of the forms of consciousness we are examining from the balanced orientation of consciousness in the "In-Between" of the *metaxy*.

The next chapter will open with an introduction to Voegelin's understanding of well-ordered consciousness. This discussion will help to clarify the general pattern of disordered consciousness and lead into an analysis of the first of the particular patterns, namely, metastatic faith. Chapter 3 will be devoted, first, to the pattern that has been categorized as prometheanism, and second, to Plato's search for a socially effective remedy for the *nosos*, or disease, of the soul. Chapter 4 will be devoted to parousiasm and an analysis of the relationship between Christianity and spiritual disorientation. Voegelin's attempt to establish an essential equivalence among ideologies will be examined in Chapter 5, along with his argument for a continuity between ideological consciousness and earlier patterns of disorder. Chapter 6 will survey and assess Voegelin's search for therapeutic responses to spiritual disorder.[50] The seventh chapter concludes this study with an evaluation of Voegelin's project as a whole.

49. On psychoanalysis, see Voegelin, *Science, Politics and Gnosticism*, 83, and *Conversations with Eric Voegelin*, 28–29.

50. Chapter 6 is premised upon the analysis in Chapter 3 of Plato's similar effort and should be read in light of that analysis.

# 2

## The Etiology of Pneumapathological Consciousness

For Voegelin the movement toward truth starts from a person's awareness of his or her existence in "untruth." Yet the process through which one gains an awareness of modes of existence in untruth is not a "given" in human experience; it is raised to the level of consciousness only during the movement toward truth. Thus, the origins of pneumapathological consciousness are difficult to distinguish from the origins of healthy or well-ordered consciousness. On the basis of Voegelin's thought it would be as correct to say that the disordered soul "discovers" the patterns of spiritual order as to say that the well-ordered soul "discovers" the nature of its disordered former existence (or its unhealthy counterparts in the surrounding environment). These discoveries are probably not distinct events so much as correlative insights from a single experience:

> From the depth of the psyche wells up life and order when historically, in the surrounding society, the souls have sunk into the depth of death and disorder. From the depth comes the force that drags the philosopher's soul up to the light, so that it is difficult to say whether the upper There is the source of his truth, or the nether There that forced him up.[1]

The disordered soul cannot be recognized as such prior to the emergence of its opposite. Its existence can be postulated retrospectively from accounts of the "leaps in being," which portray ignorance and disorientation as the background for new differentiations of the truth of the soul. But it cannot be analyzed before the differentiation is achieved, and the diagnosis cannot be justified except by comparison to the soul that is reformed by the achievement.

1. Voegelin, *Plato and Aristotle*, 62.

It was shown in the preceding chapter that Voegelin considered pneumapathological consciousness a historical constant that can be related to certain aspects of the human condition. This is, however, a conclusion and not a premise. Only rarely did Voegelin stray from analysis of historical materials to offer general observations of this kind, and then only after the materials had been set forth. His writings have a strongly empirical flavor that would be lost if we tried to examine the varieties of pneumapathological consciousness apart from the historical conditions in which they appear.[2] Voegelin's method offers no encouragement to those who would like to get at the origins of spiritual disorder *per se*. He did not, and we shall not, attempt to push the search for the origins of pneumapathological consciousness to points in time before diagnoses from positions of purportedly superior orientation emerge. Metastatic faith and prometheanism will therefore be analyzed in this chapter against the background of the specific tensions that occasioned these forms of existence-in-revolt.

With these caveats, some general comments are in order regarding Voegelin's reflections on healthy (or open or balanced) consciousness. For while Voegelin understood the particular varieties of existence-in-revolt as spiritual rebellions against particular symbolizations of truth, the Israelitic, Hellenic, and Christian symbolizations need not be strictly isolated. One of his most important theses is that these symbolisms are essentially equivalent, despite their phenotypical differences, in the sense that they refer recognizably to the same structures in reality.[3] There is only one reality;

2. Ellis Sandoz, *The Voegelinian Revolution: A Biographical Portrait* (Baton Rouge, 1981), 194: "Voegelin's noetic science rests squarely on reality experienced not as an abstract position or principle, but as a necessity dictated by the facts themselves. The reality of the discussion is the comprehensive reality of science, delimited by the insight that the only reality is the one known experientially or imaginatively extrapolated from direct experience. The symbols of *noesis*, he repeatedly stresses, are not something found floating in thin air. Rather they are tied to (engendered by) specific events reported by specific men in whom the experiences occur. . . . For this reason Voegelin's work is laden with the historiographic materials through which his "experiential analysis" (which contrasts with phenotypical analysis) proceeds in the back-and-forth zigzag of reiteration and reflective reconsideration of texts and problems."

3. Voegelin, "Equivalences of Experience and Symbolization in History," *passim*; *The Ecumenic Age*, 7–11, 188–92, 249–55. It is important to note at this point that "equivalence" does not imply identity in Voegelin's work. Something is gained— and lost—in the historical sequence that leads from cosmogonic myth to revelation

it may be symbolized in a manifold of forms, but no one form is ever fully adequate to or exhaustive of reality's rich and mysterious nature. Myth, philosophy, and revelation are examples of such symbolic forms. They vary in terms of differentiation and arise at different times in history, but the more recent and more differentiated do not simply supersede the earlier and more compact. Mythical patterns of symbolization play an important part in Platonism and Christianity and should not be regarded as regressive or untrue, because certain types of experiences cannot otherwise be expressed.[4] And just as late truths may be expressed in early forms of symbolization, an early symbolism may contain, in germinal form, a truth that is differentiated in subsequent symbolisms.[5]

The scope of this book does not permit an extended treatment of this controversial line of argument, but two points should be noted. First, the argument for essential equivalence will allow us to summarize Voegelin's perspective on balanced consciousness without violating the principles of his historiography. Second, the argument for equivalence is decisively important for (a) the generic

---

to philosophy to Christianity, and it would be a grave error to assume that, since these symbolic forms are for Voegelin structurally equivalent, they are also interchangeable. This point is made most forcefully in Voegelin's comparison of the *alethes logos* in Book I of Plato's *Laws* with the "saving tale of divine Incarnation, Death and Resurrection" from the Gospels. The "saving tale" is "richer by the missionary fervor of its spiritual universalism, poorer by its neglect of noetic control; broader by its appeal to the inarticulate humanity of the common man, more restricted by its bias against the articulate wisdom of the wise; more imposing through its imperial tone of divine authority, more imbalanced through its apocalyptic ferocity, which leads to conflicts with the conditions of man's existence in society; more compact through its generous absorption of earlier strata of mythical imagination, especially through the reception of Israelite historiogenesis and the exuberance of miracle-working, more differentiated through the intensely articulate experience of loving-divine action in the illumination of existence with truth." "The Gospel and Culture," in *Jesus and Man's Hope*, ed. D. Miller and D. G. Hadidian (Pittsburgh, 1971), 77. See also "On Christianity" (reply to a letter from Alfred Schutz, January 1, 1953), in *The Philosophy of Order: Essays on History, Consciousness, and Politics*, ed. Peter J. Opitz and Gregor Sebba (Stuttgart, 1981), 450–51.

4. Voegelin, *The Ecumenic Age*, 224–27; *Conversations with Eric Voegelin*, 27.

5. For example, Voegelin argued that "one has to recognize, and make intelligible, the presence of Christ in a Babylonian hymn, or a Taoist speculation, or a Platonic dialogue, just as much as in a gospel." Voegelin, "Response to Professor Altizer's 'A New History and a New but Ancient God?'" in *Eric Voegelin's Thought: A Critical Appraisal*, ed. Sandoz, 191.

concept of pneumapathological consciousness, (b) the thesis that such consciousness is grounded in the human condition rather than transitory circumstances, and (c) the proposition that the history of such consciousness is characterized by an unbroken continuum of movements. For if no equivalence exists between, say, Israelitic revelation and Greek philosophy, patterns of rebellion against these traditions would have to be treated as *sui generis* and the principles underlying this study could rightly be deemed arbitrary. Although this problem must be acknowledged and cannot be resolved with anything short of a book-length examination, a modest contribution will nevertheless be possible if we adopt an alternative strategy, assuming some measure of equivalence in the traditions and searching for equivalence in the corresponding patterns of revolt.

According to Voegelin, the truth of the soul, or what we have referred to as open, healthy, or balanced consciousness, was "discovered" at definite points in history by particular individuals in certain societies. It is not part of the human birthright, to be retained or squandered, nor is it created through ingenuity. Although Voegelin noted that a primitive tribal village is "materially too cramped to leave room for the *bios theoreticos*,"[6] he did not attempt to account for the emergence of the epochal, differentiating insights by reference to material or cultural preconditions. In fact, there is a sense in which he did not attempt to "explain" their emergence at all, since he regarded this as *the* mystery in the structure of history. The following questions are referred to in *The Ecumenic Age* as "the Question":

> (1) Why should there be epochs of advancing insight at all? why is the structure of reality not known in differentiated form at all times?
>
> (2) Why must the insights be discovered by such rare individuals as prophets, philosophers and saints? why is not every man the recipient of the insights?
>
> (3) Why when the insights are gained, are they not generally accepted? why must the epochal truth go through the historical torment of imperfect articulation, evasion, skepticism, disbelief, rejection, deformation, and of renaissances, renovations, rediscoveries, rearticulations, and further differentiations?[7]

---

6. Voegelin, *Israel and Revelation*, 217. See also *The Ecumenic Age*, 306.
7. Voegelin, *The Ecumenic Age*, 316. See also "History and Gnosis," 76.

These questions, Voegelin argued, "are not meant to be answered; on the contrary, they symbolize the mystery in the structure of history by their unanswerability."[8] They cannot be answered because the insights gained by the prophets, philosophers, and saints were not the result of autonomous projects of action but responses to "theophantic events" or "spiritual outbursts" or "hierophantic events" (or the persuasive communication of such events by others).[9] The human participant in a theophantic event can respond by questioning or searching, but the revelatory movement from the divine ground is not at one's command. Thus, the accounts we possess of such events spell out not methods of preparation but, rather, experiences of participation. Moses, Socrates, and Paul were acutely sensitive to their own unworthiness. Their special merit was that of openness, not of personal achievement.

If the symbols and engendering experiences of prophets, philosophers, and saints are structurally equivalent, it should be possible to turn to any of the three human types as exemplars of balanced consciousness. Because Voegelin argued, however, that "the adequate articulation and symbolization of the questioning consciousness is the epochal feat of the philosophers,"[10] we will concentrate on philosophical symbols of health, openness, and balance, especially those of Plato and Aristotle. Voegelin found within Platonic and Aristotelian thought a coherent body of language symbols that signify the various stages in the development of the philosopher's consciousness. There is, first, the group of symbols that express the initial experience of restless wondering: wondering (*thaumazein*), seeking or searching (*zetein*), search (*zetesis*), and questioning (*aporein, diaporein*).[11] The philosopher feels himself moved (*kinein*) by some unknown force to ask the questions of which the search consists; he feels himself drawn (*helkein*) into the search. This is the experience recounted in the famous cave allegory of Plato's *Republic*, where the prisoner is forced by an unknown entity to turn around (*periagoge*) and begin his ascent to the light.

Although Aristotle's account seems to place somewhat greater emphasis on the philosopher's perception of his own ignorance, in

---

8. Voegelin, *The Ecumenic Age*, 316.
9. *Ibid.*, 5, 11, 217.
10. Voegelin, "Reason: The Classic Experience," in *Anamnesis*, 93.
11. *Ibid.*

Voegelin's reading this perception is not a first piece of information acquired but a restless stirring within the soul: a person "could not know that he does not know, unless he experienced an existential unrest to escape from the ignorance (*pheugein ten agnoian*) and to search for knowledge (*episteme*)."[12] Aristotle, no less than Plato, finds the origin of the movement toward knowledge outside the seeker: "The mind (*nous*) is moved (*kineitai*) by the object (*noeton*)."[13] The object that moves the mind of the philosopher is not an object in the external world of things but the transcendent ground of those things and of the philosopher's own existence. And the ignorance that the lover of wisdom perceives, which in a sense constitutes his nature, is an ignorance not about things but about his own origins:

> The search from the human side, it appears, presupposes the movement from the divine side: Without the *kinesis*, the attraction from the ground, there is no desire to know, no questioning in confusion, no knowledge of ignorance. There would be no anxiety in the state of ignorance, unless anxiety were alive with man's knowledge of his existence from a ground that he is not himself.[14]

The movement from the divine side mentioned in this passage—the pull *from* the ground that induces a search *for* the ground—is the philosophical equivalent of the "call" answered by the prophet and the saint. Voegelin repeatedly inveighed against the medieval distinction between natural reason and supernatural revelation, which in his view was based upon a misunderstanding of the mystical character of Platonic-Aristotelian *noesis*.[15]

Although theophantic events are mysteriously reserved for prophets, philosophers, and saints, rudiments of the experiential complex that initiates the search for the ground are bestowed upon

---

12. Voegelin, *The Ecumenic Age*, 190.

13. Voegelin's translation of Aristotle, *Metaphysics*, 1072a30, in *The Ecumenic Age*, 190.

14. Voegelin, *The Ecumenic Age*, 190.

15. Voegelin, "Toynbee's History as a Search for Truth," in *The Intent of Toynbee's History*, ed. Edward T. Gargan (Chicago, 1961), 196–98; "The Gospel and Culture," 75, 77, 82; *The Ecumenic Age*, 48; *Conversations with Eric Voegelin*, 104; "Wisdom and the Magic of the Extreme," 256; "The Meditative Origin of the Philosophical Knowledge of Order," in *The Beginning and the Beyond: Papers from the Gadamer and Voegelin Conferences*, ed. Frederick Lawrence, Supplementary Issue of *Lonergan Workshop*, IV (Chico, Calif., 1984), 44–47; *In Search of Order*, 43.

all people by virtue of the natural powers of reasoning and questioning. As Aristotle stated in the first line of the *Metaphysics*, "All men by nature desire to know," and paramount among the things they wish to know is their origin. The experience of contingency, which is of decisive importance in the development of philosophical consciousness, is not the exclusive preserve of philosophers:

> Man is not a self-created, autonomous being carrying the origin and meaning of his existence within himself. He is not a divine *causa sui*; from the experience of his life in precarious existence within the limits of birth and death there rather arises the wondering question about the ultimate ground, the *aitia* or *proto arche*, of all reality and specifically his own. . . . [T]his questioning is inherent in man's experience of himself at all times.[16]

As was shown in the first chapter, Voegelin's distinction between "open" and "closed" consciousness is not based upon the assertion that the ideologist is closed to this class of experiences. Disorder is evinced in certain *reactions* to such experiences of contingency and uncertainty. If ignorance of the question of the ground were the condition of most of humanity, excepting only participants in theophanic events, disordered consciousness would be so widespread that it could not really be called disordered. And if the great majority of humanity were held culpable for not being prophetic or philosophical or saintly, these concepts would become meaningless as designations of distinct human types. The concept of ideological closure presupposes a prior exposure, and Voegelin reserved his most strident criticism for those like Marx who display both an awareness of the problem of contingency and the requisite facility for pursuing it.[17]

The experiences that orient humanity to the immanent and transcendent poles of existence in the "In-Between" of the *metaxy*, and from which the balance of consciousness may be gained or lost, are thus not beyond the ken of the majority of human beings. Although adequate symbolization of these experiences can only be achieved by those possessing extraordinary gifts, and though the experiences are an existential precondition for penetration of the symbols created by those who possess such gifts,

16. Voegelin, "Reason: The Classic Experience," in *Anamnesis*, 92–93.
17. See Voegelin, *Science, Politics and Gnosticism*, 23–28; Karl Marx, "Economic and Philosophical Manuscripts of 1844," in *Early Writings*, ed. T. B. Bottomore (New York, 1963), 165–67.

we find ourselves referred back to nothing more formidable than the experiences of finiteness and creatureliness in our existence, of being creatures of a day as the poets call man, of being born and bound to die, of dissatisfaction with a state experienced as imperfect, of apprehension of a perfection that is not of this world but is the privilege of the gods, of possible fulfillment in a state beyond this world, the Platonic *epekeina* [Beyond], and so forth.[18]

Ideologues, and pneumapaths in general, have these experiences but revolt against their finiteness and creatureliness, cannot adjust to the imperfection of their state, seek perfection without regard for divine privilege, and seek it not in a state beyond this world but rather within this world.

According to Voegelin, man experiences himself tending beyond his human imperfection toward the perfection of the divine ground that moves him. As Plato's Socrates observes in the *Symposium*, the spiritual man, the *daimonios aner*, as he is moved in his quest of the ground, moves somewhere between knowledge and ignorance. "The whole realm of the spiritual (*daimonion*) is halfway indeed between (*metaxy*) god and man."[19] Thus, Voegelin argued,

> the in-between—the *metaxy*—is not an empty space between the poles of the tension but the "realm of the spiritual"; it is the reality of "man's converse with the gods" [*Symposium*, 202–203], the mutual participation (*methexis, metalepsis*) of human in divine, and divine in human, reality.[20]

The balance of consciousness is a balance between participation in the divine and respect for the needs and limitations of the "merely" human. The balance, what Voegelin called existence in the *metaxy*, may also be symbolized as a balance between ignorance and knowledge, imperfection and perfection, time and timelessness, matter and spirit, life and death.[21] "Healthy" consciousness consists in a simultaneous attunement to the divine and worldly realities from which these dichotomous symbols arise. Human beings are more than animals and less than gods, and may (perhaps understandably) be dissatisfied with the ambiguity involved in es-

18. Voegelin, "On Debate and Existence," 146.
19. Voegelin's translation of Plato, *Symposium*, 202a, in "Reason: The Classic Experience," in *Anamnesis*, 103.
20. *Ibid.*
21. Voegelin, "Equivalences of Experience and Symbolization in History," 220; "The Gospel and Culture," 62–63; *The Ecumenic Age*, 184–88.

tablishing their identity in a negative manner by reference to realities in which they participate only partially. From such dissatisfaction emerge various forms of disorientation. For example, in Gnosticism the world and the body were regarded as demonically created prisons that restrict the divine spark in humanity.[22] The tensions arising from the fundamentally ambiguous condition of human beings have also been expressed in modern intellectual efforts to make a god of man, or to explain humanity solely in terms of animality, or to explain God as a projection of the human psyche, etc.

Those who would make a god of man or who seek to explain conceptions of divinity as projections of humanity have not simply fallen into an erroneous philosophical anthropology. The anxiety that springs from the ambiguity of the human condition cannot be alleviated by developing ever more sophisticated models of human nature, because human nature is only one element within the human condition. For Voegelin, the human condition can only be understood within the comprehensive matrix of "God and man, world and society."[23] No single element within this matrix can be fully understood unless all of its elements are fully understood. Because a full understanding of the nature of divinity is beyond the powers of humanity, and because a full understanding of humanity would require an understanding of that which is the ground of its existence, the human condition must always remain mysterious at its core.

For Voegelin the tensions associated with the mysterious relationship between God and humanity lay behind spiritual disorientation. Consequently, the earliest evidence of such disorientation is nearly as old as the awareness of such a relationship to a transcendent God. The first patterns of spiritual disorder, metastatic faith and prometheanism, follow in the wake of the discovery of spiritual order itself. According to Voegelin, the earliest conception of this order as a relationship to a transcendent God (*i.e.*, fully differentiated from the immanent realm of existence) arose with the Israelites and was made explicit in the decalogue.

Voegelin held that the prophets interpreted all types of offensive conduct—including spiritual disorder—as ultimately a violation of

22. Voegelin, *Science, Politics and Gnosticism*, 8–11.
23. Voegelin, *Israel and Revelation*, 1.

the Commandments. This interpretation was possible because the decalogue, according to Voegelin, was not only a collection of substantive rules but also an exemplification of the injunctions to restrain self-assertiveness with regard to God and man. As a consequence, Voegelin maintained, its meaning can be concentrated in one command: "Listen to my voice and I will be your God, and you shall be my people; and walk consistently in the way that I command you" (Jeremiah 7:23). The violations can, therefore, be correspondingly concentrated in the one offense: "Yet they neither listened, nor inclined their ear to me, but walked in their own counsels and the stubbornness of their evil hearts" (Jeremiah 7:24). Voegelin concluded that

> disorder in Israel thus was measured by the comprehensive order of the Decalogue. As far as persons were concerned, the rich and the poor, the king and the priests, the sage and the false prophets were equally judged by the standard of antidivine or antihuman self-assertiveness.[24]

It should be emphasized that the spiritual disorder of antidivine and antihuman self-assertiveness (known to the Greeks as hubris and to Christians as the sin of pride) has often been identified as the core of the ideological impulse in modern politics. Voegelin once defined ideology itself as "existence in rebellion against God and man."[25]

Voegelin found evidence within the Old Testament of both of the basic patterns of imbalanced consciousness introduced in the preceding chapter. The metastatic faith of Isaiah and the periodic prometheanism of the Israelites were engendered, according to Voegelin, by a unique historical dilemma. The perennial problem of maintaining a balance between openness to transcendent experience and sober attentiveness to the necessities of mundane existence was especially acute for the people as a whole. Cognizant of their unique status as a Chosen People but forced to confront the

---

24. *Ibid.*, 433.

25. Voegelin, *Israel and Revelation*, xiv. See Albert Camus, *The Rebel: An Essay on Man in Revolt*, trans. Anthony Bower (New York, 1956); Henri de Lubac, *The Drama of Atheist Humanism*, trans. Edith M. Riley (Cleveland, 1963); Karl Löwith, *Meaning in History: The Theological Implications of the Philosophy of History* (Chicago, 1949); J. L. Talmon, *The Origins of Totalitarian Democracy* (New York, 1960), *Political Messianism: The Romantic Phase* (New York, 1960), and *Romanticism and Revolt: Europe, 1815–1848* (New York, 1967); Gerhart Niemeyer, *Between Nothingness and Paradise* (Baton Rouge, 1971); Hans Jonas, *The Gnostic Religion* (Boston, 1972).

harsh realities of worldly political existence, the Israelites were involved in a continual struggle to reconcile the demands of spiritual and political life. Admonished by the prophets to entrust their fate to Yahweh and by the kings to take fate into their own hands like other peoples, "existence-in-tension" was a historical reality for the Israelites. The admonitions of the prophets were often directed against conduct essentially equivalent to what was called *hybris* among the ancient Greeks:

> You have plowed iniquity, you have reaped injustice,
> You have eaten the fruit of lies,
> in that you trusted in your chariots,
> and the multitude of your warriors.
> (Hosea 10:13)

> Let not the wise man boast of his wisdom,
> Nor the strong man boast of his strength,
> Nor the rich man boast of his riches.
> But if he boasts, let him boast of this,
> that he understands and knows me,
> How I, Yahweh, exercise mercy,
> justice, and righteousness on earth.
> (Jeremiah 9:23–24)

> For Yahweh of the hosts has a day
> Against all that is proud and high,
>     and against all that is lofty and tall:
> Against all the cedars of Lebanon, high and lofty,
>     and against all the oaks of Bashan;
> Against all the high mountains,
>     and against all the lofty hills;
> Against every tall tower,
>     and against every fortified wall;
> Against all the ships of Tarshish,
>     and against all the gallant craft.
> (Isaiah 2:12–17)

Although the prophets were acute analysts of the promethean strain in the desire of the people for military strength and self-aggrandizement, Voegelin argued that certain of the prophets were themselves prone to excess in their disregard of worldly necessities. While there may be something impious about a Chosen

People entrusting their fortune to weaponry rather than to the God of the Covenant, the intensity of the prophets' experiences of partnership with Yahweh carried the risk of obscuring the fact that a Chosen People remains, under its mundane aspect, a people like others. As such, the Israelites, like any other people, had a genuine need of an administration and an army, barring the appearance of a miraculous situation in which their spiritual assets could be directly converted into the currency of political power.

Such a situation is not conceived merely as a momentary suspension of the vicissitudes of war and political struggle. Metastatic faith is a faith that the very structure of pragmatic existence in society and history is soon to undergo a decisive transformation. Thus what is anticipated is not merely a conversion of spiritual into political assets but rather a total and permanent devaluation of the currency of political power, after which those who are rich in spirit will have the field of worldly existence to themselves. The climactic nature of the expected transformation and the belief that it is within one's power to bring it about are what distinguish metastatic faith from the simple hope that one's burdens or those of one's society will be lightened.

Voegelin's writings contain only one analysis of a case that is explicitly termed "metastatic," although, as will be argued below, it seems clear that he understood the basic experience as a perennial and widespread phenomenon. The tensions in the background of this one case, that of Isaiah in the eighth century B.C., are both social and personal. On the social level tensions confronted the Israelites, as we have seen, as a people bound by the necessities of mundane existence, like other peoples, but nevertheless cognizant of unique status as a Chosen People living in historical form under Yahweh. During the wars with Syria of 734 and with Assyria toward the end of the century, the potentially conflicting demands imposed by this dual social role came to a head, as did Isaiah's personal sense of contradiction between the order of faith in Yahweh and the apparently senseless order of power in political existence. According to Voegelin, "It became clear, in brief, that Israel, while it did not mind being a Chosen People, did not care to be chosen at the price of ceasing to be a people like the others." [26] Here was the occasion for a prophet to say what a people

---

26. Voegelin, *Israel and Revelation*, 442. See also Voegelin's brief discussion of this incident in *Autobiographical Reflections*, ed. Ellis Sandoz (Baton Rouge, 1989), 68–69.

should do in an emergency, whether reliance on an army, and even having a king and an administration, constituted an insult to Yahweh.

Isaiah, at the command of Yahweh, approached King Ahaz and counseled that the king take no defensive measures, for Yahweh had said that "it shall not stand, and it shall not be" that the designs of the enemy be crowned with success (7:9). As Voegelin interpreted it, this formula implies that "you will last, if you trust."[27] On the occasion of the Assyrian threat and the alliance with Egypt, the prophet demanded that the "House of David," *i.e.,* the king and his court, not trust in the army or the Egyptian auxiliaries, but "consult Yahweh," an injunction meaning, according to Voegelin, "consult Isaiah." Isaiah advised the king to "trust in the *ruach* [spirit] that lived in him."[28] In response to the "crucial question how the prophetic charisma can be considered by anybody an effective substitute for weapons on the battlefield," Voegelin argued:

> An aura of magic undeniably surrounds the counsel: It is due to the fact that the divine plan itself has been brought within the knowledge of man, in as much as Isaiah knows that God wants the survival of Judah as an organized people in pragmatic history. With that knowledge is given the trust, not in the inscrutable will of God that must be accepted however bitter it tastes when it does not agree with the plans of man, but in the knowable will of God that conforms with the policies of Isaiah and the Chosen People. That knowledge of the divine plan casts its paralyzing spell on the necessity of action in the world.[29]

Action in the world continues to be a necessity because the *immanent* structure of worldly existence is unaffected in any decisive way by the discovery of the transcendent ground. Voegelin held that the leap in being is not a leap out of existence; the order of this world remains autonomous, even when the one God is revealed as the ultimate source of order in humanity, society, and history.[30] An enduring recognition of this sobering truth seems almost to define what Voegelin termed the balance of consciousness.

The autonomous workings of the political realm may seem senseless to one who has participated in the leap, and they may at

27. Voegelin, *Israel and Revelation*, 451.
28. *Ibid.*, 449.
29. *Ibid.*, 451.
30. See Voegelin, *The New Science of Politics*, 156–57, and *Israel and Revelation*, 11, 452.

times be truly senseless, but they are not therefore manipulable by extra-worldly means. Voegelin found an aura of magic surrounding Isaiah's counsel because Isaiah "has tried the impossible: to make the leap in being a leap out of existence into a divinely transfigured world beyond the laws of mundane existence." This case is a matter not simply of neglect of these laws but of "rebellion against the nature of things as ordained by God," and hence a case of pneumapathological consciousness.[31] As such, it bears a resemblance to cases with which we moderns have a more immediate familiarity, and thus it is not surprising that Voegelin could argue that "the prophetic conception of a change in the constitution of being lies at the root of our contemporary beliefs in the perfection of society."[32]

Nevertheless, if there is a resemblance between this case and modern cases of ideological consciousness, there is also an important dissimilarity. To be sure, metastatic faith and ideological consciousness both arise from rebellion against the nature of things as ordained by God, but the faith that God himself will set things aright is vastly different from the declaration of an ideological project that purports to enable human beings to transform the world through their own efforts and according to their own preferences. The advice of Isaiah may represent, as Voegelin maintained, a "gnosis of transmutation,"[33] but it does not represent a human knowledge of and control over a purportedly immanent ground as in ideology. For this reason there are serious problems involved in Voegelin's identification of Isaiah and modern ideologues as "brothers under the skin" and, as we shall see, a much closer kinship exists between metastatic faith and parousiasm as forms of imbalanced consciousness.

It seems that Voegelin did not make this distinction when examining the case of Isaiah in *Israel and Revelation* because "metastatic faith" was then being used in roughly the same generic sense in which "gnosticism" increasingly came to be used in his subsequent writings. Consequently, the problems attendant to Voegelin's application of the concept of gnosticism, discussed above, attend to his reflections on metastatic faith as well. That Voegelin was employing the term in a generic sense is apparent from the

31. Voegelin, *Israel and Revelation*, 452, 453.
32. *Ibid.*, xiii.
33. Voegelin, *The Ecumenic Age*, 27.

preface to *Israel and Revelation*, where he observed that "metastatic faith is one of the great sources of disorder, if not the principal one, in the contemporary world; and it is a matter of life and death for all of us to understand the phenomenon and find remedies against it before it destroys us."[34] Surely he did not mean that the expectation of a divine intervention in Old Testament style was a massive force in our day. If we employ the somewhat more differentiated terminology introduced in the first chapter, we can see that Voegelin was arguing that modern ideological consciousness can only be understood as a variant of a broader pattern of psychic disorientation and that the evidence of pneumapathological consciousness extends deep into antiquity. This important contribution to twentieth-century political science is not diminished by problems Voegelin encountered while struggling to develop an adequate diagnostic vocabulary. In a remarkable passage in *Israel and Revelation* Voegelin demonstrated both a brilliant grasp of continuities in history and an unfortunate tendency to group under a provisional rubric movements that are best kept distinct:

> The recognition of the metastatic experience is of importance for the understanding not only of Israelite and Jewish order but of the history of Western Civilization to this day. While in the main development of Christianity, to be sure, the metastatic symbols were transformed into eschatological events beyond history, so that the order of the world regained its autonomy, the continuum of metastatic movements has never been broken. It massively surrounds, rivals, and penetrates Christianity itself through the Old Testament, as well as through the Revelation of St. John. Throughout the Middle Ages, the Church was occupied with the struggle against heresies of a metastatic complexion; and with the Reformation this underground stream has come to the surface again in a massive flood—first, in the left wing of the sectarian movements and then in the secular political creed movements which purport to exact the metastasis by revolutionary action.[35]

Insofar as a longing for the transformation of reality can be identified within each of these figures and movements, Voegelin was justified in drawing such broad parallels. Yet the passage reflects a lack of discrimination with regard to the subordinate levels of experience distinguishing those who conceive of the metastasis as an inrush of the divine from those who would transform humanity by

34. Voegelin, *Israel and Revelation*, xiii.
35. *Ibid.*, 454.

purely worldly means. Thus Voegelin was rightly taken to task by Old Testament scholar Bernhard W. Anderson: "Clearly there is no basis anywhere in prophecy for the modern illusion that man can build the kingdom of God on earth, either through technological planning or revolutionary zeal. This notion is completely alien to the prophetic understanding of history."[36] As a criticism of Voegelin's handling of the relationship between metastatic faith and ideological consciousness (at least in *Israel and Revelation*), this argument is well founded; yet it is not sufficient to establish a contention that Isaiah was not moved by metastatic faith. Obviously, the prophet did not regard technological planning or revolutionary zeal as the means by which the kingdom of God could be built on earth. But it does not follow that Isaiah regarded *any* such earthly kingdom as impossible, or that the pattern of his expectations bears no resemblance to more recent anticipations of a fundamental reordering of the world. Neither Anderson nor James M. Rhodes (who also expresses reservations about Voegelin's "attack" on Isaiah[37]) questions Voegelin's interpretation of the scriptural passages at issue. It is only the link to modern ideological movements that is disputed, and the gravity of this objection decreases markedly when metastatic faith and ideological consciousness are treated as variants of a broader pattern of psychic imbalance rather than as belonging to a single, undifferentiated class. Moreover, when the roots of this broad pattern are located in the very structure of the human condition—rather than in a chain of literary influence—it becomes clear that Voegelin's analysis need not carry the implication, as Rhodes suggests, "that the errant prophet was a prototalitarian."[38]

36. Bernhard W. Anderson, "Politics and the Transcendent: Voegelin's Philosophical and Theological Exposition of the Old Testament in the Context of the Ancient Near East," in *Eric Voegelin's Search for Order in History*, ed. Stephen A. McKnight (Rev. ed.; Lanham, Md., 1987), 88–89.

37. James M. Rhodes, "Voegelin and Christian Faith," *Center Journal*, II (Summer, 1983), 58–60, 67–68, 101.

38. *Ibid.*, 59. To quote Rhodes more fully: "Voegelin asserted that Isaiah had indulged in metastatic visions that ultimately led to modern, gnostic revolutions and, therefore, that the errant prophet was a prototalitarian" (58–59). I would take issue with this passage from Rhodes's (otherwise outstanding) article on two grounds. First, we have seen that metastatic faith is far from identical with ideological consciousness, and thus it is probably improper to suggest that Voegelin regarded Isaiah as a "prototalitarian" (a term never used by Voegelin in this con-

Although it is important, therefore, to avoid overstating the parallels between this early incident of pneumapathological consciousness and the more grandiose, ideological incidents of the nineteenth and twentieth centuries, it is equally important to emphasize Voegelin's achievement in demonstrating that the "Age of Ideology" is neither novel nor unparalleled at the level of consciousness. It is true that in Isaiah's historical situation no one could hope to overcome the vicissitudes of the human condition through the various types of intramundane manipulation foreseen by modern ideologists, for it was the rise of applied science in the modern era that made such manipulations seem plausible as means of world transformation. However, the sequence of experiential events leading Isaiah to anticipate the negation of military force in international relations is recognizably equivalent—at the level of consciousness—to the sequence that led modern ideologists to anticipate the withering away of states and an "end of history." If Voegelin's analysis of the affair is valid, Isaiah's lapse into metastatic speculation stemmed from an inability to endure the tensions of existence between the perfect order of his transcendent experience and the irrational, brutish order experienced by his people in the politics of the ancient Near East. His potentially ruinous advice to King Ahaz—no less than the actually ruinous advice of Marx—was the result of a loss of the balance of consciousness. As we shall see in the fifth chapter, Marx's ideological speculation stemmed from an inability to endure the tensions of existence between the existing "realm of necessity" (Marx's term for the phase of human history during which humanity is degraded by necessities of productive activity, such as division of labor and private property) and the future "realm of freedom" (the prophetically anticipated phase during which "socialist man" would arise through the liberating effects of labor-saving and world-transforming technology). While the particular differences

---

text). Second, since modern gnostic revolutionaries have certainly not taken either their symbolic or strategic cues from Isaiah (and since Voegelin never drew any such direct connection), it is probably improper to suggest that Voegelin asserted that Isaiah's metastatic faith "ultimately led to" modern gnostic revolutions. There is a vast and important difference between stating that Isaiah's faith "shares certain features" with the faiths of modern revolutionaries on the level of consciousness and stating that the former "led to" the latter on the level of pragmatic events in history.

between metastatic and ideological speculation should not be minimized, Voegelin's analysis of the case of Isaiah suggests that the psychic phenomena commonly associated with ideology are not exclusively modern, a suggestion to be reinforced in the following chapter, which will consider manifestations of—and possible responses to—spiritual disorientation among the ancient Greeks.

# 3

## Diagnosis and Prescription:
## The Ancient Greeks

As was noted at the outset of the previous chapter, disorders of the soul can be adequately diagnosed only by reference to the order of the soul which was achieved in what Voegelin called the leap in being and articulated most fully in philosophy. As we turn to the diagnoses of the ancient Greeks, we shall therefore focus on the analyses of Plato, but it is important to begin by indicating that the complex of disorders with which we will be working was "compactly" understood long before philosophical scrutiny became possible.

For example, Voegelin took the Homeric epics to be, among other things, studies of the causes of personal and social disorder in the Aegean-wide Mycenaean civilization. The *Iliad* and the *Odyssey* contain a study of the pathology of heroes but not of the disorders of souls because, according to Voegelin, the "men of the seventh century B.C. had no soul, immortal or otherwise." The terms *mortal* and *immortal* simply meant gods and men, and there is no word for "soul" in the epics.[1] Since the "gods" are not self-contained entities prior to the leap in being but power complexes in a compactly experienced order of being that also embraces man, the specifically human origins of psychic imbalance in the *metaxy* could not be adequately symbolized. Yet it was possible for the author or authors of the epics to recognize that the surrounding society was disordered because its members were guided by passion (*ate*) rather than by reason and the common good.

The Homeric *ate* means the blindness of passion that makes a person transgress the law in the turmoil of anger, frustration, righ-

---

1. Voegelin, *The World of the Polis*, 83, 192, 103. See also *The New Science of Politics*, 67. Presumably, this refers only to Greeks of the seventh century B.C., as Voegelin recognized an earlier leap in being in Israel.

teous pride, guilt, or anxiety.[2] Voegelin credits Homer with having created, without the aid of an adequate conceptual apparatus, a tentative psychology that could identify the symptoms of spiritual disease by reference to a transcendent order.[3] Although the divine and the human are too closely intermingled in the world of Homer for a diagnosis such as that of the prophets to have been possible, the epics do reflect a developing awareness that symptoms such as pride and uncontrollable wrath spring from antidivine and anti-human self-assertiveness. Voegelin summarizes the Homeric analysis of disorder as follows:

(1) Man is in the habit of making the gods responsible for his misdeeds, as well as for the evil consequences engendered by his misconduct.

(2) Theoretically, this habit implies that the gods are the cause of the evil which men do and suffer. This assertion is wrong. It is man, not the gods, who are responsible for evil.

(3) Practically, this habit is dangerous to social order. Misdeeds will be committed more easily if responsibility can be shifted to the gods.

(4) Historically, a civilizational order is in decline and will perish, if this habit finds general social acceptance.[4]

Homer's observation that the disorder of a society could be traced to the disordered behavior of its component members (especially the ruling class) prefigures the Platonic analyses of the fourth century. Despite "the great difference which is due to the fact that Homer wrote before, while Plato wrote after the discovery of the psyche," Voegelin regarded the Homeric diagnosis as a remarkable achievement in view of the "rather crude" symbols available to him.[5] With the development of more sophisticated symbols in the intervening centuries, Plato was able to penetrate much more deeply into psychic and social disorder, but surprisingly few of the eminent thinkers of the fourth and fifth centuries were to surpass Homer. For example, Voegelin maintained that the Homeric eti-

2. Voegelin, *The World of the Polis*, 80, 87.

3. *Ibid.*, 108–109. Darrell Dobbs, who provides no indication of having been influenced by Voegelin, has argued that Homer's principal intention in the *Odyssey* was to highlight the disordered nature of mundane rationalism when untempered by reverence before the sacred. See "Reckless Rationalism and Heroic Reverence in Homer's *Odyssey*," *American Political Science Review*, LXXXI (1987), 491–508.

4. Voegelin, *The World of the Polis*, 107–108.

5. *Ibid.*, 108.

ology of disorder was subjected to "rationalist destruction" at the hands of Herodotus, who disbelieved Homer's account of the Trojan War and preferred that of the Egyptians "because nobody would have been so foolish as to ruin a city for such a cause."[6] This dispassionate coordination of means and ends represented, in Voegelin's view, a decline from Homer's subtle attempts to explain precisely why such foolishness had happened. Moreover, Herodotus' great popularity in Athens only a few decades after the generation of Aeschylus and Marathon indicates that "the spiritual and intellectual decline" of Hellenic civilization "must have been as rapid as it was terrific." The decline became still more precipitous when Thucydides, in conformity with the temper of his time, turned to the brute facts of political power as the standard of action.[7]

By the latter years of the fifth century the strict rationality of a struggle for power without regard for the order of Hellenic society had apparently become the general standard of action in political practice. When pragmatic rationality displaces a sense of participation in right order it becomes, according to Voegelin, a dangerous indulgence that may grow into an irrational force destructive of order. Such a situation is described in the "Melian Dialogue" in Thucydides. The speeches of the Athenian ambassadors to the Melians suggest that the libidinous logic of power and conquest had eclipsed all sensitivity for justice and compassion: "You know as well as we do that in human discussion justice enters only where the pressure of necessity is equal. For the rest, the powerful exact what they can and the weak grant what they must."[8] The ambassadors open the negotiations with the request to dispense with all pretenses of justice and honorable conduct, which no one can any longer take seriously. They do not attempt to derive a right of empire from their victory over the Persians, nor do they accuse the Melians of having done any wrong. As Voegelin summarized their justification, "Empire is just empire, the ultimate reality."[9] Their course of action, which will ultimately result in the butchering of all the men of Melos and the selling of the women and children

6. *Ibid.*, 40.
7. *Ibid.*, 40, 41.
8. Voegelin's translation of passage from Thucydides, *History of the Peloponnesian War*, in *The World of the Polis*, 373.
9. Voegelin, *The Ecumenic Age*, 182.

into slavery, is said to proceed from the "necessity" imposed by nature on men and, perhaps, on the gods as well:

> Of the gods we believe, and of men we know, that by a necessity of nature they rule whenever they can. We neither made this law nor were we the first to act on it; we found it in existence before us and shall leave it to exist forever after us; we only make use of it, knowing that you and everybody else, if you were as strong as we are, would act as we do.[10]

This is more than simple political "realism"; the passage suggests that the *libido dominandi* has begun to fashion for itself a philosophy of existence detached from any divine limitation, a philosophy that will appear, full blown, in the speeches of Plato's Callicles. For Voegelin the passage signified a fictitious identification of conquest with reality, which was achieved by "identifying reality with a humanity contracted to its libidinous self."[11] Modern parallels come easily to mind, but what needs emphasis, Voegelin stated, is that unlike modern ideologists the Athenians were still conscious of the horror of this process:

> For the Athenian negotiators admit, and even stress, the horror in its starkness; they do not make the slightest attempt at smearing it over with idealisms, ideological verities, or speculative systems. It is true, they have deformed their existence and created an imaginary reality that will allow them to "do their thing," but in the background of this imaginary reality there is still the tragic consciousness of the process. They have not sunk to the untragic vileness of the ideologist who cannot commit the murder he wants to commit in order to gain an "identity" in place of the self he has lost, without moralistically appealing to a dogma of ultimate truth.[12]

If the Athenians of the time were at least straightforward about their lust for power, Thucydides nevertheless found it necessary to turn to the models of the Hippocratic school in order to describe the behavior of his contemporaries. The medical conception of disease was invoked to relate the events now known as the Peloponnesian War in terms of a *kinesis*, a feverish movement of society and a disease of political order. It is interesting to note that al-

---

10. Voegelin's translation of passage from Thucydides, *History of the Peloponnesian War*, in *The World of the Polis*, 373.

11. Voegelin, *The Ecumenic Age*, 182.

12. *Ibid.*

though we now accept it as a fact that there was such an event as the "Peloponnesian War" from 431 to 404, the contemporaries of Thucydides did not share his perception that such a great war had occurred.[13] They only knew of an Archidaman or Ten Years' War, lasting from 431 to 421, and of a Decelean or Ionian War, lasting from 414 to 404. The seven intervening years were punctuated by no more violence than was considered usual in what the Hellenes called peace among their *poleis*, and the expedition of Athens against Sicily in 415–413 was not a war against the Peloponnesians. The great war described by Thucydides was a unit of his creation based upon the Hippocratic model. When Thucydides' contemporaries said *war* they meant, according to Voegelin, a series of battles and campaigns that had a formal beginning with a declaration of war and a formal end with a treaty of peace. But "when Thucydides said war," he meant "a movement that was more than a series of diplomatic and military actions in so far as, beyond physical clashes and conflicts of passions, it had a dimension of meaning extending into the regions of moral breakdown and transfiguration."[14] It was the pressure of this pervasive moral breakdown, exerted upon the soul of Plato in the aftermath of the war and the execution of Socrates, to which Voegelin attributed the founding experiences of political philosophy.

Voegelin, who has often been labeled a Platonist,[15] flatly stated that he was "not concerned with a 'Platonic philosophy' or 'doctrine'" for the basic reason that the propagation of a doctrine was simply not, in his view, Plato's intention. The dialogues were rather a symbolic medium for Plato's resistance to the disorder of the surrounding society and his effort to restore the order of Hellenic civilization through love of wisdom. Thus, for Voegelin,

> [Plato's] philosopher does not exist in a social vacuum, but in opposition to the sophist. Justice is not defined in the abstract but in opposition to the concrete forms which injustice assumes. The right order of the polis is not presented as an "ideal state," but the elements of right order are developed in concrete opposition to the elements of dis-

13. Voegelin, *The World of the Polis*, 350, 358.
14. *Ibid.*, 358.
15. *E.g.*, Hannah Arendt, *Between Past and Future* (Harmondsworth, U.K., 1977), 127; Frederick D. Wilhelmsen, *Christianity and Political Philosophy* (Athens, Ga., 1978), 201. Compare with Fred Dallmayr, "Voegelin's Search for Order," in Dallmayr, *Margins of Political Discourse* (Albany, 1989), 84.

order in the surrounding society. And the shape, the Eidos, of Arete in the soul grows in opposition to the many *eide* of disorder in the soul.[16]

One would search in vain for a distinction in Voegelin's writings between philosophy and political philosophy because he regarded all true philosophizing as a historically rooted act of resistance to the disordering of the soul and society by spiritual disease. He took this to have been Plato's conception of philosophy as well, and the importance of Voegelin's diagnostic efforts within his thought as a whole should be understood in this light. It is not as though Voegelin simply digressed from time to time in his writings on ancient conceptions of order to offer an observation on the crisis of the present; the historical search itself was expressly intended as part of his own act of resistance.[17]

It was noted in Chapter 1 that Voegelin's response to the civilizational crisis of modernity can be described as a search for the wellsprings of the crisis, for the analytical tools required to render it intelligible, and for sources for an appropriate therapy. This set of projects, like his conception of philosophy, appears to have been influenced greatly by Plato:

> Philosophy . . . has its origin in the resistance of the soul to its destruction by society. Philosophy in this sense, as an act of resistance illuminated by conceptual understanding, has two functions for Plato. It is first, and most importantly, an act of salvation for himself and others, in that the evocation of right order and its reconstitution in his own soul becomes the substantive center of a new community which, by its existence, relieves the pressure of the surrounding corrupt society. Under this aspect Plato is the founder of the community of philosophers that lives throughout the ages. Philosophy is, second, an act of judgment. . . . Since the order of the soul is recaptured through resistance to the surrounding disorder, the pairs of concepts [in the *Republic*] which illuminate the act of resistance develop into the criteria (in the pregnant sense of instruments or standards of judgment) of social order and disorder. Under this second aspect Plato is the founder of political science.[18]

The Platonic dialogues are the most helpful materials for understanding why Voegelin interpreted the mass movements of the

16. Voegelin, *Plato and Aristotle*, 63.
17. Voegelin, *Israel and Revelation*, xiv; *Plato and Aristotle*, 302; *The Ecumenic Age*, 38; *Anamnesis*, 137–38.
18. Voegelin, *Plato and Aristotle*, 68–69.

twentieth century as political manifestations of spiritual (as distinct from institutional or intellectual) disorder. As will become clear in later chapters, the foundation of this line of interpretation was set by Voegelin's appropriation of what he called Plato's "anthropological principle." We shall also see that the direction of Voegelin's search for sources of spiritual and societal therapy was strongly influenced by Plato's parallel effort.

Just as Voegelin's diagnostic, conceptual, and therapeutic projects were in a sense restorations of the Platonic analysis, Plato drew upon the symbols and methods of his own predecessors. He incorporated the characterization by Heraclitus of conceit as a "sacred disease" and the distinction of Xenophanes between proper and improper representations of the gods.[19] He also utilized the medical models of the Hippocratic school as adapted by Thucydides, along with Aeschylus' understanding of *authadia* as a madness or disease (*nosos*) characterized by "brazen, shameless, conceited, self-reliant self-satisfaction."[20] Building upon the Aeschylean understanding of society as an order of the soul, and of the soul as a social order of forces, Plato could formulate the principles of the *Republic* that social disorders are traceable to psychic disorders and that the right order of the soul is the source of order in society.

For Plato, justice and injustice are in the soul what health and disease are in the body.[21] Bodily health is defined as the establishment of a natural order among the parts of the organism, whereas disease is a disturbance of the natural order of rule and subordination among the parts. Similarly, the condition of justice in the soul is conceived as a natural, harmonious order of the parts in which each fulfills its function without interfering with the functions of the others. *Dikaiosyne*, or justice, is contrasted to *polypragmosyne*, which Voegelin understood as "the readiness to engage in multifarious activities which are not a man's proper business." When applied to the soul, *polypragmosyne* refers to the tendency of appetites and desires to dictate human action and claim the rulership of the soul that properly belongs to wisdom.[22] The ruler-

19. *Ibid.*, 260, 67; Voegelin, *The World of the Polis*, 171–80, 184–88.

20. Aeschylus, *Prometheus Bound*, lines 977, 1012, 1037; Voegelin, *The World of the Polis*, 258–60. See also *The New Science of Politics*, 66.

21. Plato, *The Republic of Plato*, trans. Allan Bloom (New York, 1968), 444c–d.

22. Voegelin, *Plato and Aristotle*, 64. Ignorance is also described in these terms

ship of wisdom consists in the ordering of one's life toward contemplation of divine being and the preparation of the soul for its existence beyond this life. Injustice is a diseased inversion of this order, manifested in *hybris* and *pleonexia* (unjust will to power), which are the basic characteristics of the complex we have termed prometheanism.

The connection between spiritually disordered individuals and the disorder of a community is set forth most directly in the principle, stated at *Republic* 368d–e, that society is man written in larger letters. The broadening of the *Republic* from a dialogue on the just life of the individual to an inquiry into political order and disorder is dependent upon the proposition that the order of the individual psyche is manifested in a corresponding state of society. At 435e, Plato's Socrates asks, "Isn't it quite necessary for us to agree that the same forms and dispositions as are in the city are in each of us?" and answers that "surely they didn't get there from any other place." At 544d–e Glaucon is told that "it is necessary that there also be as many forms of human character as there are forms of regimes" and is asked, "or do you suppose that the regimes arise 'from oak and rocks' and not from the dispositions of men in the cities, which, tipping the scale as it were, draw the rest along with them?" Thus it is not only the good *polis* that is man written large, but every *polis* writes large the type of person that is socially dominant in it. As Voegelin succinctly summarized the thesis derived from this "anthropological" principle, "a polis is in order when it is ruled by men with well-ordered souls; it is in disorder when the souls of the rulers are disordered."[23]

In keeping with this anthropological principle, Plato analyzed the concrete disorders of his time on both the individual and social level and thus was able to relate a sophisticated understanding of the reciprocal causal relationships involved in the corrupting pro-

---

at *Laws* 689b–c, which accords with the Socratic identification of knowledge and virtue: "So when the soul opposes knowledge, or opinions, or reason—the natural rulers—this I call lack of intelligence: in a city, when the majority refuses to obey the rulers and laws, and in one man, when the noble arguments in the soul achieve nothing, but indeed go contrary to these things." Plato, *The Laws of Plato*, trans. Thomas L. Pangle (New York, 1980).

23. Voegelin, *Plato and Aristotle*, 70. On Plato's anthropological principle see *The New Science of Politics*, 61–63, 67–70; *Plato and Aristotle*, 67–70, 85–88, 124–29.

cess. Plato was not lapsing into inconsistency when he had his Socrates cast the sophists, poets, and politicians as not only the corruptors of society but also mere creatures of an already corrupted society. In the *Gorgias* Socrates takes the famous sophist to task for empowering men who lack knowledge of the health of the *polis* with persuasive techniques that can make them powerful in the city. Yet Plato goes on to show that the effectiveness of these techniques is dependent on the debasement of the public at large, which prefers sophistic flattery to the sobering critical inquiry of philosophers. Socrates grants to Gorgias that one trained in rhetoric by a sophist will best a physician in public competition for a post like that of our Surgeon General, but only when the competition takes place before a public ignorant of the art of medicine and preferring the pleasant but ineffective remedy of a confectioner to the painful treatment of a physician. The medical metaphor emerges again at 519, where Socrates accuses the "great" politicians of Athenian history of having "bloated" the city with docks and harbors and tribute money while leaving no room for justice and temperance. He holds Themistocles, Pericles, Cimon, and Miltiades culpable, but by the same token he attributes the political "success" of these figures to their willingness to deliver at the behest of a populace riddled with hubris and *pleonexia*.

As Plato's diagnosis proceeds in the *Gorgias* he is able to avoid a blurring of the lines of responsibility in this situation—without losing sight of the pervasiveness of the disorder—by clearly defining the essential task of the statesman, who is again likened to a physician. A statesman is good if under his care the citizens become better; he is bad if under his rule the citizens become worse, in terms of existential order.[24] Socrates declares this to be the true art of politics, of which he is the only practitioner.[25] With this standard set, it becomes apparent that the supposedly great statesmen of Athens were not statesmen at all but exemplars of *polypragmos-*

---

24. Plato, *Gorgias*, 504e, in *The Collected Dialogues of Plato*, ed. Hamilton and Cairns. See also *Statesman*, 296b–297b, in *The Collected Dialogues of Plato*, ed. Hamilton and Cairns; *Laws*, 960c–d; and Voegelin, *Plato and Aristotle*, 38.

25. Plato, *Gorgias*, 521d. Voegelin interprets this striking passage as a claim on the part of Plato—not Socrates—to the moral authority for which the corrupted public realm of Athens was no longer fit. Given the decidedly un-Socratic tone of the section, this seems plausible as an interpretive point. See Voegelin, *Plato and Aristotle*, 36–39.

*yne,* dilettantish meddlesomeness in matters for which they were radically unsuited. Suitability for founding or ruling a political community is not a function of mundane political "know-how," but of the order established in the soul through the transformative vision of the *Agathon* or Good-in-Itself. And as the *Republic* makes clear, the goodness of a *polis* originates not from its institutional pattern but from the psyche of the founder or ruler who will stamp the pattern of his soul on the institutions. Thus Socrates is quite elaborate in his description of the education that will form the souls of the guardians in his good *polis,* but, as Voegelin observed, Socrates

> roundly refuses to go into details, not only of customs and mores, but even of civil, commercial, and criminal law, because such matters will take care of themselves if only the souls of the legislative rulers are in good order (425a–d). Moreover, he restrains himself deliberately at this point in order not to give the false impression that good order in a polis can be created through institutional devices. He considers it, on the contrary, a symptom of disease in a polis when the citizens are fever- ishly active with patching up this or that gap in the law, but do not dare to touch the well-known source of the multitude of minor evils. [26]

Since it is the animating spirit of a regime and not its institu- tional form that determines the nature of political order, Plato can speak of a sophistic or philosophic *polis* according to the nature of the ruler whose psyche determines its character. The philosophic *polis* is constituted by the rule of a philosopher king or a number of philosophers, and it is a matter of indifference to Socrates whether the institutional form will in fact be monarchical or aris- tocratic. [27] The sophistic *polis* may also take on a variety of forms, none of which is strictly dictated by the nature of sophistry. Thus, the problem with democracy for Plato may not have been technical or structural, except in the restricted sense that sophistic flatterers are somewhat more likely to rise to power (for the same reason that the dubious art of the sophist works best in a crowd). In this case, which was of course the case in Athens at the time of the compo- sition of the *Republic,* the blame for the resulting degradation of

---

26. Voegelin, *Plato and Aristotle,* 87. This is, in essence, the reason why Voegelin considered "constitutionalism" an ideology.

27. Plato, *Republic,* 445c–e. See also Voegelin, *The New Science of Politics,* 62; *Plato and Aristotle,* 70.

politics must be shared between the sophists and the crowd—rather than being ascribed to procedural problems.

The blame must be shared because the sophists, like politicians of the type encountered above, were as much the products as the causes of a spiritually corrupt society. It is less likely that Protagoras corrupted the Hellenes by declaring man to be the measure than that he became famous for articulating an orientation to which they had gradually become accustomed. In Book VI of the *Republic* Socrates argues that it is not the sophists who corrupt the youth but society, which is described as "the greatest of all sophists."[28] Individual sophists are likened to a man who learns by heart the desires and dislikes of a great beast that he is rearing. Having learned which sounds indicate ferocity or tameness in the beast, and which stimuli bring forth these states, the man organizes his observations, calls them wisdom, and proceeds to teach others. Knowing nothing of what is actually good or bad for the beast but only what pleases or displeases it, the man is obviously a charlatan at the art of animal husbandry. Such is the relation of sophist to society. The sophistic politician merely observes and satisfies the desires of the "many-headed beast," as Socrates had stated to the great discomfiture of Callicles in the *Gorgias*.[29] Men such as Callicles only *seem* to call the tune; in truth they mimic "the greatest of all sophists." But again, the blame must be shared because individual sophists and their students have, like the allegorical handler of the beast, unjustly taken it upon themselves to practice an art for which they are wholly unsuited.

Neither the greatness nor the limitations of Plato's diagnosis can be fully appreciated unless we depart from Voegelin's analysis to consider Plato's search for forms of personal and social therapy. This topic will also prove to be of great importance when we turn, in the sixth chapter, to Voegelin's own therapeutic project. What is most noteworthy about Plato's search is the development of an awareness that it was profoundly unlikely (although not impossible) that the transcendent pattern of order experienced in his soul could be made authoritative in the order of society. We know from the *Seventh Letter* and other sources that Plato, like Isaiah, was

28. Plato, *Republic*, 492b; *cf.* Voegelin, *Plato and Aristotle*, 70.
29. Plato, *Gorgias*, 513.

acutely sensitive to the pressures exerted by the corruption of the surrounding society. We are also told that he was the recipient of mystical insights into the transcendent source of order of such magnificence that they could not be distilled into the structure of language.[30] Yet even in this extraordinary tension between the horror of the mundane and the beauty of the transcendent—the same existential tension that gave rise to the metastatic faith of Isaiah and, as we shall see, the parousiasm of the millenarian sects of the Middle Ages—Plato was able to maintain the balance of consciousness. Voegelin regarded the Platonic response to this tension as a model of "noetic control" and contrasted it favorably to the Isaianic response:

> When Plato lets his analysis of right order in society culminate in the symbols of the Philosopher King and the Royal Ruler, he is fully aware of the obstacles presented by human nature and the course of pragmatic history to the event of a paradigmatic polis ever becoming the institution of a society; he stresses both the improbability of its establishment and the inevitability of its decline if it ever should be established. When Isaiah lets his faith culminate in the vision of the Prince of peace who will set the act of faith which the pragmatic king rejects, he believes in the magic power of an act that will transmute the structure of reality, as well as in his own advice as a Gnosis of transmutation.[31]

The *Seventh Letter* indicates that even as a young man Plato was aware that the *poleis* of his time could only be redeemed by an "effort of an almost miraculous kind" (326a). But unlike Isaiah, Plato seems never to have thought such a miracle forthcoming, nor did he think it within his power to bring about a metastasis. This is shown by his perception that even such a miraculous effort would have to be "accompanied by good luck" (326a).

A reform of the Hellenic world along the lines of the *Republic* or *Statesman* was not anticipated for a variety of reasons. We have seen that Plato discounted the possibility that a restructuring of political institutions could penetrate to the spiritual roots of the crisis of the *polis*. Thus there is little reason to believe that the *Republic* was intended as a blueprint for the institutional reform of the *polis*. It is more likely that Plato's intention was to warn against

30. Plato, *Letter VII*, 324c–326b, 341b–e, 343a–344c, in *The Collected Dialogues of Plato*, ed. Hamilton and Cairns.
31. Voegelin, *The Ecumenic Age*, 27.

attempts to embody the Idea through social engineering, by illustrating the unnatural and outlandish means necessary to bring about a perfectly rational and harmonious society. The hypothetical necessity of measures such as a program of eugenics and a thoroughgoing communism would seem to suggest that there is an inherent resistance in the matter of political life to the imposition of the form of transcendentally or philosophically grounded order, and the closing books of the *Republic* make clear Plato's opinion on whether such a regime, if it could come into being, would be able to stand forever against the forces of corruption in the realm of Becoming.[32]

Because Plato understood political disorder as a spiritual rather than as a procedural phenomenon, a reform at the level of institutions would be of no avail unless the spiritual authority of the philosopher could set the pattern for a general spiritual reform. This second option is also highly problematic, as Plato shows with great subtlety. It is conceivable that philosophers might have been able to effect such a reform in at least four ways: (1) by means of the forcible isolation and education of the uncorrupted youth, (2) by means of the propagation of a new religious dogma to replace the corroded cults popularized by epic and tragic poetry, (3) by means of a general appeal from the authority of philosophy to the populace, or (4) by means of a reform of individual leaders through the cathartic effects of Socratic dialectic. These possibilities will be taken up in order.

At the end of Book VII of the *Republic* Socrates suggests that in the event that true philosophers should come to power in a *polis*, the whole population over ten years of age should be sent out to the countryside. He and Glaucon agree that this would be the quickest and easiest way to institute the regime. With the rule of the philosophers established, they could raise the children under ten years of age according to their own manners and laws.[33] Voegelin agreed that the program is ingenious and eminently practical, with the one flaw that it cannot be executed by true philosophers. For as Plato had also seen, "Any attempt to realize the order of the idea by violent means would defeat itself. The authority of the spirit is an authority only if, and when, it is accepted in free-

32. See esp. Plato, *Republic*, 546a.
33. *Ibid.*, 541a.

dom."[34] While Plato evidently did not intend that the program be put into practice, Voegelin observed that

> we see it followed almost to the letter in our own time when bands of sectarians gain power in a country and begin to reconstruct the people according to their own manners and character by eliminating the older generation from public life and bringing up the children in a new creed.[35]

There is ample evidence of this in the Hitler Youth of Nazi Germany, the Komsomol and Young Pioneers of the Soviet Union, the Red Guards of the Cultural Revolution, and in the wholesale slaughter of the older generation in Cambodia by children under the direction of the Khmer Rouge. Each of these grotesque attempts at the forcible embodiment of a creed has proven what Plato already knew: "The disorder of the polis cannot be repaired by descending to the level of disorder, by adding a new faction to the existing ones. The tyranny of the rabble cannot be transformed into freedom by countering it with a tyranny of the spirit."[36]

Even if it is recognized that a creed cannot be forcibly embodied, it would still be conceivable that a restorative creed could be publicized in such a way that through *peitho*, existential persuasion, the souls of the citizens would be reordered. The problem here is that philosophy, as understood by both Plato and Voegelin, can issue in no such creed, political or religious. The communicable results of philosophizing are symbols of experience, not dogmas or doctrines. In fact, the latter are produced by hypostatizing philosophical symbols, which in simpler terms means transforming them into something they are not—for purposes to which they should not be put.[37] We can again consult the *Seventh Letter* for Plato's assessment of public doctrine as a medium for the transmission of philosophical experience:

> I certainly have composed no work in regard to it, nor shall I ever do so in the future, for there is no way of putting it in words. . . . If I thought it possible to deal adequately with the subject in a treatise or a

34. Voegelin, *Plato and Aristotle*, 135.

35. *Ibid*.

36. *Ibid.*, 143.

37. The problem of the hypostatization of philosophical symbols will be taken up in the final chapter. This is precisely the fate that befell Plato's philosophy at the hands of Dionysius. See Plato, *Letter VII*, 341b. For a brief overview of Voegelin's views regarding hypostatization see Barry Cooper, "Voegelin's Concept of Historiogenesis," in Cooper, *The Political Theory of Eric Voegelin* (Lewiston, 1986), 129–34.

lecture for the general public, what finer achievement would there have been in my life than to write a work of great benefit to mankind and to bring the nature of things to light for all men? I do not, however, think the attempt to tell mankind of these matters a good thing, except in the case of some few who are capable of discovering the truth for themselves with a little guidance. In the case of the rest to do so would excite in some an unjustified contempt in a thoroughly offensive fashion, in others certain lofty and vain hopes, as if they had acquired some awesome lore (341c–342a).[38]

Voegelin therefore simply denied the existence of anything that could rightly be called a religious "doctrine" in Plato's work and insisted with regard to political "doctrine" that "if Plato's evocation of a paradigm of right order is interpreted as a philosopher's opinion about politics, the result will be hopeless nonsense, not worth a word of debate."[39]

Plato did not attempt a reform of Hellas by concocting a theology that would be sufficiently crude so that it *could* be absorbed by everyone, even though it seems that he did attempt a reform of Hellenic theology. This latter effort appears to be one of the objectives underlying the myths of *Gorgias, Republic,* and *Timaeus,* and throughout the dialogues Plato is clearly in competition with the epic and tragic poets over representations of the gods. But an *alethinos logos* or "true story" can provide orientation only to those with experiences of truth; the disoriented soul must be told a *gennaion pseudos,* a "Big Lie," and thus Plato was forced to decide whether to attempt to slip such a lie past his contemporaries in the hope that it could provide enough in the way of spiritual reform to make a political reform possible. He decided not to do so: he called it a lie. The content of the lie or Phoenician Tale in *Republic* III is the truth that all men are brothers.[40] It is called a "big" lie—a "whopper," as Voegelin translates—because it was so little appreciated in Plato's disordered environment. Voegelin suggested that "the introduction of the supreme truth as an unbelievable Big Lie is one of the bitterest passages in a work that heaps so much scorn on Athens."[41]

Thus Plato rejected the possibility of effecting a spiritual reform

38. See also Plato, *Phaedrus,* 275c–e, in *The Collected Dialogues of Plato,* ed. Hamilton and Cairns.
39. Voegelin, *Plato and Aristotle,* 70.
40. Plato, *Republic,* 414b–415b. *Cf.* Voegelin, *Plato and Aristotle,* 105.
41. Voegelin, *Plato and Aristotle,* 105–106.

by means of a dogmatic, public theology. He chose to do no more than to create, in the *Laws*, a minimum set of dogmas for the mass of men whose spiritual orientation was so weak that they would otherwise fall prey to the *nosos* or disease of the soul introduced by misconceptions of the gods.[42] The set is of particular interest because it was not, any more than Plato's work as a whole, an act of abstract speculation but a response to concrete spiritual disorder. At *Republic* 365d–e, and throughout Book X of the *Laws*, Plato calls attention to a contrary set of propositions that apparently were commonly advanced at the time:

> (1) It seems that no gods exist;
> (2) Even if they do exist, they do not care about humanity;
> (3) Even if they care, they can be bribed with gifts and sacrifices.[43]

To these Plato opposes the propositions that the gods do exist, that they do care about humanity, and that they cannot be appeased with bribes. In the *Laws* the creed is to be enforced by the Nocturnal Council. There is no suggestion that the creed can serve by itself as an adequate theology, or that it will even be effective as an antidote against the *nosos* when it has taken root in a soul. If we may pursue the metaphor, the creed represents a purely preventive prescription. As creeds go it is certainly not very detailed—in keeping with the dim view taken by Plato of doctrinal representations of transcendent truth for mass consumption.[44]

A direct appeal for spiritual reform by philosophers would pose equally intractable problems. There is first the difficulty that it is impossible for a multitude to be philosophic, as Socrates asserts in the *Republic*, and that those who do philosophize are, therefore, necessarily blamed by the multitude.[45] In the *Statesman*, the young Socrates agrees with the Eleatic Stranger that no large group of men will indeed be capable of acquiring *any* art, much less the art of ruling (300e). Since the political art does not come within the range of their personal experience, they cannot recognize it even when it is being practiced before their eyes. If a ruler appears who wishes to reform the *polis*, the people cannot know whether he is a true ruler or a tyrant; his appeal will be rejected as a dangerous

---

42. Plato, *Laws*, 888b.
43. See Voegelin, *The World of the Polis*, 274; *Plato and Aristotle*, 263–67.
44. See Plato, *Phaedrus*, 275d–278d.
45. Plato, *Republic*, 494a.

pretension because they cannot believe that anybody is able to rule in the spirit of wisdom and virtue (301c–d).[46]

The tone of these passages is empathetic rather than misanthropic. That the people cannot recognize the authority of the philosopher is disastrous, but it is not, according to Plato, simply the fault of the people. When Socrates proposes that the city should be turned over to philosophers at *Republic* 487d, Adeimantus balks, apparently out of fear that he has been led to an absurd conclusion by dialectical trickery. For after all, Adeimantus suggests, everyone says that those who linger in philosophy become queer and useless to the cities. Surprisingly, Socrates agrees, though he then tries to show that this uselessness is not the fault of true philosophers; philosophers are useless to the cities because the people have no good reason to believe that the practices of the philosopher have anything to do with ruling. Acquainted as they are with the daily activities of rulers, they find it difficult to believe that one who spends his time in contemplation of eternal being will be well equipped for such tasks. This is perfectly sensible on their part. The pilot of a ship must appear quite mad to a passenger who is unaware that the art of navigation requires the pilot to look toward the heavens. Both the pilot and the philosopher will be called stargazers.

The situation is complicated further by the fact that most of those who purport to be philosophers are mere imitators of the philosophic nature.[47] The result is that true philosophers, who seem odd enough as things stand, are innocently associated with a genuinely contemptible lot. That the people are innocent in making this association can be shown by returning to the perspective of the passenger aboard ship. If pilots were widely known to be quacks who continually run their ships aground, we could not help but sympathize with a passenger who would prefer someone at the helm who concerned himself with what lay immediately before the ship. The people cannot be blamed for preferring politicians who concern themselves with what lies immediately before the *polis*. The people can recognize the need for docks and harbors and revenues but have not an inkling of the journey of the soul beyond death, and thus they turn to a Pericles (if they are lucky)

46. See Voegelin, *Plato and Aristotle*, 163.
47. Plato, *Republic*, 491a.

and not to the philosopher who could prepare their souls for that ultimate voyage.

The politicians who preside over the spiritual corruption of society are formidable opponents despite (and to some extent because of) their infirmities of character, as is grudgingly admitted even in the sharpest of Plato's attacks:

> He acquires a tense and bitter shrewdness; he knows how to flatter his master and earn his good graces, but his mind is narrow and crooked. An apprenticeship in slavery has dwarfed and twisted his growth and robbed him of his free spirit, driving him into devious ways, threatening him with fears and dangers. . . . [S]o, turning from the first to lies and the requital of wrong with wrong, warped and stunted, he passes from youth to manhood with no soundness in him and turns out, in the end, a man of formidable intellect—as he imagines.[48]

The philosopher is no match for such a person in political struggle, at least not as long as the most efficient techniques of combat are disdained. Plato seems to have studied this character type intently, and it is probably safe to assume that he articulated the world view of a Thrasymachus or a Callicles with greater clarity than their historical counterparts, if such there were, could have done. Plato could easily have exposed such men to a devastating critique, not in writing but in the Assembly prior to a public appeal for reform, if he had thought this potentially fruitful. But the moral appeal would likely be publicly ridiculed, because the philosopher tends to cut a ridiculous figure in public.

In the *Apology*, Socrates denies the charge of Aristophanes that he is engaged in the study of things below the earth and in the sky, yet he does not deny that philosophers are as bizarre from the perspective of the uninitiated as the *Clouds* had suggested.[49] In *Theaetetus* Socrates admits that although the philosopher spends all of his time inquiring into human nature he is hardly aware of whether his next-door neighbor is man or animal. The inattentiveness that lands Thales in the legendary well is not a quirk limited to an individual but is characteristic of philosophers as a type, and the laughter of the Thracian maidservant will be raised to a din if the philosopher enters the public arena:

48. Plato, *Theaetetus*, 173a–b, in *The Collected Dialogues of Plato*, ed. Hamilton and Cairns.

49. Plato, *Apology*, 18a–19d, in *The Collected Dialogues of Plato*, ed. Hamilton and Cairns; Aristophanes, *Clouds*, in *The Complete Plays of Aristophanes* (Toronto, 1962).

On a public occasion or in private company, in a law court or anywhere else, when he is forced to talk about what lies at his feet or is before his eyes, the whole rabble will join the maidservants in laughing at him, as from inexperience he walks blindly and stumbles into every pitfall. His terrible clumsiness makes him seem so stupid. (174b–c)

If Plato's philosopher is forced to join in the disputations of the Cave he will become a source of laughter; if he actively attempts to free others from their bonds and to take the lead on the way of ascent, they will kill him when an opportunity is presented.[50] As Allan Bloom has argued, Plato's understanding of the difficulties confronting the public dissemination of knowledge stands in stark contrast to the view of the leading figures of the Enlightenment:

> The Enlightenment, taken literally, believed that the light could be brought into the cave and the shadows dispelled. . . . This Socrates denies; the philosopher does not bring light to the cave, he escapes into the light and can lead a few to it; he is a guide, not a torchbearer. . . . The Enlightenment teaches that the cave can be transformed; Socrates teaches that it must be transcended and that this transcendence can be accomplished only by a few.[51]

Thus a public appeal for spiritual reform would be ineffective at best.

One final possibility remains. If a philosopher can guide at least a few souls toward a transcendent orientation that could permit them to resist the attractions of power and passion, perhaps the reform of a number of important citizens could mitigate the corruption of the general public. At the disposal of the Socratic educator is "the art of turning around . . . the whole soul" toward knowledge and justice.[52] Although Socrates insists in the *Republic* that it is impossible for a multitude to be philosophic, it is also asserted that the potential for reorientation exists in the soul of each individual (518c). Moreover, this potential is not exhausted when the malleability of youthful behavior hardens into the habits of adulthood. Thus it would not be necessary to expel the older generation from the city in order to perform the art of turning around indi-

50. Plato, *Republic*, 517a.

51. Allan Bloom, "Interpretive Essay," in *The Republic of Plato*, trans. Bloom, 403. See also John Wild, *Plato's Modern Enemies and the Theory of Natural Law* (Chicago, 1953), 24.

52. Plato, *Republic*, 518c–e.

vidual souls. Even the hardest cases, such as the sophistic politician just described, are susceptible to the cathartic effects of Socratic dialectic.

Shortly after the soul of this politician is described in *Theaetetus* as "dwarfed and twisted, . . . warped and stunted," Socrates acknowledges that a public exhortation to avoid evil "will sound like foolishness to such strong and unscrupulous minds" (177a). Yet this outcome is not inevitable:

> But there is one thing about them; when you get them alone and make them explain their objections to philosophy, then, if they are men enough to face a long examination without running away, it is odd how they end by finding their own arguments unsatisfying. Somehow their flow of eloquence runs dry, and then they become as speechless as an infant. (177b)

In public, the politician can reduce the philosopher to an object of laughter, but in private philosophical inquiry, the situation is reversed:

> Now it is he who is dizzy from hanging at such an unaccustomed height and looking down from mid-air. Lost and dismayed and stammering, he will be laughed at, not by maidservants or the uneducated—they will not see what is happening—but by everyone whose breeding has been the antithesis of a slave's. (175d)[53]

The superior cunning of the sophists and rhetoricians can be overcome in private. The pride that encases their souls can be pierced by dialectical questioning, and if their souls can be opened it is possible that the pattern within the souls could be changed. As we have seen, Plato held that the pattern of public order is largely a function of the pattern that exists in the souls of the leading citizens, and thus it would appear that reform could be brought about by means of inquiry and persuasion.

The problem is that the closed soul can and will resist philosophical therapy, usually with an impressive array of rhetorical tricks, with support from the surrounding environment, and with ultimate success. Not for long will the proud public person be willingly subjected to an inquiry that induces dizziness and stammering. One can simply refuse to enter into discussion, or enter with such prolixity that nothing is accomplished. In the *Protagoras*

53. See also *Gorgias*, 527a.

Socrates complains that politicians and orators are only willing to speak in endless disquisitions: "Ask them the smallest thing supplementary to what they have said, and like a gong which booms out when you strike it and goes on until you lay a hand on it, so our orators at a tiny question spin out a regular Marathon of speech."[54] Voegelin recognized that, given the fragile nature of rational discussion, the politicians' tactic is likely to meet with success:

> It is impossible to pin the speaker down to the subject; it is submerged in a flood of amusing but quite irrelevant digressions, of authoritative quotations, of aptly chosen examples, and of pretentious verbiage. Scrutiny of an idea, discussion in the form of terse argument and counter-argument, which necessitates perhaps fifty exchanges of assertion and retort before the issue is settled, becomes impossible if one of the protagonists replies to every argument with a speech lasting half an hour.[55]

If the philosopher is nevertheless able to unsettle an unwilling partner, inquiry and persuasion can still be defeated by other tricks exposed by Voegelin. "Back-stair psychology" or pejorative labels can ascribe a sinister intention to others or dismiss them altogether. Retreating into a systematic dogmatism or skepticism is another effective means of evasion.[56] If backed into a corner, one can claim that trickery has made the weaker argument the stronger, and if all else fails one can admit defeat but later claim to have been insincere in doing so.[57]

In brief, Plato recognized both the potential and the inherent limitations of rational discussion as a means for spiritual reorientation. His Socrates is often able to lead other characters into embarrassing admissions, and occasionally into a deeper anxiety that might blossom into humility and reverence. Yet instances of deep existential conversion are conspicuously absent from the dialogues.[58] Thrasymachus is charmed into docility in the *Republic*, but

54. Plato, *Protagoras*, 329a–b, in *The Collected Dialogues of Plato*, ed. Hamilton and Cairns.

55. Voegelin, "On Readiness to Rational Discussion," in *Freedom and Serfdom*, ed. Edward T. Gargan (Dordrecht, Netherlands, 1961), 276.

56. *Ibid.*, 279–81. See also *Plato and Aristotle*, 26, 29–30, 43–44.

57. *Cf.* Plato, *Gorgias*, 505c.

58. Because it is a basic principle of Socratic and Platonic thought that pride is the single most important barrier to the development of wisdom, one should not minimize the importance of the Socratic practice of drawing the partner in dialogue

one suspects that the spell will wear off quickly and that, as with Alcibiades, a reversion to old ways is almost assured. In the *Gorgias* Callicles is drawn to admit: "I don't know how it is that your words attract me, Socrates. Yet I feel as most people do: You can't quite convince me" (513c).

This passage is especially illuminating because, at three distinct points in the preceding pages, Socrates had stated that his only objective in the discussion was to obtain the personal assent of Polus and Callicles: "But for my part, if I fail to produce you yourself as my sole witness to testify to the truth of my statements, I shall think that I've accomplished nothing of importance toward solving the matter under discussion" (472b–c).[59] It is made abundantly clear in the dialogue that Socrates fails to meet his own standard of success. Gorgias, Polus, and Callicles are indeed defeated at the dialectical level; each is drawn into a sulky admission related to a contradiction of his initial argument. Socrates is able to do this by showing the monstrous logical conclusions to which their positions lead. Each character chooses to contradict himself rather than embrace such conclusions before an audience, but these choices are not dictated by a recognition of the monstrosity of their positions. All three are exposed as deliberate deceivers of the people whose single aim is to enhance their personal power and pleasure. If they were to admit this, and avoid the embarrassment of self-contradiction, the game would be over; better to accept defeat in one of Socrates' little quibbles and live to plunder on the morrow. All three maintain a consistency on the existential level that is unaffected by their dialectical inconsistency.[60]

---

into doubt or bewilderment (*aporia*). Nevertheless, there is a great difference between making another aware that he is heading up a blind alley and actually putting him on the right track; Socrates seems confident of his ability to perform the former service but expressly disclaims any ability to perform the latter. See *Apology*, 23a–d; *Meno*, 80a–c, 84a–d, in *The Collected Dialogues of Plato*, ed. Hamilton and Cairns; *Theaetetus*, 151c–d; *Sophist*, 230b–233d, in *The Collected Dialogues of Plato*, ed. Hamilton and Cairns.

59. See also Plato, *Gorgias*, 474a, 486e–487b.

60. This interpretation of the dramatic structure of this section of the *Gorgias* is largely owed to James L. Wiser. See his "Philosophy as Political Action: A Reading of the *Gorgias*," *American Journal of Political Science* XIX (1975), 313–22, and "The Force of Reason: On Reading Plato's *Gorgias*," in *The Ethical Dimension of Political Life: Essays in Honor of John H. Hallowell*, ed. Francis Canavan (Durham, N.C., 1983), 49–60.

Socrates seems to recognize that his purpose has not been ful-filled. After Callicles has decided to cut his losses through self-contradiction and to make Socrates proceed on his own, Plato has Socrates change tactics and tell a story of the judgment of the dead. Because rational discussion has failed to penetrate to the deeper consciousness of his patients, Socrates can only attempt to find common experiential ground by eliciting the dreadful pathos that attaches to the apprehension of death. Callicles cannot otherwise be shaken because he knows the way to what he wants within the contracted reality of worldly struggles for power and pleasure, and he is sure that he will not be called to account for his actions. This is assured by his rhetorical training and by the gullibility of his prey. Only the prospect of death can cast a pall over what looks like a very bright future of power after power. The death of the body will entail the death of all that is real for Callicles, who cannot even hope that he is wrong in denying the existence of a spiritual realm. For if the soul were to live on it would come before judges in Hades who are not as gullible as Athenian jurors: stripped of his eloquence and reputation, the rottenness of his soul would be ex-posed, and justice would finally be done.

The beautiful exhortation to virtue that closes the dialogue goes unanswered, but there is little suspense as to the outcome. Socrates began the story with the plea that it is a true one, but he acknowledges that Callicles will take it for a myth. We can safely assume that a character such as Callicles would have found a way to quell whatever disturbance the story might have caused in his soul. The moment of dread will almost always pass and be forgot-ten, with the soul left unreformed. Owing to the persistent corrup-tion of its dominant element, the city will also go unreformed. Socrates does not lead the eminent citizens to a life of reverence and self-examination; he drives them to murderous anger.

Plato would seem to have led us to an impasse. As a physician of the soul and society he was able to diagnose and conceptualize the sources of psychic *nosos* (disease) and *ataxia* (disorder) as *hy-bris, pleonexia, thymos, epithymia, amathia,* and *polypragmosyne.* He was also able to set forth patterns for the right order of the soul and society. Yet remedies that patients cannot stomach are not cures, regardless of their hypothetical effectiveness. It is surely to Plato's credit that during his passionate search for a cure in the midst of a profound social crisis he could calmly instruct his readers about the intricate difficulties that confront such a project.

It must also be remembered that a diagnosis is not invalidated because the remedy for which it calls turns out to be unworkable in practice. As a remedy, *periagoge* is not *simply* unworkable; the turning around of the soul is a symbol developed to recount an actual experience of Plato and possibly of others in his circle as well, but the remedy cannot be socially effective because the *periagoge* cannot be compelled at the behest of the philosopher. Even if the eminent citizens were less unwilling, there would remain the problem that the *periagoge* is not merely a matter of will. As Plato describes the experience in the *Republic*, it is by the agency of some *external* force that a person is "released and suddenly compelled to stand up, to turn his neck around, to walk and look up toward the light" (515c). The Platonic philosopher does not know the force that compelled his own ascent and does not know why he was chosen rather than the others.

In the language of Christianity it is as though the *periagoge* is mysteriously granted by grace, and the recipient of grace does not also receive the capacity to extend it to others. According to Plato's Socrates in the *Republic*, "You should be well aware that, if anything should be saved and become such as it ought in regimes in this kind of condition, it won't be bad if you say that a god's dispensation saved it" (493a). Plato ultimately recognized that only divine dispensation could save his contemporaries. This was also the conviction of certain medieval sectarians, with the difference that unlike Plato they thought themselves capable of calling forth such a dispensation. The impasse at which we are left is the impasse of the *metaxy*. The impasse is set by our inability to either perfect or flee the world and is rich with the tensions of being in—but not of—the world.

For Voegelin these tensions became even more acute with the epiphany of Christ, as will be seen in the following chapter. In parousiasm we will encounter the consciousness in which worldly reality is eclipsed by an apprehension of transcendent perfection. In ideological consciousness it is the transcendent that is eclipsed by the passion for worldly perfection. These post-Christian mutations of metastatic faith and prometheanism stem from the same experiential basis in the human condition—from tensions that Plato could articulate but could not "solve." Plato did not find a socially effective "cure" for pneumapathological consciousness, and in the sixth chapter we shall see whether Voegelin's similar effort met with any greater success. Plato did, however, have advice to offer. In *Theaetetus* the wisdom of the mature Plato is crystallized in a speech of Socrates that simultaneously shows the way and shows that the way is perilous. It is remarkable that a passage that could stand as a stern warning against either basic form of psychic imbalance could also be used to express either form of imbalance:

> Evils, Theodorus, can never be done away with, for the good must always have its contrary; nor have they any place in the divine world, but they must needs haunt this region of our mortal nature. That is why we should make all speed to take flight from this world to the other, and that means becoming like the divine so far as we can, and that again is to become righteous with the help of wisdom. (176a–b)

With modifications no greater than a touch of reification here and there, this passage could be cited with approval either by the gnostic who regards the world as the preserve of an evil second god or by the ideologist who would deify humanity through systematic knowledge. Plato did not, of course, succumb to these temptations, but their presence at the center of his thought suggests that the tensions in the field of consciousness are heightened as one moves toward the point of balance. This in turn shows the ultimate reason why Platonic philosophy cannot provide a socially effective cure for the *nosos* of the psyche. Imbalanced consciousness of either basic variety is a movement *away* from the tension of consciousness in the "In-Between"; Plato's philosophy leads precisely *toward* the tension which the pneumapath would flee.

# 4

## A New Heaven and a New Earth

One of the most remarkable aspects of Voegelin's work was his ability to break with his own theoretical programs. Writers are frequently said to be their own toughest critics, but of course we know that they are also frequently their own greatest admirers. This latter tendency was not to be found in Voegelin, whose integrity led him to criticize, in the strongest of terms, the theoretical structures that he had outgrown. Voegelin remarked that he abandoned the "History of Western Political Thought," a four-thousand page manuscript that has yet to be published, after "it dawned on me that the conception of a history of ideas was an ideological deformation of reality."[1] A new program, announced in *The New Science of Politics* and carried halfway to completion in the first three volumes of *Order and History*, was in turn rejected. Voegelin discovered that his own conception of the process of history was vitiated by the very flaw that characterized the ideological philosophies of history he had sought to surpass.[2] This second major break was announced when Voegelin was in his seventies, after *Order and History* had met with lavish praise. He was his own

1. Voegelin, *Autobiographical Reflections*, 63. On this initial break see also Webb, *Eric Voegelin: Philosopher of History*, 6–7; William C. Havard, "Voegelin's Changing Conception of History and Consciousness," in *Eric Voegelin's Search for Order in History*, ed. McKnight, 14–16, 24; Gregor Sebba, "Prelude and Variations on the Theme of Eric Voegelin," in *Eric Voegelin's Thought: A Critical Appraisal*, ed. Sandoz, 15–17.

2. Voegelin's coinage for this flaw is "historiogenesis," or the conception of history as a sequential, unilinear process of advancement from a point of cosmic-divine origin to the present. Voegelin broke with the initial program for *Order and History* after realizing that the five basic types of order with which he was working could not be aligned in any time sequence that would permit the conception of history as a "course." See Voegelin, *The Ecumenic Age*, 1–11, 57–113, and Cooper, "Voegelin's Concept of Historiogenesis," 125–60.

toughest critic in part because his readers simply could not keep up. Commentators are confronted with a body of writings that is not only intrinsically difficult but also internally divided, and because Voegelin was more inclined to explore new directions than to explain precisely what could or could not be salvaged from prior paths, great care must be exercised when pronouncing any thesis a constant in Voegelin's work.

One such constant is Voegelin's view that Christianity is of fundamental importance in the generation and expansion of ideological consciousness. This view informs all of his major writings from *Political Religions* (1938) to *In Search of Order*, despite several intervening shifts in emphasis.[3] Yet it is not immediately apparent how this fact can be squared with the interpretation of the preceding chapters, *viz.*, that Voegelin's last works trace the deepest roots of spiritual disorder into the human condition itself. Why should such special importance be accorded to Christianity, which arose in a particular place at a particular time, if the sources of pneumapathological consciousness are held to be universal and perennial?

We can begin to work toward an answer by recalling the distinction in Chapter 1 between ideological and pneumapathological consciousness. The constant theme in Voegelin's writings is that ideological consciousness is a post- or anti-Christian phenomenon, one that can only be understood by reference to the background of Christian consciousness against which it arose in rebellion. But ideological consciousness is only one variant of pneumapathological consciousness, just as Christianity is only one among a number of modes in which the tensions of existence in the *metaxy* have been symbolized (albeit the most fully differentiated of these modes). Thus it is possible to maintain that the sources of pneuma-

---

3. Voegelin, *Die politischen Religionen* (Vienna, 1938; reprinted with new foreword, Stockholm, 1939; trans. T. J. DiNapoli and E. S. Easterly III as *Political Religions* [Lewiston, N.Y., 1986]). The principal shift in emphasis was away from the view that a series of unfortunate ecclesiastical decisions in the Catholic Church created a vacuum in spiritual leadership and toward a focus on the inherently unstable dynamics of Christian faith itself. On the former, see John A. Gueguen, "Voegelin's *From Enlightenment to Revolution*: A Review Article," *Thomist*, XLII (1978), 128–30. On the latter, see Voegelin, *The New Science of Politics*, 122–26, 129; *The Ecumenic Age*, 17–22, 239–41, 300–304. The former view did not disappear completely in Voegelin's late writings. *Cf.*, *e.g.*, "Response to Professor Altizer's 'A New History and a New but Ancient God?'" in *Eric Voegelin's Thought: A Critical Appraisal*, ed. Sandoz, 191.

pathological consciousness are universal and perennial, in the sense of being derived from tensions that inhere in the human condition, while still maintaining that Christianity is the central formative force behind particular manifestations of spiritual disorder.

The *conditio humana* (in Voegelin's very broad sense of existence in the *metaxy*) has always been what it is—but has not always been recognized for what it is.[4] According to Voegelin, human nature does not change.[5] Yet human understanding of human nature does indeed change, in the process that Voegelin called the differentiation of the truth of existence, and different forms of self-understanding entail differing levels of the tensions inherent in the human condition. The human condition *per se* is not a sufficient condition for the development of pneumapathological consciousness; a variety of circumstances ranging from the personal to the civilizational spheres of existence must coalesce for such a development to occur. The necessary conditions for spiritual disorder arise as soon as human beings become aware of the mystery of divine presence in reality, and Voegelin's analysis of the petroglyphic symbols of the Palaeolithicum suggests that this awareness dates from at least as far back as *ca.* 20,000 B.C.[6] Yet the dim apprehension that humanity does not sit atop the hierarchy of being is not sufficient to bring forth the consciousness that hates the gods or seeks to enlist them in worldly struggles, much less the consciousness that would divinize humanity through the manipulation of immanent reality.

One need not find a Palaeolithic equivalent to Marx to confirm Voegelin's thesis on the perennial nature of the sources of spiritual disorder, because the thesis does not imply that each type of pneumapathological consciousness is somehow built into the hu-

---

4. This simple insight provides the key to understanding why Voegelin sought to develop a philosophy of consciousness *within* a philosophy of history. The principle also helps to explain how Voegelin could maintain that human nature does not change and yet make the statement quoted in the preceding chapter that the men of the seventh century B.C. had no souls, immortal or otherwise. The statement serves the twofold function of illustrating the idea that a soul is not really a soul until it is experienced as the "sensorium of transcendence," while also criticizing those who reify the symbol of *psyche*. On human nature as a historical discovery see *Conversations with Eric Voegelin*, 81.

5. Voegelin, *The New Science of Politics*, 165.

6. Voegelin, "Response to Professor Altizer's 'A New History and a New but Ancient God?'" in *Eric Voegelin's Thought: A Critical Appraisal*, ed. Sandoz, 190.

man organism and may break out at any time. One such as Marx cannot be imagined in the absence of a Judeo-Christian culture that de-divinizes nature by locating the ground of being in a transcendent realm, thus making possible the notion that not only nature but reality itself is without divine forces of order. And even this civilizational atmosphere is not a sufficient condition that will give rise to the advent of elaborate Second Realities such as that offered by Marx. For this to occur the Judeo-Christian culture must be in a phase of decomposition so that the symbols developed to express experiences of the First Reality can be misunderstood by a thinker as untrue propositions about "things."[7] Science and technology must also have developed to the point that a thinker could fall into the illusion that these are sufficient for the creation of supermen. In addition there must appear a deeply alienated individual with vast intellectual powers and an absence of certain virtues of character, and if his Second Reality is not to be a hermitage, he must appear at a time when the critical instruments of philosophy are so little known that "opinions which would have been laughed out of court in the late Middle Ages or the Renaissance"[8] can attain general respectability.

This list of necessary conditions involved in the phenomenon of Marxism could be expanded further, but the point should already be clear. Although the sources of pneumapathological consciousness are rooted in the human condition, which does not change in its essentials, the manifestations of such consciousness have a history because they are shaped by historical events. For Voegelin the single most important event in the history of spiritual order *and* disorder is the epiphany of Christ, which is not to say that Christianity is the "cause" of pneumapathological consciousness, but rather that it has been the most salient of a broad set of catalytic factors that help to explain the particular patterns we have termed parousiasm and ideological consciousness.

Yet the resolution of this problem leads only to another, more difficult issue. Even if it is allowed that a particular "leap in being," such as Christianity, may stand as a catalytic factor independent of the tensions imposed by the human condition itself, it remains to be seen how certain "leaps" can have a greater catalytic effect than

7. See Voegelin, *The Ecumenic Age*, 36–43.
8. Voegelin, *Autobiographical Reflections*, 49.

others. If all of the great conceptions of human existence in the *metaxy* are held to be, in some sense, equivalent, why would certain conceptions pose greater dangers than others? If the human condition is essentially unchanging, and if the various modes of the "opening of the soul" are openings onto the same divine reality, why might the balance of consciousness be more precarious for a Christian than for a Platonist or a Jew? These questions are especially troubling in light of Voegelin's repeated assertions that Christianity at its best provides the most fully differentiated understanding of human existence in the *metaxy*.[9] Voegelin held that the ancient search for the true order of being culminates in the Christian recognition of Jesus as the divine/human mediator between the poles of the *metaxy*. How, then, can this advance in human understanding of the order of being be seen as the great catalyst behind medieval and modern disorders of the soul?

A direct answer is not immediately apparent in any of Voegelin's writings, but it is possible to clarify his argument by extrapolating from his account of the experiential dynamics of the search for order. It will be recalled that for Voegelin it was the experience of contingency—and the anxiety that attends to this experience—that prompts the search for the ground of being. The questions of "where-from" and "what-for" arise from the human condition itself, and Voegelin, following Aristotle, held that the search for understanding is a constant in human history. Voegelin's description of the events in consciousness that initiate the search suggests a plurality of motivations: the seeker desires a true understanding of the ontological structure of reality but also a release from the pressure of anxious uncertainty and the prospect of meaninglessness. These motivations will have been present, according to Voegelin, regardless of whether the results of the search are subsequently expressed mythologically, philosophically, theologically, or even ideologically. Both truth and certainty are sought, but if the truth turns out to be that the order of being is essentially mysterious, the anxiety of uncertainty may be deepened rather than alleviated in the course of the search. Thus, we can make sense of Voegelin's observation that Christianity brought to light the fully differentiated truth of the soul while simultaneously offering less

9. Voegelin, *The New Science of Politics*, 77–79, 164; "On Christianity" (letter to Alfred Schutz of January 1, 1953), in *The Philosophy of Order: Essays on History, Consciousness and Politics*, ed. Opitz and Sebba, 450ff.; "The Gospel and Culture," 77; *The Ecumenic Age*, 303–304.

certainty than more compact understandings. A particular representation of the order of being can be both *more* accurate than prior representations, when measured against maximally differentiated experiences of reality, and yet *less* assuaging of the anxiety that prompts every search for order.

A truth that requires faith for its confirmation will leave many a seeker unsatisfied. Those who do not have or cannot maintain the capacity for gracefully accepting a truth that does not slake the natural human thirst for certainty will have ample motivation to strike out again in search of something more tangible and less trying. This is the sense in which parousiasm and ideological consciousness were regarded by Voegelin as post- or anti-Christian phenomena. The drive for certainty was inflamed rather than calmed by Christianity because "uncertainty is the very essence of Christianity." This well-known observation from *The New Science of Politics* opens a passage in which Voegelin set forth his understanding of the connection between Christian experience and spiritual disorientation with greater conciseness, clarity, and beauty of expression than he achieved in any later work:

> The feeling of security in a "world full of gods" is lost with the gods themselves; when the world is de-divinized, communication with the world-transcendent God is reduced to the tenuous bond of faith, in the sense of Heb. 11:1, as the substance of things hoped for and the proof of things unseen. Ontologically, the substance of things hoped for is nowhere to be found but in faith itself; and, epistemologically, there is no proof for things unseen but again this very faith. The bond is tenuous, indeed, and it may snap easily. The life of the soul in openness toward God, the waiting, the periods of aridity and dullness, guilt and despondency, contrition and repentance, forsakenness and hope against hope, the silent stirrings of love and grace, trembling on the verge of a certainty which if gained is loss [*sic*]—the very lightness of this fabric may prove too heavy a burden for men who lust for massively possessive experience. The danger of a breakdown of faith to a socially relevant degree, now, will increase in the measure in which Christianity is a worldly success, that is, it will grow when Christianity penetrates a civilizational area thoroughly, supported by institutional pressure, and when, at the same time, it undergoes an internal process of spiritualization, of a more complete realization of its essence. The more people are drawn into the Christian orbit, the greater will be the number among them who do not have the spiritual stamina for the heroic adventure of the soul that is Christianity.[10]

10. Voegelin, *The New Science of Politics*, 122–23.

For Voegelin the truth of Christianity was essentially mysterious,[11] and thus, unlike forms of truth that impose a finality upon the process of questioning, Christian consciousness was understood as an ongoing struggle that required great spiritual stamina. Accordingly, Voegelin seemed to take it as natural or inevitable that a Christian culture would produce an almost continual stream of efforts to develop less arduous modes of orientation.[12] Although these forms vary widely in terms of their specific content,[13] two basic tendencies can be observed: one may dispense with the mysteries of transcendent truth by collapsing reality into its immanent dimension, or one may distort Christianity in such a way as to make its truth appear to be certain, immediate, and tangible. Out of the former tendency flow the histories of materialism, scientism, and ideology; out of the latter tendency flow the histories of chiliasm, millenarianism, and apocalyptic hysteria or, put more generally, the history of the phenomena we have termed parousiasm.

The wealth of recent studies of "heretical" Christian groups would seem to corroborate Voegelin's argument, at least to the extent that the apparent pervasiveness of parousiastic phenomena suggests a more than accidental connection between the rigors of

11. This did not become fully clear prior to Voegelin's increasingly frequent references to "the Unknown God" in his late work. In a 1977 article, Voegelin's long-time friend Gregor Sebba explained what a surprise it had been for him to learn of the essentially mystical character of Voegelin's philosophical activity: "To me," Sebba wrote, "Eric Voegelin has always been an exemplary representative of rationality in the Greek sense, but when I argued that against a statement calling him a mystic philosopher he wrote back: 'This will shock you, but I *am* a mystic philosopher.'" Sebba, "Prelude and Variations on the Theme of Eric Voegelin," *Southern Review*, n.s., XIII (1977), 662. On Voegelin's references to "the Unknown God" see Frederick D. Wilhelmsen, "Professor Voegelin and the Christian Tradition," in Wilhelmsen, *Christianity and Political Philosophy* (Athens, Ga., 1978), 193–208; John A. Gueguen, "Voegelin's *From Enlightenment to Revolution*: A Review Article," 125–26; Rhodes, "Voegelin and Christian Faith," 84–89. On Voegelin's mysticism see Russell Nieli, "Eric Voegelin: Gnosticism, Mysticism, and Modern Radical Politics," *Southern Review*, n.s., XXIII (1987), 340–46.

12. *Cf.* Voegelin, *Science, Politics and Gnosticism*, 108–10.

13. Cohn, *The Pursuit of the Millennium*, 2nd page of unpaginated Introduction: "Millenarian sects and movements have varied in attitude from the most violent aggressiveness to the mildest pacifism and from the most ethereal spirituality to the most earthbound materialism. And they have also varied greatly in social composition and social function." One of the central tenets of Cohn's work, however, is that in its essentials the vision of the millenarian is remarkably consistent from movement to movement.

Christianity and a widely discernible pattern of disorientation. This pervasiveness is not only geographical and chronological but also social, insofar as no segment of the population would seem to have been immune to outbreaks of parousiasm.[14] This is not an unimportant point, despite the fact that Voegelin's argument gives us reason to doubt that social class has much to do with spiritual disorder, because much of the recent literature has been produced by Marxist writers who endeavor to show that heretical movements were actually forms of class struggle.[15] There is indeed a strong historical correlation between various types of hardship or catastrophe and outbreaks of parousiasm, and certain of these types, such as famine, are indeed stratified in their effects along class lines. Yet this is not the case with most types of natural disaster, nor are class distinctions particularly important when plague strikes or an empire is destroyed. Had Voegelin deigned to join in the controversy on the question of whether the roots of heresy are psychic or material, he would probably have argued that both are important but that parousiasm (as distinct from simple doctrinal error) must ultimately be recognized as a phenomenon in consciousness. To be more precise, he might have argued that though purely mundane hardships do lead to acute forms of distress, they only lead to spiritual disorientation when these hardships cannot be reconciled within a consciousness of the world as providentially ordered. The dissonance occasioned by hardship is surely greater for one who must square the indifference of nature and the senseless succession of empires with a providential understanding of the world than for one who need not; in the latter case we might expect reactions such as cynicism or ruthlessness but not the fervent expectation that things must soon be set aright by powers divine.

Christianity has from its inception provided fertile ground for such expectations, but it is important to stress once again that this class of phenomena antedates Christianity and is not a simple "effect" of a Christian "cause." Although the debate as to how far Christ's own teaching was influenced by Jewish apocalypticism has continued since the problem was formulated over eighty years ago

14. *Ibid.* See also Bernard McGinn, *Visions of the End: Apocalyptic Traditions in the Middle Ages* (New York, 1979), 29–30.

15. *Cf.* Cohn, Foreword to *The Pursuit of the Millennium.* This area of Marxist "scholarship" can be traced to Engels. See *The Peasant War in Germany* (Moscow, 1972).

by Johannes Weiss and Albert Schweitzer, there is no longer much doubt that messianism and millenarianism are prominent features of Jewish history.[16] Norman Cohn's account of millenarianism in Jewish history dovetails with Voegelin's view that parousiasm results from the pressure exerted by senseless events *in* history on the consciousness imbued with a sensitivity to the divinely ordained nature *of* history:

> Precisely because they were so utterly certain of being the Chosen People, Jews tended to react to peril, oppression and hardship by phantasies of the total triumph and boundless prosperity which Yahweh, out of his omnipotence, would bestow upon his Elect in the fulness of time. Already in the Prophetical Books there are passages—some of them dating from the eighth century—that foretell how, out of an immense cosmic catastrophe, there will arise a Palestine which will be nothing less than a new Eden, Paradise regained. . . . It will be a just world, where the poor are protected, and a harmonious and peaceful world, where wild and dangerous beasts have become tame and harmless. The moon will shine as the sun and the sun's light will be increased sevenfold. There will be an abundance of water and provender for flocks and herds, for men there will be an abundance of corn and wine and fish and fruit; men and flocks will multiply exceedingly. Freed from disease and sorrow of every kind, doing no more iniquity but living according to the law of Yahweh now written in their hearts, the Chosen People will live in joy and gladness.[17]

It was expected that this paradise would be preceded by pestilence, war, captivity, and the proliferation of every sort of abomination. Thus, the righteous are provided with an explanation of how such tribulations could befall the Chosen People: the tribulations can be seen as portents of the day of Yahweh, a Day of Wrath when the wicked within and the enemy without will be cast down, when the sun and the moon will be darkened, when the heavens will be rolled together and the earth shaken. In this way the senselessness

16. See Johannes Weiss, *Jesus' Proclamation of the Kingdom of God*, ed. and trans. Richard H. Hiers and David L. Holland (Philadelphia, 1971) and Albert Schweitzer, *The Quest for the Historical Jesus*, trans. W. Montgomery (New York, 1968). For texts see James H. Charlesworth, ed., *Apocalyptic Literature and Testaments*, Vol. I of *The Old Testament Pseudepigrapha* (New York, 1983). See also George W. E. Nickelsburg, *Jewish Literature Between the Bible and the Mishnah* (Philadelphia, 1981) and Michael Stone, *Scriptures, Sects, and Visions: A Profile of Judaism from Ezra to the Jewish Revolts* (Philadelphia, 1980).

17. Cohn, *The Pursuit of the Millennium*, 19–20.

of worldly catastrophe becomes not only sensible but even desirable, as a sign that the Day of Yahweh will soon come to pass.

This prophetic vision was to arise again and again, at least in its essential aspects, throughout ancient Jewish history.[18] The Apocalyptic "dream" that occupies chapter 7 of the book of Daniel was composed at the height of the Maccabean revolt, which resulted from the banning of Jewish religious observances by the Seleucid monarch Antiochus IV Epiphanes. Reflecting on the symbolism of this apocalyptic vision, Cohn noted that:

> Already one can recognize the paradigm of what was to become and remain the central phantasy of revolutionary eschatology. The world is dominated by an evil, tyrannous power of boundless destructiveness—a power moreover which is imagined not as simply human but as demonic. The tyranny of that power will become more and more outrageous, the suffering of its victims more and more intolerable—until suddenly the hour will strike when the Saints of God are able to rise up and overthrow it. Then the saints themselves, the chosen, holy people who hitherto have groaned under the oppressor's heel, shall in turn inherit dominion over the whole earth. This will be the culmination of history; the Kingdom of the Saints will not only surpass in glory all previous kingdoms, it will have no successors.[19]

It bears pointing out that when Cohn refers here to a paradigm that became and remained the central phantasy of revolutionary eschatology he refers not only to the later apocalypses of Ezra and Baruch, nor only to that of John or those of medieval times inspired by the Book of Revelation, but also to the revolutionary eschatology of modern ideological movements.[20]

Difficult as it may be to disentangle the Jewish and Christian apocalypticism of the first century A.D., experts generally agree that Christianity gave rise to an independent body of apocalyptic literature.[21] To be sure, a considerable number of Jewish apocalyp-

18. See D. S. Russell, *The Method and Message of Jewish Apocalyptic* (Philadelphia, 1964) and R. H. Charles, *Eschatology: The Doctrine of a Future Life in Israel, Judaism, and Christianity* (New York, 1963).

19. Cohn, *The Pursuit of the Millennium*, 21. For text and commentary see Andre Lacoque, *The Book of Daniel*, trans. David Pellauer (Atlanta, 1979).

20. On the apocalypses of Ezra and Baruch, see Nickelsburg, *Jewish Literature Between the Bible and the Mishnah*, 281–303, and Charles, *Eschatology*, 323–53.

21. Christopher Rowland, *The Open Heaven: A Study of Apocalyptic in Judaism and Early Christianity* (New York, 1982), 358ff.; Russell, *The Method and Message of Jewish*

tic texts were incorporated into the early Christian canon with the adoption of the LXX translation of the Old Testament, many of which were taken over just as they stood and continued to enjoy a widespread popularity well into the third century.[22] Other texts were revised by Christian editors who made them more suitable for their purposes or interpolated them with new material expressing specifically Christian doctrines. The Sibylline Oracles and 2 Esdras, for example, were freely augmented.[23] The popularity of these writings among Christians is not difficult to understand, since the hopes and claims of the early Christian Church were enhanced in their authority by the teachings of these texts concerning "the two ages," the imminent coming of the Messiah, the messianic kingdom, the woes of the last days, the judgment of the world, the resurrection of the dead, the future lot of the wicked and the righteous, etc. Yet it is well established that many apocalyptic texts were composed by Christians. Although some of these are known to us only by name or in fragmentary allusions, many others have survived, among the most important of which are the Apocalypse of Peter, the Shepherd of Hermas, the Epistle of the Apostles, the Apocalypse of Paul, and the Ascension of Isaiah. It was only through a long and controversial process that scriptural authority was denied to these apocryphal writings, which nevertheless retained influence in various Christian communities. It seems that apocalyptic and millenarian writings and movements sprang up as quickly as the Patres could put them down.

Of these movements Montanism is the most widely known. Around A.D. 156 a certain Montanus, who claimed to be the incarnation of the Holy Ghost, began to surround himself with a number of ecstatics whose visionary experiences were brought together to form a "Third Testament."[24] It was asserted that the New Jerusalem foretold in Revelation would soon descend onto Pepuza, an

---

*Apocalyptic*, 34; McGinn, *Visions of the End*, 11–16; Charles, *Eschatology*, 362–400; Cohn, *The Pursuit of the Millennium*, 23–29.

22. Russell, *The Method and Message of Jewish Apocalyptic*, 33–35; W. D. McHardy, Introduction to *The New English Bible: The Apocrypha* (Oxford, 1970), xi–xiii.

23. McGinn, *Visions of the End*, 43–50; Russell, *The Method and Message of Jewish Apocalyptic*, 54–55.

24. Cohn, *The Pursuit of the Millennium*, 25. See also McGinn, *Visions of the End*, 21–27.

obscure Phrygian town, and thus all Christians were summoned there to await the Second Coming. The Montanists were ascetical to the point of inviting martyrdom, which probably resulted from the passage in the Book of Revelation where it is said that those who "were beheaded for the witness of Jesus and for the word of God" are the ones who would reign in the new realm with Christ for a thousand years. Consequently, Cohn has written,

> Nothing was so propitious to the spread of Montanism as persecution; and when, from the year 177 onwards, Christians were being once again persecuted in many provinces of the Empire, Montanism suddenly ceased to be merely a local movement and spread far and wide, not only through Asia Minor but to Africa, Rome, and even Gaul. Although Montanists no longer looked to Phrygia, their confidence in the imminent appearance of the New Jerusalem was unshaken; and this was true even of Tertullian, the most famous theologian in the West at that time, when he joined the movement.[25]

Cohn argues that in expecting the Second Coming from day to day and week to week the Montanists were "following in the footsteps of many, perhaps most, of the earliest Christians."[26]

This judgment appears to be supported both by the writings of certain apocalyptically inclined Fathers of the early Church, such as Lactantius, as well as by the disparaging accounts of heretical sects written by others, such as Eusebius and Augustine.[27] In *The Unmasking and Refutation of False Gnosis* by Irenaeus there can be found a lengthy attack on a variety of movements, along with a telling strain of apocalypticism in Irenaeus' own theology.[28] Although the issue of the orthodoxy of the vast majority of apocalyptic writings was ultimately decided in the negative, the Book of

25. Cohn, *The Pursuit of the Millennium*, 25–26.

26. *Ibid.*, 26.

27. Lactantius, *On the Deaths of the Persecutors* (*De Mortibus Persecutorum*), trans. Mary Francis McDonald, in *Lactantius: The Minor Works* (Washington, D.C. 1965), 137–203; see also McGinn, *Visions of the End*, 23–25; Eusebius; *The History of the Church from Christ to Constantine*, trans. G. A. Williamson (Harmondsworth, U.K., 1965), esp. 149–53; Augustine, *City of God*, trans. Henry Bettenson (Harmondsworth, U.K., 1984), 20:7. Note Augustine's uncharacteristic approval of the prophecies of the Erythraean Sibyl, 18:23.

28. See Irenaeus, *The Unmasking and Refutation of False Gnosis*, esp. 5:25–35. Chapters 25–29 are concerned with the Antichrist; chapter 30 is a bridge section, and chapters 31–35 treat of the chiliastic kingdom. See also Jean Danielou, *The Theology of Jewish Christianity* (Chicago, 1964), 386ff.

Revelation was included in the canon despite misgivings about its compatibility with the idea and mission of the Church. Additional fuel for continued millenarianism was available in the Gospels themselves, most notably in the parallel passages of Matthew 24–25, Mark 13, and Luke 21, as well as in 1 Thessalonians (4: 13–5:11).[29] According to Voegelin, "the life of the early Christian communities was not fixed but oscillated between the eschatological expectation of the parousia that would bring the Kingdom of God[,] and the understanding of the church as the apocalypse of Christ in history."[30]

The conflict between apocalyptic and eschatological Christianity was correctly drawn by Voegelin in this passage, but it is helpful to reverse his usage of these adjectives in deference to the conventions of more recent literature. Following Alois Dempf, Voegelin applied the term *apocalyptic* to the doctrine that the divine will is revealed in history and in the Church, creating a new historical consciousness, in opposition to the *eschatological* millenarianism of the Book of Revelation.[31] While this was an improvement over earlier treatments, which often invoked the terms interchangeably, more recent works generally regard apocalypticism as a species of the genus eschatology.[32] All Christian conceptions of history are eschatological in the sense that history is understood as a teleological process toward a scripturally revealed End, but there is a vast difference between viewing the events of one's time in the light of the End of history and seeing them as the last events themselves. Augustine provides the classic example that it is possible to be deeply eschatological and yet distinctly anti-apocalyptic. The conflict between these orientations, or what Voegelin called the "oscillation" between them, was not resolved with doctrinal finality until Augustine was able to "de-apocalypticize" the Book of

29. For a close reading of other brief passages see Rowland, *The Open Heaven*, 358–402.

30. Voegelin, *The New Science of Politics*, 107–108. The comma in this sentence (which greatly adds to its clarity) does not appear in the original due, according to Gregor Sebba, to an error in typesetting. See "Prelude and Variations on the Theme of Eric Voegelin," in *Eric Voegelin's Thought: A Critical Appraisal*, ed. Sandoz, 23, n. 40.

31. Alois Dempf, *Sacrum Imperium* (Darmstadt, 1962), 77ff. Voegelin's usage of the term *apocalyptic* on p. 33 of *In Search of Order* suggests that he ultimately recognized the need for this reversal.

32. McGinn, *Visions of the End*, 3–5.

Revelation with his highly allegorical interpretation in *City of God* 20:7–17. Augustine dismissed literal beliefs in the imminence of the millennium as "ridiculous fables" and declared that "the Church even now is the kingdom of Christ and the kingdom of heaven. And so even now his saints reign with him. . . . For those people reign with Christ who . . . are in his kingdom in such a way that they *are* his kingdom."[33] Augustine held that the Book of Revelation was to be understood not as a prophecy of impending events but rather as an allegory of the struggle between good and evil in the present life of the Church and in the life of individual souls.

According to Voegelin, "The Augustinian conception of the church, without substantial change, remained historically effective to the end of the Middle Ages."[34] Literalist interpretations of Revelation were thenceforth pushed beyond the pale, but not by any means out of existence. Despite what Voegelin called Augustine's "tour de force of interpretation," an unbroken stream of millennial, apocalyptic, and parousiastic literature was turned out between the years 400 and 1100; that is, in the years prior to the writings and sects that have become widely known through Cohn's *The Pursuit of the Millennium*. Much of this literature has now been compiled and translated into English.[35] Its very existence helps to corroborate Voegelin's assertion, quoted above, that "the continuum of metastatic movements has never been broken"—an assertion that in turn is central to the corroboration of Voegelin's phenomenology of spiritual disorientation. The entire range of symbols engendered by the chiliastic excitement of certain early Christians, and preserved within the canon in Revelation, continued to appear in the interim between Augustine's work and the first serious challenge to it, that of Joachim of Fiore in the twelfth century. The apocalyptic literature of the period abounds with the setting of dates for the apocalypse, visions of a descending New Jerusalem, the strange lore of Gog and Magog, and continual identifications of this or that figure as the Antichrist. The persistent reappearance of these symbols suggests that they were important for conveying

33. Augustine, *City of God*, 20:9. Emphasis in original.
34. Voegelin, *The New Science of Politics*, 109.
35. See the texts and commentary in McGinn, *Visions of the End*, 37–125, and his bibliography.

experiences that may grow out of Christianity itself and not merely out of the persecutions or prophecies of early times.

Although the millennial movements of the Middle Ages are simply too numerous—and the literature about them too extensive[36]—to be described in any detail, we can at least get a sense of Voegelin's understanding of the experiential dynamics of these movements from his analysis of why Augustine's philosophy of history and doctrine of the Church could not effectively prevent continued outbreaks of parousiasm. Augustine was indeed successful in turning Church doctrine away from chiliasm and apocalypticism by forwarding a view of the present as the *saeculum senescens*, the time of waiting for the Parousia, which would last for an unknowable period of time.[37] The present age was cast as the last of six historical epochs, which were not demarcated by mundane events because such events were, by definition, devoid of true meaningfulness.[38] The first epoch extends from Adam to the Flood, the second to Abraham, and the third to David. The fourth extends from David to the Babylonian Exile, and the fifth to the birth of Christ. With the birth of Christ the succession of truly meaningful events in history comes to an end. The meaning of history as salvation is revealed with a finality such that for Augustine the historical task of the Church is not to develop the Christian truth through successive stages (as with Joachim) but simply to spread it.[39] While this understanding of the Christian mission served as something of a barrier against heretical innovations, it also served, according to Voegelin, as a barrier to creativity that could not long stand against the human penchant for novelty.[40] Also restricted was the still more powerful penchant of humans to endow their mundane or political activity with a sense of mission—a penchant so strong that it is probably better described as a psychological need. Although Voegelin held that this need can give rise to such delusions as the notion that history culminates in one's

---

36. See the excellent bibliographies in Gordon Leff, *Heresy in the Later Middle Ages* (Manchester, 1967); Walter L. Wakefield and Austin P. Evans, *Heresies of the High Middle Ages* (New York, 1969); McGinn, *Visions of the End*; Cohn, *The Pursuit of the Millennium.*

37. Augustine, *City of God*, 22:30. See also Voegelin, *Science, Politics and Gnosticism*, 92–93, and *The Ecumenic Age*, 172, 268.

38. See Löwith, *Meaning in History*, 166.

39. *Ibid.*, 145, 166.

40. See Voegelin, *From Enlightenment to Revolution*, 14.

own efforts, he also held that the tendency to conceive of one's political activity as an expression of a particular understanding of transcendent order is not, in and of itself, pathological.[41] He found evidence of this tendency in the earliest historical records of major (*i.e.*, post-tribal) political societies:

> All of the early Empires, Near Eastern as well as Far Eastern, under-stood themselves as representatives of a transcendent order. . . . Whether one turns to the earliest Chinese sources in the *Shu King* or to the inscriptions of Egypt, Babylonia, Assyria, or Persia, one uniformly finds the order of the empire interpreted as a representation of cosmic order in the medium of human society. The empire is a cosmic ana-logue, a little world reflecting the order of the great, comprehensive world.[42]

When the implications of the discovery of the human soul were finally clearly drawn in the work of Plato, it was recognized that "a political society should be not only a microcosmos but also a ma-croanthropos."[43] With this shift in accent the pattern for political order is found not in the rhythms of the cosmos but rather in the pattern of the souls of the leading citizens. Yet the element of tran-scendent representation was not lost, since a political order was understood to be healthy to the extent that the patterns of these souls were attuned to the transcendent pattern of order. But with Augustine's rigid articulation of Christian society into distinct spir-itual and temporal orders, the political realm was de-divinized to the point of being devalued. Augustine provided a valuable correc-tive against the more grotesque manifestations of the human ten-dency to attach transcendent significance to mundane activity, but for Voegelin this accomplishment was at the cost of virtually ob-scuring the significance of political activity *per se*.[44] In support of Voegelin's contention we might consider this passage from Book V of the *City of God*: "As for this mortal life, which ends after a few days' course, what does it matter under whose rule a man lives, being so soon to die, provided that the rulers do not force him to impious and wicked acts?"[45] If human beings have a need (or at least a continual tendency) to understand their worldly po-

41. Voegelin, *The New Science of Politics*, 27–28, 168–69.
42. *Ibid.*, 54.
43. *Ibid.*, 61.
44. See Voegelin, "World Empire and the Unity of Mankind," 184–88.
45. Augustine, *City of God*, 5:17.

litical activity as transcendentally meaningful, as Voegelin's analysis suggests, then we may expect that, when a civilization no longer leaves room for the expression of this need, the need will make room for itself. In a striking passage that Voegelin admitted was somewhat drastic, he seems to have drawn precisely this conclusion:

> If we formulate the deepest sentiment that causes the spiritual tensions of the West since the Middle Ages somewhat drastically, we might say that the bearers of Western civilization do not want to be a senseless appendix to the history of antiquity; they want to understand their civilizational existence as meaningful. If the Church is not able to see the hand of God in the History of mankind, men will not remain satisfied but will go out in search of gods who take some interest in their civilizational efforts. The Church has abandoned its spiritual leadership insofar as it has left post-medieval man without guidance in his endeavors to find meaning in a complex civilization which differs profoundly in its horizons of reason, nature and history from the ancient that was absorbed and penetrated by the early Church. In the face of this abandonment of the *magisterium* it is futile when Christian thinkers accuse the *superbia* of modern man who will not submit to the authority of the Church. There is always enough *superbia* in man to bolster the accusation plausibly, but the complaint dodges the real issue: that man in search of authority cannot find it in the Church, through no fault of his own.[46]

Augustine's symbolization of the era after Christ as the *saeculum senescens* remained effective only on the doctrinal level. As we have seen, parousiastic ideas and movements were pushed beyond the pale of orthodoxy but not out of existence, and by the twelfth century the expansion of medieval civilization and the rise of monastic orders led to such reinterpretations of history as the *Chronica* of Otto of Freising and the writings of Joachim of Fiore.[47] According

---

46. Voegelin, *From Enlightenment to Revolution*, 22–23.

47. Voegelin, *The Ecumenic Age*, 268. Otto and Joachim were not alone in their unwillingness to conceive of their own age as a mere time of waiting, nor were they alone in regarding the rise of monastic orders as a portent of an impending advance in a historical process of spiritual fulfillment. In a chapter on Joachim from Voegelin's unpublished "History of Western Political Thought," three other writers are also mentioned in this connection: Rupert of Deutz (*De sancta trinitate et operibus eius*, ca. 1110); Honorius of Autun (*Summa Gloria*, ca. 1120); Anselm of Havelberg (*Liber de una forma credendi et multiformitate vivendi*, ca. 1135). The tremendous enthusiasm with which Joachim's writings were received by figures such as Hugh of

to Voegelin, both Otto and Joachim interpreted the flowering of the monastic life as an event that indicated a meaningful advance in the process of transfiguration after the age of Christ and before the end of the world.[48] Joachim broke with the Augustinian conception of Christian society by applying the symbol of the Trinity to the course of history in such a way that the impending era could be understood not as a mere time of waiting but as the time of ultimate spiritual consummation. The history of mankind was divided into three ages, which were said to correspond to the three Persons of the Trinity. The first period of the world, the age of the Father, was succeeded upon the appearance of Christ by the age of the Son. According to Joachim's calculations (based principally on Rev. 11:3 and 12:6, along with Matt. 1:17), the third age would appear within two generations. The age of the Spirit would entail the ultimate revelation of God's purpose on earth and in time, and inasmuch as the papacy and clerical hierarchy were institutions of the second epoch, Joachim held that the existing Church would have to yield to the coming Church of the Spirit.[49]

Joachim did not claim himself to be the *Dux e Babylone* who would usher in the coming era, nor did he, as a man of the second era, criticize the contemporary Church or draw revolutionary conclusions from his visions. His followers were not nearly so circumspect, and as the year 1260 drew near there broke out an unusually intense and widespread rash of parousiastic excitement.[50] That the events prophesied by Joachim and Otto failed to materialize does not negate the importance of their reinterpretations of history, for the pattern of a three-age history that leads to a final, perfected epoch was to act as a powerful influence in post-medieval symbolizations of ideological consciousness.[51] For Voegelin these reinter-

---

Digne, Gerard of Borgo San Domingo, and John of Parma suggests that the Augustinian conception of the *saeculum senescens* had worn thin as a deterrent to millenarianism. See Leff, *Heresy in the Later Middle Ages*, 68–83.

48. Voegelin, *The Ecumenic Age*, 268; *The New Science of Politics*, 110–13, 119. See also Löwith, *Meaning in History*, 150–51.

49. *Cf.* Löwith, *Meaning in History*, 149–51, and Leff, *Heresy in the Later Middle Ages*, 77–79.

50. Cohn, *The Pursuit of the Millennium*, 110–18, 128–31.

51. Voegelin, *From Enlightenment to Revolution*, 11–12; *The New Science of Politics*, 111–12. Joachim's was not the only three-age conception of history during medieval

pretations of history are crucial for an understanding of the continuity that binds medieval parousiasm and modern ideological consciousness:

> Though Otto's and Joachim's metastatic expectations were no more fulfilled than Paul's, their symbolisms marked a decisive step in the self-interpretation of Western society, because they created a new pattern of expectations: The age of perfection, the *teleion*, would be an age of the Spirit beyond the age of Christ; it would bring the free association of spiritualists, of men of the new monastic type, unencumbered by institutions; and it would be an age, therefore, beyond the establishment of church and empire. The potentialities of the new type of expectations became apparent in the fourteenth century, when Petrarca (1304–1374) symbolized the age that began with Christ as the *tenebrae*, as the dark age, that now would be followed by a renewal of the *lux* of pagan antiquity. The monk as the figure promising a new age was succeeded by the humanist intellectual. Hegel, finally, brought the potential to fruition by identifying revelation with a dialectical process of consciousness in history, a process that reached its *teleion* in his own "system of science." . . . The Parousia, at last, had occurred.[52]

As we turn in the following chapter to modern ideological consciousness, we will find that expectations of an age of perfection were as compatible with movements stressing reason and enlightenment as with those grounded in revelation and mysticism. Yet the differences between these movements must not be minimized. The apocalyptic, millenarian movements associated with parousiastic consciousness were emphatically religious in character (regardless of the question of orthodoxy), whereas modern ideologies are uniformly and explicitly anti-religious. The perfected realm anticipated by the parousiast is envisioned either as a heavenly state beyond the imperfections of the world or as a new world made heavenly through a massive influx of transcendent order. Conversely, the perfected realm anticipated by the ideologist is envisioned as a worldly paradise achieved through a flowering of purely human potentialities hitherto stunted by the worship of imagined gods. Parousiasts look to God as the agent who will transform reality, with perhaps a bit of preparatory assistance from

---

times. See Norman Cohn's account of the doctrines of the Amaurians in *The Pursuit of the Millennium*, 154–56.

52. Voegelin, *The Ecumenic Age*, 268.

the Elect; ideologists look to immanent historical laws or the inevitable ascendancy of a particular class, race, or methodology.

In light of these dramatic dissimilarities, we must anticipate the question of whether the elements of continuity between parousiasm and ideological consciousness are sufficiently strong to warrant a positive evaluation of Voegelin's attempt to link ideological movements to a trans-historical pattern of spiritual disorientation. There can be little doubt that this attempt would prove unpersuasive if analysis were restricted to the level of surface manifestations, and thus we can at least say that it was prudent for Voegelin to couch the attempt in terms of a theory of consciousness. A comparison of the lives and writings of particular ideologists and parousiasts—even of apparently kindred spirits such as Marx and Thomas Muntzer—would likely lead one to the conclusion that any apparent similarities are vastly outweighed by differences in their thought and activity. If it could be demonstrated that both had fallen prey to forms of disorientation, but not that these forms are in some sense intelligibly equivalent, then Voegelin's objective of finding historical precedents for the disorders of our time would not have been met. Rather than comparing individuals directly, a more promising (if less ambitious) approach is to identify broad patterns of consciousness and then search the writings of individuals for symbols and indications of experiences that fit the general pattern. If we could be convinced that Marx was indeed an ideologist and that Muntzer was a parousiast, and furthermore that ideological consciousness and parousiasm are intelligibly linked as variants of a more general, pneumapathological consciousness, we might then be prepared to conclude that the differences between the two figures are not as daunting as direct comparison would suggest.

Thus, as the focus of our investigation of Voegelin's analysis shifts from parousiasm to ideological consciousness, and as we draw nearer to the task of evaluation, we would expect to find two types of underlying continuity: one suggestive of patterns of experience and symbolization common to various ideologists and another suggestive of a connection between ideologists and pneumapaths in general. If it cannot be shown that the widely varying forms of ideological movements enumerated in Chapter 1 are expressions of a common pattern of consciousness, we would be forced to question the value of Voegelin's diagnostic project as a whole, for if we cannot find good reason to equate ideologies with one another, we cannot legitimately speak of an ideological consciousness at all, much less locate it within the general category of pneumapathological disorientation. To push this line of speculation one stage further, if we find that there are important similarities between metastatic faith, prometheanism, and parousiasm but that we must stop here, we will have found conclusions that may be interesting but that are quite irrelevant to Voegelin's intentions. His excursions into the history of spiritual disorder were not undertaken because this class of phenomena was thought to be of particular value in its own right. As a historian of order, Voegelin would have been content to leave analysis of the materials we have encountered to this point to those who are interested in the history of various types of disorder; but as a political scientist and a man of the twentieth century, he regarded the task of understanding the ideological disorders of his age as a matter of obligation.[53] It was the pursuit of this objective that led him to search for historical precedents. The question that must ultimately determine our evaluation of Voegelin's diagnostic project is whether earlier patterns of disorder can be related not to each other but specifically to ideological consciousness. This question will be taken up in the following chapter.

53. Voegelin, *Science, Politics and Gnosticism*, 22–23, 49; *From Enlightenment to Revolution*, 247.

# 5

# Ideology, Consciousness, and History

Since the concept of "ideology" was first used by Antoine Destutt de Tracy at the time of the French Revolution, it has taken on a broad array of connotations.[1] Initially conceived simply as the science of ideas, the term has generally come to be reserved for political ideas in particular. Contemporary political scientists utilize the term in a bewildering variety of contexts, but four basic patterns of usage can be discerned. Analysts of international politics—especially those of the "realist" school—often use the term to denote any set of principles that serves to justify or conceal the true aims of a nation-state's leaders in their struggle for power.[2] Public-opinion researchers and empirically oriented students of political behavior are more likely to refer to ideology as a characteristic of the political outlook of individuals, in which sense an ideology is an internally consistent set of opinions and beliefs. Individuals who exhibit greater degrees of consistency are said to possess greater "ideological constraint" than those who adopt conflicting views in an *ad hoc* manner.[3]

Among political theorists the concept of ideology is almost always used in one of two senses, both of which are pejorative. Writers in the Marxist tradition generally refer to ideology as a type of false consciousness that results from either a limited histori-

1. For brief histories of the concept, see George Lichtheim, *"The Concept of Ideology" and Other Essays* (New York, 1967), 3–46; Karl Manheim, *Ideology and Utopia* (New York, 1936), 55–108; David McLellan, *Ideology* (Minneapolis, 1986), 1–63.

2. *E.g.*, Hans J. Morgenthau, *Politics Among Nations: The Struggle for Power and Peace* (6th ed.; New York, 1985), 101–104, 243–47.

3. *E.g.*, W. Lance Bennett, *Public Opinion in American Politics* (New York, 1980), 48–56; Kenneth M. Dolbeare and Linda J. Medcalf, *American Ideologies Today* (London, 1988), 4–7.

cal perspective, distortions imposed by class interest, or intellectual domination by a ruling elite.[4] Among non-Marxist theorists, ideology is viewed as a form or style of political thought distinct from—and by nature inferior to—authentic political philosophy.[5] That the emphasis here is more on form than on content is evinced by the fact that mutually hostile creeds or "isms" are grouped under a single overarching rubric. Since those whose doctrines are classified in this way can easily point to elements that differentiate their creeds from others in the set, it would seem that the very use of the term in this sense presupposes an identification of common elements that unite widely disparate bodies of thought.

Although it is not possible here to track down aspects of ideology that have been proposed as these common elements by analysts other than Voegelin, it is important to note the general agreement among contemporary theorists that the last two hundred years have witnessed a proliferation of novel political orientations that conform to some shared pattern. In this respect Voegelin's analysis of ideological consciousness is situated in the mainstream of current conceptions. His departure from the mainstream consisted most directly in the assertion that ideologies are the products not of fallacious thinking on modern problems, but rather of a deeper disturbance in consciousness bearing only an inessential connection to the specifically modern aspects of the political world. For Voegelin it was not the atheistic, systematic, quasi-scientific, progressivist, or activist tendencies of modern ideologies that represented their common, central elements. He indeed recognized these tendencies, but only as epiphenomenal manifestations of a revolt against the human condition within the order of being. From Voegelin's perspective, an ideology was less a body of propositions about things in the world than an effort to conjure up a new and improved world. Thus, since ideologies are constructed for the purpose of enacting such a transformation, activism and progressivism are inherent to their character. Moreover, since the very idea of a transformed world would be senseless if not accompanied by a rejection of the notion that the "old world" is divinely

---

4. For the most extensive presentation of Marx's concept see Marx and Engels, *The German Ideology*, 33–83. See also Bhikhu Parekh, *Marx's Theory of Ideology* (London, 1982).

5. *Cf., e.g.*, Dante Germino, *Beyond Ideology: The Revival of Political Theory* (New York, 1967), 45–67; Elizabeth M. James, *Political Theory: An Introduction to Interpretation* (Chicago, 1976), 6–7.

created and sustained, it is to be expected that ideologies would tend toward atheism. Finally, since the preferred means for predicting and effecting the transformation will be those that appear most promising at a given time, it is equally unsurprising that nineteenth- and twentieth-century ideologists would at least have affected the systematic form of the modern natural sciences.

Voegelin's late work suggests that the fundamental motivations for a project of world transformation arise from the human condition as such, rather than from the historical circumstances of a particular period.[6] This does not imply, however, that the characteristics of a period will play no part in determining the phenomenal aspects or the popular appeal of such projects. Although Voegelin's analysis does have the effect of "de-modernizing" the essence of ideology, it would be incorrect to state that his understanding of ideology is ahistorical. We have already seen that the spiritual demands imposed by Christianity are of decisive importance in Voegelin's account of the consciousness in search of comprehensive and final certainty, and that this holds true for ideologists as well as parousiasts. The historical axis of the typology introduced in Chapter 1 is based on a historical event, the epiphany of Christ, and the subsequent history of the Church's struggle to maintain itself through dogmatization and social compromise forms the immediate background for ideological rejections of Christianity.[7]

6. Voegelin's late work (at least with regard to his diagnostic analyses) would include those writings published after the release of Volumes II and III of *Order and History* in 1957. It is clear that Voegelin had once seen a more intimate connection between ideology and modernity, because the first chapter of *The New Science of Politics* (1952), which treats of ideological movements, was entitled, "Gnosticism—The Nature of Modernity" (p. 107). By 1959 Voegelin was already speaking of an "essential sameness of attitudes and motives in ancient and modern gnosticism." See the English translation of *Wissenschaft, Politik, und Gnosis* (Voegelin's inaugural lecture at the University of Munich)—*Science, Politics and Gnosticism*, 40. It appears that in the 1970s Voegelin came to doubt whether modernity had a distinct nature at all. The essence of gnosticism (or pneumapathological consciousness) seems to have been completely dissociated with modernity in *The Ecumenic Age* (1974). Nowhere is this more forcefully suggested than in two rhetorical questions from that work: "What exactly is modern about modernity?" and "What is modern about the modern mind?" (7, 68). In neither instance is an answer proposed. Note also Voegelin's references to "the so-called Modern Age" ("On Hegel: A Study in Sorcery," 337), "the so-called modern period" ("Wisdom and the Magic of the Extreme: A Meditation," 268), and "the so-called modernity" (*Autobiographical Reflections*, 102).

7. Voegelin, *Anamnesis*, 191, 194: "The Churches as social organizations . . . historically did everything that could provoke the ideological rebellion, under which

The influences exerted by the historic advances in the natural sciences are also of more than coincidental significance. Ideologies were unscientific by definition for Voegelin,[8] but in his view the relationship amounted to more, as we shall see, than mimicry on the part of ideologists. There can be little doubt that the successes of science in turning natural powers toward human objectives had much to do with ideological conceptions of a worldly paradise. Voegelin recognized that the longing for such a paradise is not simply the result of uncontrolled imagination, but rather of genuine hardship and social trauma:

> The population shifts, the deportations and enslavements, and the interpenetration of cultures reduce men who exercise no control over the proceedings of history to an extreme state of forlornness in the turmoil of the world, of intellectual disorientation, of material and spiritual insecurity. The loss of meaning that results from the breakdown of institutions, civilizations, and ethnic cohesion evokes attempts to regain an understanding of the meaning of human existence in the given conditions of the world.[9]

The broader context of this passage is a discussion of the events in the ancient world that gave rise to Stoicism, the mystery religions, the Heliopolitan slave cults, Hebrew apocalyptic, Christianity, Manichaeism, and Gnosticism. Voegelin was similarly prepared to connect ideological attempts at a recovery of meaning with

---

they suffer today. . . . The antiphilosophical resentment of the ideologist thus is not directed against the classical noesis, of which they know nothing, but against Thomas's design of a propositional 'metaphysics' treating of universals, principles and substances. The ideological rebellion, as I already said, was indeed strongly provoked." See also "Siger de Brabant," *Philosophy and Phenomenological Research*, IV (1944), esp. 523–25; *From Enlightenment to Revolution*, 19–23; "Autobiographical Memoir," quoted in Sandoz, *The Voegelinian Revolution*, 80–81; "Response to Professor Altizer's 'A New History and a New but Ancient God?' " in *Eric Voegelin's Thought: A Critical Appraisal*, ed. Sandoz, 191; John Kirby, "Symbolism and Dogmatism: Voegelin's Distinction," *Ecumenist*, XIII (1975), *passim*.

8. However, this is not to say that ideologies are simply untrue, or that none embodies important truths. Voegelin repeatedly stressed the critical accomplishments of the great ideologists. See *From Enlightenment to Revolution*, 299–301; "History and Gnosis," 65, 82–83; "On Hegel: A Study in Sorcery," 343–44; "The Eclipse of Reality," 189–90.

9. Voegelin, *Science, Politics and Gnosticism*, 8. See also the more extensive enumeration of historical sources of pneumapathological disorientation (which also includes reference to modern sources) in *In Search of Order*, 35–36.

tangible sources of discontent.[10] Thus, with regard to the etiology of particular movements, Voegelin cannot be charged with ignoring events in history in favor of events in consciousness.[11]

Nevertheless, while there is rarely if ever a shortage of tangible sources of discontent in human life, there is also no natural necessity whereby discontent brings forth projects for transforming reality:

> There is enough "darkness" in reality to provide the grievances from which a revolt can start. The life of man is really burdened with the well-known miseries enumerated by Hesiod. We remember his list of hunger, hard work, disease, early death, and the fear of injustices to be suffered by the weaker man at the hands of the more powerful—not to mention the problem of Pandora. Still, as long as our existence is undeformed by fantasies, these miseries are not experienced as senseless. We understand them as the lot of man, mysterious it is true, but as the lot he has to cope with in the organization and conduct of his life, in the fight for survival, the protection of his dependents, the resistance to injustice, and in his spiritual and intellectual response to the mystery of existence. The burden of existence loses its sense, and becomes absurd, only when a dreamer believes himself to possess the power of transfiguring imperfect existence into a lasting state of perfection.[12]

A cataloging of the upheavals of the past two hundred years would certainly provide us with important information for understanding

10. An important case in point, which has perhaps been given insufficient attention by Voegelin's more conservative admirers, is that of Marxism: "Marx has laid his finger on the sore spot of modern industrial society, on the cause of serious trouble (even if the trouble should not take the form of a general communist revolution), that is the growth of economic institutions into a power of such overwhelming influence on the life of every single man, that in the face of such power all talk about human freedom becomes futile. . . . That no economic theorist after Marx was sufficiently interested in the philosophical foundations of his science to explore this problem further, that no modern school of economic theory exists that would understand and develop the very important beginnings of Marx, casts a significant light on this whole branch of science." Voegelin, *From Enlightenment to Revolution*, 299–300.

11. This is, in substance, the charge once leveled against Voegelin by Hannah Arendt: "I think that what separates my approach from Professor Voegelin's is that I proceed from facts and events instead of intellectual affinities and influences." "A Reply" (to Voegelin's review of *The Origins of Totalitarianism*), *Review of Politics*, XV (1953), 80. For Voegelin's response see his "Concluding Remark," esp. 85. In fairness to Arendt it should be noted that her charge was closer to the mark at the time of writing, since Voegelin's break from the methodology of his early studies in the history of ideas was not yet fully apparent.

12. Voegelin, "Wisdom and the Magic of the Extreme," 237–38.

modern ideological movements. But if we are to penetrate to the essence of ideology we must, according to Voegelin, move from the level of pragmatic events to an analysis of consciousness.

In one sense, we find ourselves on familiar ground in the analysis of ideological consciousness. The tensions experienced in the "in-between" reality of the *metaxy* are not susceptible to change; once the divine Beyond of reality has been differentiated from the immanent realm of human existence, the person who searches for meaning and orientation will participate in the same field of tensions as his predecessors.[13] The questioning consciousness in our time, as always, will find that its own existence must be contingent upon a reality that lies beyond its immediate experience. Modern man has no more reason than ancient man to believe that he has caused himself, and hence no less reason to ask the question of the ground. The range of conceivable "answers" to the question will not have changed much since ancient times, and none of the possibilities will offer much hope that the transcendent ground can be known with certainty or compelled to do our bidding.

Even a hard-boiled enemy of metaphysical speculation like Marx recognized that the question of the ground will arise naturally— along with its attendant implications—out of our basic experiences:

> A being only counts itself as independent when it stands on its own feet and it stands on its own feet as long as it owes its existence to itself. A man who lives by the grace of another considers himself a dependent being. But I live completely by the grace of another when I owe him not only the maintenance of my life but when he has also created my life, when he is the source of my life. And my life necessarily has such a ground outside itself if it is not my own creation. The idea of creation is thus one that it is very difficult to drive out of the minds of people. They find it impossible to conceive of nature and man existing through themselves since it contradicts all the evidences of practical life.[14]

In this passage Marx has let his guard down long enough for one to glimpse the inner logic of an ideological rebellion. It is apparent that his problem is not simply one of spiritual obtuseness, for he is reflective enough to perceive that his own existence must have a ground beyond itself. One might ask why this observation does

13. Voegelin, "Equivalences of Experience and Symbolization in History," 216–17.

14. Marx, "Economic and Philosophical Manuscripts of 1844," in *Karl Marx: Selected Writings*, 94.

not prompt him to inquire into the nature of the ground, or to explore the extent to which he could know or participate in its order, but the answer is already before us. Marx knows in advance that the very presence of such a ground will necessitate the recognition of his status as a dependent being, and thus the revolt must begin at this point. Humanity cannot be independent—cannot be the measure—unless Marx can find a way to depict it (however implausibly) as having created itself.

Perhaps Marx's philosophical conscience as a former student of philosophy induced a bit of anxiety at this point. If so, he must have found a way to quell the disturbance, possibly by driving the idea of creation from his own mind. Consistent with his self-appointed role as the modern Prometheus, he then sets out to save others from the anxiety by attempting, difficulties notwithstanding, to drive the idea of creation from their minds as well. If it is objected that we are now reading too much into the passage, and that we have no evidence of any anxiety on Marx's part, we must still ask why he should care whether the idea of creation occurs to people. Is it because he knows that his theory, in which humanity creates itself through productive activity, begs rather than answers the question of the ground? If he believed that his theory could pass scrutiny when measured against "all the evidences of practical life," would he have any reason to wish that the idea of creation might be driven from people's minds? The succeeding paragraph makes it abundantly clear that Marx does not have persuasion in mind when speaking of a "driving out," since his final response to an imaginary critic (who pursues the Aristotelian argument for a *proto arche*) is, "Give up your abstraction and you will give up your question. . . . [D]o not think, do not ask me questions."[15]

This model case of existential closure reveals the sequence of events that, according to Voegelin, typifies the development of ideological consciousness.[16] By using terms such as "revolt," "rebellion," and "closure," Voegelin sought to stress the reactive nature of the ideological impulse. In his view, it is not as though

15. *Ibid.*, 95.

16. Voegelin identifies Marx as a model case in "Wisdom and the Magic of the Extreme," 238. This section of Marx's "Economic and Philosophical Manuscripts of 1844" was regarded by Voegelin as something of a model case within a model case. For his analysis see *Science, Politics and Gnosticism*, 23–28, and *From Enlightenment to Revolution*, 289–91.

an ideologist first discovers some neglected class of phenomena, builds a system explaining its ubiquitous effects, and then, after finding that his system conflicts with classical and Judeo-Christian writings, proceeds to rebel against the latter. It is rather the case that the confrontation with the reality depicted in Christianity and classical philosophy comes first; the system that announces a preferable Second Reality is the product of a prior rebellion. Voegelin's writings would lead us to believe that this reactivity holds true for all of the great ideologists, since none is exempted from the general characterization. This contention would certainly have been strengthened if Voegelin had provided a broad set of particular examples of the phenomenon, but he may have thought that treatments of Marx and Hegel would be sufficient for an understanding of the dynamics of ideological closure.[17]

We have noted that the concept of personal closure against the transcendent ground presupposes a prior exposure. In some instances this exposure will have been more authentic than in others. For example, Voegelin credited Hegel with having penetrated beneath the dogmas and propositional metaphysics of his day to the experiential roots of Christianity and philosophy, unlike thinkers such as Helvetius and Vauvenargues who revolted only against the opaque symbols of traditions they could not fathom.[18] Nevertheless, a certain hostility toward Christianity and classical Greek philosophy would seem to stand as a constant in modern ideologies. One would be hard-pressed to think of a major ideologist who was simply indifferent to these traditions. We must ask, therefore, why these modes of existential orientation would have proven so unsettling.

If it is accepted that aggression is usually preceded by frustration of some sort, the hostility of the ideologist will become intelligible as a response to two characteristics of Christianity and classical philosophy: both run counter to the *libido dominandi* and the longing for ultimate certainty. Perhaps it would be better to say that

17. Voegelin also refers to Hegel as a "prototypical case." See *The Ecumenic Age*, 21; *Science, Politics and Gnosticism*, 40; "Response to Professor Altizer's 'A New History and a New but Ancient God?' " in *Eric Voegelin's Thought: A Critical Appraisal*, ed. Sandoz, 196.

18. On Hegel see *In Search of Order*, 48, 53, 61–62. On Helvetius and Vauvenargues see *From Enlightenment to Revolution*, 36–42, 59. See also "On Classical Studies," *Modern Age*, XVII (1973), 4.

these are experiential characteristics of the human condition or of reality itself, and not of particular traditions of symbolization, but we must account for those cases in which the experience of the ideologist is mediated by a body of hypostatized symbols. In any event, the fundamental alternatives are clear. One may respond to the tensions of the *metaxy* with humility and reverence, faith and the love of wisdom, or one can attempt to eliminate the tension outright by falsifying reality so that the love of wisdom can become its possession.[19] The act of falsification is itself an expression of the will to power, but one that will also pave the way for still more ambitious projects. A transcendent ground cannot be manipulated in pursuance of immanent objectives, and Plato's *sophon* can only be loved, not redirected. But if faith and philosophy could become *gnosis*, a new world filled with manipulative possibilities could be opened.

The new world that is sought in the speculation of the ideologist will necessarily be a truncated world. Philosophy cannot become *gnosis* unless the realm of transcendent experience is cast adrift from the immanent sphere of life, and thus the personal closure of the ideologist will give rise to a stubborn theoretical immanentism. Once the intramundane has eclipsed the divine, the order of the world can, at least conceivably, be known with certainty. If an immanent counterpart to the transcendent ground can be located (as for instance in productive relations or racial composition or scientific rationality), it will then become possible not only to fully understand reality but also to manipulate it to one's liking. The drive for certainty and the will to power will both have gotten their way, simultaneously, through the single act that Voegelin called "the decapitation of being" or the "murder of God."[20]

The speculative murder of God can be accomplished in a more or less subtle manner, but it must be accomplished if man is to emerge as the measure of all things. Hegel, Feuerbach, Marx, and

19. Voegelin, *Science, Politics and Gnosticism*, 42: "Philosophy springs from the love of being; it is man's loving endeavor to perceive the order of being and attune himself to it. Gnosis desires dominion over being; in order to sieze control of being the gnostic constructs his system." On the importance of the distinction between love and possession of wisdom, see "On Hegel: A Study in Sorcery," 342–43; "The Meditative Origin of the Philosophical Knowledge of Order," 43; *In Search of Order*, 54–55.

20. Voegelin, *Science, Politics and Gnosticism*, 54.

Nietzsche are fairly explicit about their intentions, whereas others perform the feat indirectly. Thinkers such as Bacon and Descartes do not mount a frontal assault but push the transcendent ground out of the back door by isolating nature as a self-contained object of inquiry. When nature is declared to be nothing but matter-in-motion, devoid of design and purpose, God can be reduced to the status of a hypothesis and relegated to theologians so that scientists and philosophers can get on with the "real" business of enhancing human power and longevity.[21] Hobbes abolished the tension between love of self and love of God in an equally efficient way.[22] By stating that "there is no such *Finis ultimus* (utmost ayme) nor *Summum Bonum*, (greatest Good,) as is spoken of in the Books of the old Morall Philosophers," Hobbes makes the passions the center of the person.[23] Voltaire simply exchanges the transcendental *pneuma* of Christ for an intramundane *esprit humain* as the object of general history, and the change of heart is replaced by a progress toward ever more enlightened opinions.[24] Helvetius discards the traditional understanding of the growth of the soul as an internal process that is nourished by communication with transcendent reality in favor of the formation of conduct through external management by an enlightened legislator.[25] Turgot, Saint-Simon, and Comte relegate spiritual experience to a bygone phase of human immaturity, with the obvious implication that those who still order their existence by reference to such experiences are unfit for the new age of positivistic rationality.[26] Finally (or at least most re-

21. See Francis Bacon, *The Great Instauration* (Arlington Heights, Ill., 1980), 15–17; René Descartes, "Discourse on the Method of Rightly Conducting the Reason and Seeking Truth in the Field of Science," in Descartes, *Discourse on Method and Meditations*, trans. Lawrence J. Lafleur (Indianapolis, 1960), 44–47.

22. Voegelin wrote that Augustine's analysis of this tension (which is roughly equivalent to Voegelin's characterization of the tension of existence in the *metaxy*) is "philosophically perfect." See Augustine, *St. Augustine on the Psalms*, trans. Scholastica Hebgin and Felicitas Corrigan (Westminster, Md., 1960), Psalm LXIV, and Voegelin, "Configurations of History," in *The Concept of Order*, ed. Paul G. Kuntz (Seattle, 1968), 33; *The New Science of Politics*, 178–84.

23. Thomas Hobbes, *Leviathan* (Harmondsworth, U.K., 1968), Book I, ch. xi, p. 160.

24. Voegelin, *From Enlightenment to Revolution*, 10.

25. *Ibid.*, 70.

26. On Turgot see Voegelin, "Philosophies of History: An Interview with Eric Voegelin," *New Orleans Review*, II (1973), 135–36; *From Enlightenment to Revolution*, 135–36. On Saint-Simon and Comte see *ibid.*, 136–94.

cently), in what Voegelin called the ideologies of biologism and psychologism, the direction in which the *realissimum* of existence is to be sought is inverted from the transcendent realm to genetic coding or psychological conditioning.[27] Voegelin characterized this sequence of deformations as a

> movement of intramundane religious sentiments, pressing the interpretation of history and politics downward from the spirit to the animal basis of existence. Neither the "model" of the secular "sacred history," nor the dogmatic symbols on the level of the "thesis of generality" remain constant; they change continuously in accordance with the stratum of human nature that commands the attention of the time and becomes the object of the process of deification. The rapid descent from reason, through technical and planning intellect, to the economic, psychological and biological levels of human nature, as the dominants in the image of man, is a strong contrast to the imposing stability of the Christian anthropology through eighteen centuries. Once the transcendental anchorage is surrendered, the descent from the rational to the animal nature, so it seems, is inevitable.[28]

In each of the cases discussed above the thinker has, according to Voegelin, defined nature or humanity in such a way that the transcendent ground of spiritual experience is eclipsed. For Voegelin this equivalence on the level of results arose from a deeper equivalence at the level of motivating experiences. Each of these projects was engendered by an inordinate drive for certainty and power, and thus Voegelin could argue for an intelligible unity among these efforts, despite their phenotypical differences. Yet there is also another, rather more obvious commonality that runs through the writings in question. All of these thinkers understood themselves as scientists, regardless of what we might have to say about the value of their work as science. We must be wary of mistaking overenthusiasm or simple errors in judgment for a murderous will to replace God. At what point does science shade over into a scientism that bespeaks a pneumapathological disorder?

In an important article published in 1948, "The Origins of Scientism," Voegelin set forth a characterization of the ideological na-

---

27. Voegelin, *From Enlightenment to Revolution*, 69. Voegelin did not deny that these are important factors in human nature; biology and psychology become biologism and psychologism only when these factors are said to be all there is to human nature. See "Reason: The Classic Experience," in *Anamnesis*, 113–15.

28. Voegelin, *From Enlightenment to Revolution*, 13.

ture of scientism that is strikingly consistent with the views he was expressing some forty years hence. He associated three principal dogmas with the scientistic creed: (1) the assumption that the mathematized science of natural phenomena is a model to which all other sciences ought to conform; (2) that all realms of being are accessible to the methods of the sciences of phenomena; and (3) that all reality that is not accessible to the sciences of phenomena is either irrelevant or, in the more radical form of the dogma, illusionary. Voegelin held that the creed implies two great denials: "it denies the dignity of science to the quest for substance in nature, in man and society, as well as in transcendental reality; and, in the more radical form, it denies the reality of substance." Scientism was defined as "the attempt to treat substance (including man and society and history) as if it were phenomenon."[29] Its origins, according to Voegelin,

> began in a fascination with the new science to the point of underrating and neglecting concern for experiences of the spirit; they developed into the assumption that the new science could create a world view that would substitute for the religious order of the soul; and they culminated, in the nineteenth century, in the dictatorial prohibition, on the part of scientistic thinkers, against asking questions of a metaphysical nature.[30]

In contrast to his definition of scientism, Voegelin once defined science in the following manner:

> Science is a search for truth concerning the nature of the various realms of being. Relevant in science is whatever contributes to the success of this search. Facts are relevant in so far as their knowledge contributes to the study of essence, while methods are adequate in so far as they can be effectively used as means for this end. Different objects require different methods. . . . If the adequacy of a method is not measured by

29. Voegelin, "The Origins of Scientism," *Social Research*, XV (1948), 462–64.

30. *Ibid.*, 462. Voegelin treated these as three distinct phases in the development of scientism as an intellectual movement. The first he traced to the second half of the sixteenth century, the second to the middle of the seventeenth century, and the third to the first lecture of Comte's *Cours de philosophie positive* in 1830. With regard to Comte's prohibition of metaphysical questioning, Voegelin presumably had in mind a passage where Comte describes the positive philosophy, "whose leading characteristic it is to regard as interdicted to human reason those sublime mysteries which theology explains. . . . Theologians and metaphysicians may imagine and refine about such questions; but positive philosophy rejects them." Auguste Comte, *The Positive Philosophy*, trans. Abraham S. Blumberg (New York, 1974), 27, 29.

its usefulness to the purpose of science, if on the contrary the use of a method is made the criterion of science, then the meaning of science as the orientation of man in his world, and as the great instrument for man's understanding of his own position in the universe is lost.[31]

Scientism is the ideological perversion of science through reduction to a single method, a method that does indeed have much to offer in the way of enhanced certainty and power—but that also, if declared to be the only legitimate mode of inquiry, entraps the practitioner within the closed and flattened world of an ideology. For the architects of scientism this closure is not an unfortunate side effect of rigor. Rather, it is precisely because the ideologists of science seek refuge from the tensions and mysteries of an open consciousness that an immanentist method is enshrined.

Scientism is thus an ideology or type of pneumapathological consciousness in its own right, as well as an undercurrent that runs through most modern ideologies. On the basis of Voegelin's analysis, one could say either that scientism is a form of ideology or that ideologies are forms of scientism. This does not mean, however, that those in our day who confine their inquiries to the methods of the natural sciences are pneumapaths. We can observe that work within these methods, which for one such as Comte was a shield against the tensions of open existence, may at the other extreme be nothing more momentous than a job that pays the bills. The clear implication of Voegelin's "The Origins of Scientism" is that the rank and file of modern science are not the active agents of a pneumapathological scientism but, rather, its victims.[32]

31. Voegelin, *The New Science of Politics*, 4–5.

32. Voegelin, "The Origins of Scientism," 491: "The spreading belief [that human existence can be oriented in an absolute sense through the truth of science] has had the result that the magnificent advance of science in western civilization is paralleled by an unspeakable advance of mass ignorance with regard to the problems which are existentially the important ones. . . . Once the scientistic pathos has penetrated the educational institutions of a society, it has become a social force which cannot easily be broken, if it can be broken at all. The problem is no longer one of mere ignorance; if the belief in the self-sufficient ordering of existence through science is socially entrenched, it has become a force which actively prevents the cultivation of human substance and corrodes the surviving elements of cultural tradition still further. The spiritual desire, in the Platonic sense, must be very strong in a young man of our time to overcome the obstacles which social pressure puts in the way of its cultivation." The bracketed interpolation is from the preceding page. For Voegelin's views on contemporary universities, see "On Classical Studies," *passim*.

Voegelin argued that scientism, from its very origins, was the offshoot of an obsession with power. This is apparent enough in Bacon's declaration, "I am laboring to lay the foundation, not of any sect or doctrine, but of human utility and power," and in Descartes' praise of the method by which we will "make ourselves masters and possessors of nature."[33] Yet Voegelin held that the idea of power through science is neither intrinsically pathological nor exclusively modern:

> The idea of power through science has a rational core: if we have knowledge of causal relations we can form means-ends relations; if we have the means we can achieve the end; hence knowledge in this sense is eminently useful. The rational, utilitarian core in itself is of necessity present in all human existence, both personal and social; utilitarian rationality determines a segment of life in primitive as well as advanced civilizations; in itself it is not the specific determinant of any particular society. Under the impact of the modern advance of science, however, this core has acquired the characteristics of a cancerous growth. The rational-utilitarian segment is expanding so strongly in our civilization that the social realization of other values is noticeably weakened. This expansion is carried by the mass creed that the utilitarian domination over nature through science should and will become the exclusive preoccupation of man, as well as the exclusive determinant for the structure of society. In the nineteenth century this idea of utilitarian exclusiveness crystalized in the belief that the dominion of man over man would be replaced by the dominion of man over nature, and that the government of men would be replaced by the administration of things. . . . Here we can see in the raw the fascination with power that exudes from the new science: it is so overwhelming that it blunts one's awareness of the elementary problems of human existence; science becomes an idol that will magically cure the evils of existence and transform the nature of man.[34]

It is the obsession with power, the yearning for a magical cure for the evils of existence, and the desire to transform human nature that stand as equivalences on the level of consciousness among ideologies (and, for that matter, among ideology and metastatic faith, prometheanism and parousiasm).

These projects of magical transformation cannot, of course, be effected until the realm of human nature and society can be brought within the grasp of the methods of the natural sciences.

33. Bacon, *The Great Instauration*, 16; Descartes, "Discourse on Method," 45.
34. Voegelin, "The Origins of Scientism," 486–87.

Although Bacon and Descartes ostensibly disclaimed any intention to take this step, Comte, among others, was clear about its necessity and desirability:

> This general revolution of the human mind is nearly accomplished. We have only to complete the Positive Philosophy by bringing Social phenomena within its comprehension, and afterward consolidating the whole into one body of homogenous doctrine. . . . When it has become complete, its supremacy will take place spontaneously, and will reestablish order through society. . . . All our fundamental conceptions having become homogeneous, the Positive state will be fully established. It can never again change its character, though it will be for ever in course of development by additions of new knowledge.[35]

Although Comte's distinctly millennialist hopes for a positivistic science of society were to take root most dramatically in totalitarian movements, Voegelin argued that they continue to find expression in Western social science and in "the so-called liberal and progressive movements."[36] Here the obsession with power and the longing for a transformed existence takes the form of the belief that the calamities that accompany the age of science must be cured by still more science. The argument runs that, since we have gained dominion over nature through science, we must avoid the misuse of this power by gaining control over our social environment through a corresponding advancement of social science.[37] While Voegelin regarded such a project as impossible on principle, he found more than a simple misconception of science operating within this movement:

> Scientists of more social prestige than human wisdom stand up before large audiences and tell them in all seriousness that social scientists will have to emulate the natural scientists and do their share in order to realize the perfect society. There seems to be no suspicion that the effects of natural science, both beneficial and destructive, are not due to the genius of scientists but to the objective structure of the realm of phenomena which permits the introduction of human action into the chain of cause and effect once the law of the chain has been discovered; [there is] no suspicion that this objective structure does not prevail in the realm of substance. . . . The knowledge of phenomena is certainly the key to their utilitarian mastery, but the understanding of human substance is not the key to the mastery of society and history. The ex-

---

35. Comte, *The Positive Philosophy*, 30, 36.
36. Voegelin, "The Origins of Scientism," 487.
37. *Ibid.*

pansion of the will to power from the realm of phenomena to that of substance, or the attempt to operate in the realm of substance as if it were the realm of phenomena—that is the definition of magic.[38]

It would certainly be incorrect to state that all (or even many) of those who foresee fruitful avenues for the application of quantitative methods in the social sciences have fallen prey to the consciousness of the sorcerer. Indeed, behavioralists in the social sciences are more vulnerable to the charge that their researches are simply irrelevant to questions of substance than to the charge that they have mishandled such questions. The grandiose claims of the 1940s and 1950s seem to have fallen by the wayside, largely due to the self-correcting character of the movement as one that sought not only progressivist objectives but also analytic rigor.[39]

Nevertheless, if the heyday of scientism in the human sciences has passed, the great prestige of the methods of the natural sciences has not, and thus it would be premature to discount Voegelin's observations. His principal fear in the late 1940s was not that scientistic projects would work, but rather that the general infatuation with the natural sciences would lead to atrophy in the historical and philosophical sciences to the extent that traditional sources of sobriety and reorientation would be lost to Western civilization.[40] Although this danger has yet to pass, Voegelin found encouraging signs even before the end of the 1950s. As he moved beyond his early studies in the history of political ideas and into other disciplines, he was led to state that "we are living today in a period of progress in the historical and philosophical sciences that hardly has a parallel in the history of mankind":[41]

38. *Ibid.*, 487–88.

39. Voegelin shifted his criticism in this direction only four years after the publication of "The Origins of Scientism." See *The New Science of Politics*, 1–13. The more grotesque forms of scientism have been pushed into relatively insignificant private institutes for "futuristic studies." On occasion one hears talk of immortality through cryonics or cloning from certain quarters in the academic community, but by and large science as magic has fallen to writers of science fiction. This genre of "literature" is surely significant, as it preserves scientistic consciousness within the popular imagination, but it has failed to eclipse older sources of disorientation such as communal romanticism, astrology, apocalypticism, or popularized forms of Oriental mysticism.

40. See "The Origins of Scientism," 489–94.

41. Voegelin, "Autobiographical Memoir," quoted in Sandoz, *The Voegelinian Revolution*, 82. For evidence that Voegelin found cause for such optimism even in the early 1950s see *The New Science of Politics*, 2–4. In these pages Voegelin identified three parallel periods of progress, each of which arose as a response to crisis: "On

The enormous enlargement of our historical horizon through archaeo-
logical discoveries, critical editions of texts, and a flood of monographic
interpretation is so well known a fact that elaboration is superfluous.
The sources are already at hand; and the convergent interpretations by
orientalists and semitologists, by classical philologists and historians of
antiquity, by theologians and medievalists, facilitate and invite the attempt to use the primary sources as the basis for a philosophical study
of order. . . . We have gained a new freedom in science, and it is a joy
to use it.[42]

While we might question whether this renaissance has become an
important force among the general public, or even within the academic community, the optimism of this passage stands in stark
contrast to the fears expressed by Voegelin in 1948:

As a consequence of the interlocking of science and social power, the
political tentacles of scientistic civilization reach into every nook and
corner of an industrialized society, and with increasing effectiveness
they stretch over the whole globe. There exist only differences, though
very important ones, in the various regions of the global asylum with
regard to the possibility of personal escape into the freedom of the
spirit. What is left is hope—but hope should not obscure the realistic
insight that we who are living today shall never experience freedom of
the spirit in society.[43]

Yet we should not make too much of the finding of a shift
around 1950 from "pessimism" to "optimism" regarding the future
course of scientism, for these passages do not adequately convey
the extent to which Voegelin expressed both sentiments before and
after this time. We shall have occasion in the following chapter to
examine Voegelin's prognoses from the 1970s and 1980s, but here
it will be helpful to note that in the same article from which the
preceding quotation was drawn he implied that civilization would
survive scientism and that historians would survive to view it in
retrospect:

In retrospect the age of science will appear as the greatest power orgy
in the history of mankind; . . . at the bottom of this orgy the historian

---

the largest scale of Western history three such epochs occurred. The foundation of
political science through Plato and Aristotle marked the Hellenic crisis; St. Augustine's *Civitas Dei* marked the crisis of Rome and Christianity; and Hegel's philosophy of law and history marked the first major earthquake of the Western crisis."
    42. Voegelin, *Israel and Revelation*, xii-xiii.
    43. Voegelin, "The Origins of Scientism," 494.

will find a gigantic outburst of magic imagination after the breakdown of the intellectual and spiritual form of medieval high-civilization. The climax of this outburst is the magic dream of creating the superman, the man-made being that will succeed the sorry creature of God's making.[44]

This passage provides us with a point of transition. Having seen the grounds on which Voegelin could argue for an essential equivalence among modern ideologies at the level of consciousness, we must now (and also in the final chapter) ask whether this equivalence can be extended to earlier manifestations of pneumapathological disorientation. Was it legitimate for Voegelin to speak of scientism in the modern world in terms of magic and sorcery? Can modern ideologies be intelligibly connected to gnosticism, hermeticism, and alchemy? Is it really the case that "the prophetic conception of a change in the constitution of being," metastatic faith, "lies at the root of our contemporary beliefs in the perfection of society"?[45]

The first thing that must be said in response to these questions is that Voegelin has simply not provided us with a sufficient amount of material upon which to conclusively decide the issue in his favor. In fairness it should be noted that Voegelin never presumed to have settled the issue so decisively that only irrational persons could fail to be convinced by his account. Nevertheless, the fact remains that one can do much more in the way of corroborating Voegelin's basic thesis if the analysis is conducted at the level of patterns in consciousness rather than at the level of specific traditions and movements in history.

Despite the importance of the concept of gnosticism in his work, Voegelin's discussions of the historical Gnostics and their writings do not amount to more than a few pages. Late in life Voegelin attributed great importance to magic, hermeticism, and alchemy, and yet he provided virtually no explicit treatment of these traditions or of their specific points of connection to modern ideology. His account of metastatic faith was developed from a description of one event involving one prophet, and we are not told why Voegelin did not choose to interpret Isaiah's actions as prompted by God in this one instance when he was willing to do so in others. With regard to the phenomena we have termed prometheanism,

44. *Ibid.*, 488–89.
45. Voegelin, *Israel and Revelation*, xiii.

Voegelin argued from a more fully articulated foundation by dint of his analyses of Homer, Aeschylus, Thucydides, Plato, and Aristotle. Yet his references to a similar diagnosis of the *nosos* of the *psyche* by the Stoics and Cicero are, at least as far as I have been able to follow them, disappointing. What little Voegelin wrote on parousiasm was completed in the 1940s and has yet to be published. Aside from a brief section in *The New Science of Politics* on the radical Puritans in the English revolutions of the seventeenth century, Voegelin's writings in this area are largely confined to a chapter entitled "The People of God" from the abandoned history of political ideas, which, though it provides a number of interesting insights, still falls short of a work like Cohn's *The Pursuit of the Millennium* in terms of developing explicit connections to modern political movements.[46] In brief, those who may wish to establish connections between modern ideological consciousness and specific traditions from the past will discover not only that they must move beyond Voegelin's accounts to the original sources, but that they must also go beyond the materials mentioned by him.

But with all of this said, I am still of the opinion that Voegelin has made a contribution of the greatest importance for our understanding of modern ideological movements—a contribution that can be, moreover, quite persuasive if properly understood. It is at least conceivable that, if enough monographic studies were performed in support of Voegelin's project, we might one day be able to connect ideological consciousness with earlier forms of disorientation in the manner of the comparative study of literature. Several such studies have already been published and others are forthcoming.[47] As I interpret Voegelin, however, the key to the discovery and confirmation of continuities in the history of disordered consciousness is to find such continuities at the level of experiences rather than literary expressions.[48] Stated differently, one who

46. See esp. the concluding chapter to the first edition, published by Secker and Warburg (London, 1957).

47. *E.g.*, David Walsh, "Revising the Renaissance: New Light on the Origins of Modern Political Thought," *Political Science Reviewer*, XI (1981), 27–52; Robert G. Waite, *The Mysticism of Innerworldly Fulfillment: A Study of Jacob Boehme* (Gainesville, 1983). See also Stephen A. McKnight, "The Renaissance Magus and the Modern Messiah," *Religious Studies Review*, V (1979), 81–88; "Understanding Modernity: A Reappraisal of the Gnostic Element," *Intercollegiate Review*, XIV (1979), 107–17; *Sacralizing the Secular: The Renaissance Origins of Modernity* (Baton Rouge, 1989).

48. The issue is not quite this simple, and an example is in order. One such

wished to establish the essential equivalence of, say, ideological consciousness and medieval millenarianism would do better to articulate and compare the general ideological and parousiastic experiences than to attempt a direct comparison of texts. To pursue this example, one can only connect the parousiast's symbol of the "Kingdom of God" with the Marxist "realm of freedom" by showing that both were engendered by an alienated dissatisfaction with worldly conditions and an inordinate longing for a perfected realm that would be, strictly speaking, "otherworldly." Those who anticipate a revolution of the saints are anticipating something very different from a revolution of proletarians, but it is entirely possible that both types of speculation arise from a similar condition in the soul. The student of comparative literature is likely to object if we attempt to draw a literary connection between these two types of revolutionary texts; the historian, on the other hand, may find Voegelin's experiential analysis extremely helpful in the struggle to understand the relationship between movements that are so similar and yet so different.

---

continuity at the level of literary expression would be the symbol of history as a sequence of three ages, of which the third age is the final and ultimate fulfillment of an underlying design or progressive process. As examples of this symbol Voegelin mentioned Joachim of Flora's conception of history as the ages of the Father, Son, and Spirit; Turgot's and Comte's theory of a sequence of theological, metaphysical, and scientific phases; Hegel's dialectic of the three stages of freedom and self-reflective spiritual fulfillment; the Marxian dialectic of the three stages of primitive communism, class society, and final communism; the National Socialist symbol of the Third Realm; and the identification of Moscow as the Third Rome. It would be extraordinarily difficult, if not impossible, to demonstrate that the symbols that appeared later in time were the result of influences exerted by earlier symbolizations, or that the identification of three stages in each case was not a matter only of coincidence. For instance, Marx speaks of five historical stages in *The German Ideology*, 38–44, and of only two in *A Contribution to the Critique of Political Economy* (Moscow, 1970), 20–22. While it may therefore be fruitless to attempt to demonstrate an equivalence among these particular symbols, it is possible to provide a plausible explanation for the continued appearance of the basic symbol by reference to engendering experiences (such as the desire to understand one's efforts as transcendentally significant or one's era as that of final victory or enlightenment, which are in turn engendered by the experiences of uncertainty and the senselessness of mundane events in history). This point is by no means intended to depreciate the efforts of those who are applying the principles of Voegelin's diagnostic project to particular texts, however, because the important experiences can only be articulated by reference to the symbols in which they are expressed.

What is certain is that the historian will also object if we do not disaggregate Voegelin's concept of gnosticism so that we can account for the very real differences in patterns of spiritual disorder in history. The problem here is not that the extent of the literary influences exerted by the historical Gnostics will be doubted, for as I have argued, that was not what Voegelin was driving at when speaking of gnostic tendencies in modern thinkers.[49] The real problem is that, if we can do no better than to subsume the likes of Marx and Muntzer within only one concept, we invite skepticism because we obscure the line between common and distinct elements. It was one of Voegelin's great achievements to have highlighted the commonalities; it is a minor and correctable flaw that his terminology does not do justice to the distinctions.[50]

Because it was Voegelin's intention to draw lines of continuity between patterns of consciousness rather than genres of literature, the lack of extended treatments by Voegelin of writings that would correspond to certain of the patterns is less problematic than it might seem. For example, while we would be in a much better position to evaluate his comments on the enduring significance of metastatic faith if he had cited evidence of its presence in other prophets and provided a more elaborate treatment of the case of Isaiah, we have little reason to believe that no priest or prophet or soothsayer in the ancient world ever thought it possible to invoke divine powers in order to win worldly struggles or transform the conditions of life. We can have reason to doubt that metastatic faith existed in Isaiah without having reason to doubt that it existed at all. If we have cause to believe that millennialism has existed in the ancient, the medieval, and the modern world, we also have cause to welcome a project such as Voegelin's that attempts to account for this continuity through an analysis of consciousness. If it turns out that this continuity can be persuasively traced to certain experiences of the human condition that also help to account for the

49. See Chapter 2 above.

50. The typology set forth in Chapter 1 is intended as a first step toward a solution for this problem. Any such solution must necessarily accomplish three distinct objectives: (1) differentiate between types of spiritual disorientation marked by a desire either to perfect or to flee the world, (2) account for the decisive catalytic effects of Christianity, and (3) embrace all of the resulting varieties of disorientation under a generic concept that, like Voegelin's concept of gnosticism, can reflect their underlying commonalities and perennial appearances.

character of ideological thought and activity, then the political scientist in particular has cause to welcome such a project.

In conclusion, Voegelin's analysis of consciousness is instructive not only for an understanding of the underlying commonalities among ideologies but also for an understanding of the patterns of continuity within the general history of pneumapathological disorientation. In fact, the very experiences Voegelin found essential in making the first type of connection are also those that permitted him to make the second type. These are the experiences of contingency, uncertainty, and alienation, along with the corresponding longings for absoluteness, final certainty, and control. It is the hubristic revolt against the human condition and the will to power in a transfigured reality that unite modern ideologies—and that unite ideological consciousness with metastatic faith, prometheanism, and parousiasm.

# 6

## The Search for Therapeutic Wisdom

It was noted at the outset of this study that Eric Voegelin's response to the civilizational crisis of modernity can be described as a search for the wellsprings of the crisis, for the analytical tools required to render it intelligible, and for appropriate sources of therapy. A number of passages in Voegelin's writings seem to suggest that this might also serve as an accurate description of his theoretical activity as a whole. One objection that would likely be leveled against such a general description would be that it overemphasizes the importance of Voegelin's diagnostic and therapeutic projects, or that Voegelin's quest was first a search for psychic order and only secondarily an attempt to understand and resist the forces of disorder.

While it is certainly not true that Voegelin's philosophy of order was secondary or merely functional to his analysis of disorder, it can be stated with equal certainty that Voegelin's search for order cannot be rightly understood if treated as distinct from his analysis of psychic disorder. Such a statement would run contrary not only to Voegelin's reflections on his own philosophical activity but also to his understanding of philosophy *per se*:

> I have spoken of remedies against the disorder of the time. One of these remedies is philosophical inquiry itself. . . . Philosophy is the love of being through love of divine Being as the source of its order. The Logos of being is the object proper of philosophical inquiry; and the search for truth concerning the order of being cannot be conducted without diagnosing the modes of existence in untruth. The truth of order has to be gained and regained in the perpetual struggle against the fall from it; and the movement toward the truth starts from a man's awareness of his existence in untruth. The diagnostic and therapeutic functions are inseparable in philosophy as a form of existence. And ever since Plato, in the disorder of his time, discovered the connection, philo-

sophical inquiry has been one of the means of establishing islands of order in the disorder of the age. *Order and History* is a philosophical inquiry concerning the order of human existence in society and history. Perhaps it will have its remedial effect—in the modest measure that, in the passionate course of events, is allowed to Philosophy.[1]

These lines, which conclude Voegelin's preface to the first volume of *Order and History*, indicate the centrality of his diagnostic/therapeutic project within his work as a whole.

What is not made clear in these lines, or for that matter in any of the pertinent passages in Voegelin's writings, is what he had in mind when speaking of a "remedy" or "therapy."[2] This is quite surprising in light of Voegelin's stated intentions for *Order and History* and in light of the remark in *Science, Politics and Gnosticism* that "our presentation of the phenomenon [of the spiritual crisis of a society], therefore, will at the same time furnish the remedy for it through therapeutic analysis."[3] The bracketed phrase here, which is interpolated from the preceding sentence in the text, would seem to suggest that Voegelin was considering the possibility of a remedy that might prove effective against both individual disorientation and social crisis. But when read in its entirety, the passage could also suggest that a society in disorder cannot be "cured" but only escaped through an individual reordering.[4]

1. Voegelin, *Israel and Revelation*, xiv. Of his own work, Voegelin said: "It is not simply an academic problem, or a problem in the history of opinion and so on, that evokes my interest in this or that issue in the theory of consciousness, but the very practical problem of mass murder in the twentieth century." Voegelin, "Autobiographical Statement at Age Eighty-Two," in *The Beginning and the Beyond*, ed. Lawrence, 117. See also "The Meditative Origin of the Philosophical Knowledge of Order," in *The Beginning and the Beyond*, ed. Lawrence, 43; Voegelin, *In Search of Order*, 39; and David Walsh, "Voegelin's Response to the Disorder of the Age," *Review of Politics*, XLVI (1984), 266.

2. The most important of these pertinent passages include "Nietzsche, the Crisis, and the War," *Journal of Politics*, VI (1944), 195; "The Origins of Scientism," 488; *Science, Politics and Gnosticism*, 22–23; "On Readiness to Rational Discussion," 283–84; "On Debate and Existence," *Intercollegiate Review*, III (1967), 152; "The Gospel and Culture," 101; "On Hegel: A Study in Sorcery," 349; *Anamnesis*, 188; *The Ecumenic Age*, 184; "Autobiographical Statement at Age Eighty-Two," 118; *In Search of Order*, 39.

3. Voegelin, *Science, Politics and Gnosticism*, 23.

4. The passage runs as follows: "The spiritual disorder of our time, the civilizational crisis of which everyone so readily speaks, does not by any means have to be borne as an inevitable fate; . . . on the contrary, everyone possesses the means of overcoming it in his own life. And our effort would not only indicate the means,

The latter reading seems to receive decisive support from statements such as the following:

> Nobody can heal the spiritual disorder of an "age." A philosopher can do no more than work himself free from the rubble of the idols which, under the name of an "age," threatens to cripple and bury him; and he can hope that the example of his efforts will be of help to others who find themselves in the same situation and experience the same desire to gain their humanity under God.[5]

The issue cannot, however, be settled so easily. Voegelin repeatedly suggested that certain types of philosophical activity could provide a remedy for disoriented individuals, and since he never broke from the Platonic "anthropological principle" that the order of a society is a function of the order in the souls of its leading citizens, it is entirely possible that even if Voegelin discounted the idea of a "social remedy" he searched nonetheless for an individual remedy that could prove socially effective. This possibility raises another: If disoriented individuals can be reoriented, including individuals who are situated in such a way that through them order might be restored to an entire society, is it possible that the history of pneumapathological consciousness might one day come to an end?

Voegelin's references to "remedies" and "therapies" are often puzzling, but with regard to this last possibility it can be said with confidence that he rejected the notion that spiritual disorder could ever be done away with. This rejection was tacit rather than explicit, since Voegelin never wrote on the issue, but the implication of his analysis is no less clear for that reason. To be more pointed, if we accept Voegelin's argument that pneumapathological consciousness is rooted in reactions to the most basic experiences of the human condition (which are unaffected by the accoutrements

---

but also show how to employ them. No one is obliged to take part in the spiritual crisis of a society; on the contrary, everyone is obliged to avoid this folly and live his life in order. Our presentation of the phenomenon, therefore, will at the same time furnish the remedy for it through therapeutic analysis." *Ibid.*, 22–23.

5. Voegelin, "On Hegel: A Study in Sorcery," 349. Lest it be thought that Voegelin was being so blunt in the first sentence of this quotation because he thought that an "age" could not be spiritually disordered, it might be noted that Voegelin once referred to his own time as "a diseased age." See his "History and Gnosis," 81.

of social change or technological progress), we would have to conclude that the very expectation of an era free from spiritual disorientation would itself be an expression of spiritual disorientation.

To use a pair of current phrases, we could say that whenever an "End of Ideology" might come to pass, and whatever a "postmodern era" might be like, an absence of pneumapathological consciousness will not be among its characteristics. Paradoxical as it may seem, there is reason to doubt that Voegelin would have thought such an absence to be desirable even if he had thought it possible. This is explained by the further paradox that well-ordered and disordered consciousness spring from the same sources in human experience. Both patterns of consciousness, according to Voegelin, arise in response to a condition of contingency, uncertainty, mortality, and imperfection. Although these experiences supply the background for either a revolt against such a condition or an attempt to escape it into a transfigured paradise, they also stand as essential preconditions permitting the differentiation of the transcendent from the mundane realm of existence. A humanity that lost the capacity for a revolt against the ground of being would simultaneously lose the philosophical or religious capacity for "turning-toward" the ground. To complicate matters further, it is not as though balanced and imbalanced consciousness share only their moment of origin and then go their separate ways.[6] For Voegelin, it was rather the case that every advance in the historical process of differentiation of the transcendent from the immanent realm will tend to make the point of balance in the *metaxy* that much more precarious:

> The differentiating experience, either noetic or pneumatic, can be so intensive that the man to whom it occurs feels transformed into a new being. The new image of the world resulting from the experience can be misunderstood as a new world; and the process of change itself can be extrapolated into the future. As that changeability mutates into images of a changeable reality comprising the poles of participation, we have the roots of the phenomenona of metastatic beliefs: The gradual-

6. Voegelin, "The Gospel and Culture," 100–101: "The structural possibility of the derailment is present whenever the existential Movement of differentiating the Unknown God from the intra-cosmic gods has begun. . . . Though the possibility of the Gnostic derailment is inherent to the Movement from its beginning, only the full differentiation of the truth of existence under the Unknown God through his Son has created the cultural field in which the extra-cosmic contraction of existence is an equally radical possibility."

istic idea of infinite progress in the time of the world, the apocalyptic visions of the catastrophe of an old world and its *metastasis* into a new one resulting from divine intervention; the revolutionary ideas of a *metastasis* manipulated by human action; and so on.[7]

As the cosmological "world full of gods" gives way to a transcendent realm beyond objective knowledge (but not beyond experience), the uncertainties of our condition are multiplied even as the truth of existence is discovered; the apprehension of our contingency deepens as the absolute status of the source of order is sensed, and our mortality and imperfection become ever more difficult to bear as the immortality and perfection of the divine is revealed.

The process that Voegelin called the "de-divinization" of the world is the source of disorder as well as order in the soul.[8] A ground that is progressively revealed as transcendent will require a progressively greater opening of the soul, which in turn will exacerbate the stimuli leading to existential closure. The closing of the soul is no more an intellectual error that can be corrected by means of instruction than the opening of the soul is a condition that results from following a formula.[9] Since the history of spiritual experience (at least as read by Voegelin) has witnessed not a diminution but rather an inflammation of disorders of the soul, and since the essential sources of spiritual disorder are rooted in the very structure of human life, there is precisely no reason to expect that pneumapathological consciousness can be relegated to the past.

This bracing insight need not issue in quietism or pessimism, as was evinced by Voegelin's continued search for effective avenues of reorientation after he first sensed a symbiotic relationship between differentiation and disorder. Spiritual disorientation cannot be uprooted, but it does not follow that it cannot be cut back. Indications of a hopefulness concerning the remedial capacity of philosophy as a response to social disorder can be found in Voegelin's

7. Voegelin, *Anamnesis*, 166.

8. See Voegelin, *The New Science of Politics*, 100–10.

9. Voegelin, "Remembrance of Things Past," in *Anamnesis*, 6: "The reasons why the various ideologies were wrong were sufficiently well known in the 1920s, but no ideologist could be persuaded to change his position under the pressure of argument. Obviously, rational discourse, or the resistance to it, had existential roots far deeper than the debate conducted on the surface." See also *In Search of Order*, 39.

writings at least up until the late 1960s. However, it would be grossly misleading to suggest that Voegelin was *simply* hopeful; his response to the political crisis of modernity was tempered, almost from the start, by a clear perception of the enormity of the obstacles that confront a philosophical attempt to reorder a society. Voegelin knew well that philosophers have not established a particularly impressive record on this score. In 1948 Voegelin wrote that "no wisdom of a Plato could prevent the suicide of Athens and no climactic synthesis of a St. Thomas the end of imperial Christianity."[10] We might add that the efforts of the Hebrew prophets, of Irenaeus and Augustine, of Hooker and Hobbes, and of Baur, Neander, and Matter met with no greater success.[11]

A review of Voegelin's comments on social and individual therapy shows no discernable trend toward greater or lesser optimism in the thirty years between the publication of *Political Religions* and *Anamnesis*. Such a review could indeed lead one to conclude that he was downright inconsistent, since Voegelin seems to rise to the challenge of reform in one piece and deny in the next that reform by means of philosophy is even possible. Nevertheless, it is difficult to believe that Voegelin was simply inept in his treatment of the problem or that his temperament was so uneven as to fluctuate according to the events of the day. I believe that the apparent inconsistency in his views is best explained by a striking, seemingly autobiographical passage from 1944:

> Platonism in politics is the attempt, perhaps hopeless and futile, to regenerate a disintegrating society spiritually by creating the model of a true order of values. . . . The position of Santayana implies the resignation, probably quite justified, that such an attempt at the present juncture would be vain. But resignation cannot be achieved by everybody; the man with the Platonic temper will try the impossible.[12]

10. Voegelin, "The Origins of Scientism," 488.

11. For Voegelin's fascinating account of Richard Hooker's analysis of the Puritans see *The New Science of Politics*, 134–44. On resistance to parousiasm as a fundamental motivation in Hobbes see *ibid.*, 152–62, 179–84. Voegelin credits Ferdinand Christian Baur (*Die christliche Gnosis*, 1835), Johann August Neander (*Genetische Entwicklung der vornehmsten gnostischen Systeme*, 1818), and Jacques Matter (*Historie critique du Gnosticisme et de son influence sur les sectes religieuses et philosophiques des six premiers siècles de l'ère chrétienne*, 1928) with having been among the first to call attention to gnostic tendencies in the Enlightenment and German idealism. See *Science, Politics and Gnosticism*, 3–5.

12. Voegelin, "Nietzsche, the Crisis, and the War," 195.

It was Nietzsche that Voegelin went on to identify as a man with the Platonic temper, but it seems indisputable that Voegelin also fit the pattern.[13] Undaunted by his early awareness of the difficulties surrounding an effort to provide a socially effective remedy by means of spiritual analysis and evocation, Voegelin did indeed try the impossible.

Of course, it was not entirely clear in 1944 that the task could not be successfully carried out, since much remained to be done on the diagnostic front. Voegelin knew that, by following Thucydides and Plato in adopting the medicinal model of diagnosis and prescription, he was obligated to let the latter be dictated by the former. Since his diagnostic work continued to develop and deepen over the course of the next twenty-five years, the therapeutic project was often mentioned but always left in abeyance. No extended analysis of therapeutic possibilities was ever published because, by the time that his mature diagnosis had taken shape, the diagnosis itself indicated that any social remedy would almost surely be unworkable. Disappointing as this outcome may be, it is still the case that Voegelin, like Plato before him, has bequeathed to us a profound set of insights into the intractability of spiritual disorder when it has penetrated the order of a society.

It would appear that Voegelin's early reading in Plato provided instruction on which paths to reform would most likely prove fruitless. It is perhaps surprising that Voegelin, who always referred to politics as his field of study, would never have entertained the possibility of institutional remedies against the crisis that provided the motivation for his choice of scholarly discipline. Mention of issues

13. This is not to say that Voegelin can easily be labeled a Platonist (or anything else, for that matter), since he frequently stressed Plato's limitations and included the label among those with which he had incorrectly been saddled: "On my religious 'position', I have been classified as a Protestant, a Catholic, as anti-semitic and as a typical Jew; politically, as a Liberal, a Fascist, a National Socialist and a Conservative; and on my theoretical position, as a Platonist, a Neo-Augustinian, a Thomist, a disciple of Hegel, an existentialist, a historical relativist and an empirical sceptic; in recent years the suspicion has frequently been voiced that I am a Christian. All these classifications have been made by university professors and people with academic degrees. They give ample food for thought regarding the state of our universities." Voegelin, "On Readiness to Rational Discussion," 280. See also *Autobiographical Reflections*, 46. Pages 89–93 of *Plato and Aristotle* are highly suggestive of the parallels that run through the attitudes of Voegelin and Plato on questions of political reform.

of form or procedure or policy are conspicuous by their absence from his works. Voegelin was persuaded that Plato was correct in regarding institutional problems as epiphenomenal manifestations of an underlying loss of spiritual orientation, and his view seems to correspond to that which we saw him ascribe to Socrates in the second chapter:

> He roundly refuses to go into details, not only of customs and mores, but even of civil, commercial, and criminal law, because such matters will take care of themselves if only the souls of the legislative rulers are in good order. Moreover, he restrains himself deliberately at this point in order not to give the false impression that good order in a polis can be created through institutional devices. He considers it, on the contrary, a symptom of disease in a polis when the citizens are feverishly active with patching up this or that gap in the law, but do not dare to touch the well-known source of the multitude of minor evils.[14]

In *The New Science of Politics*, Voegelin expressed this same fear that a preoccupation with form instead of spiritual substance would deflect attention from the root causes of social disorder: "The more fervently all human energies are thrown into the great enterprise of salvation through world-immanent action, the farther the human beings who engage in this enterprise move away from the life of the spirit."[15]

Voegelin could not indulge in the notion that an institutional reordering could effect a spiritual reordering for the simple reason that he did not share the Enlightenment view that human behavior is a product of institutional environment. He accepted the perspective of Plato and Aristotle that a human nature exists, that it is comprised of a complex set of competing forces that can be arranged in a variety of hierarchical orders, and that a social order can exert a limited influence on the outcome of this competition but cannot abolish it or impose at will a preconceived hierarchy. He also accepted the classical insight that certain institutional arrangements are better than others (insofar as they may tend to encourage the flourishing of those elements such as wisdom and moderation that permit a healthy ordering of other elements and forces), but that no institutional patterns exist that cannot be perverted so as to hinder the proper formation of character and en-

---

14. Voegelin, *Plato and Aristotle*, 87. It bears pointing out that Voegelin's formal training and most of his early articles were in the area of public law.
15. Voegelin, *The New Science of Politics*, 131.

courage the social ascendancy of infirm character types. Indeed it was the case for Voegelin that institutions and cultural environments have greater potential, owing to the peculiarities of the process of character development, for generalizing a pattern of personal disorder than for nourishing a healthy order in individual souls. Since a healthy personal order is in large part the outgrowth of an orientation by reference to the transcendent aspects of human experience, and since these experiences are either granted by grace to individuals or are evoked through a non-volitional responsiveness to symbols that articulate the experiences of others, it is not possible for society to bring forth with a formula a citizenry characterized by the balance of consciousness. By contrast, societies can exert pressures that are quite effective in muting human responsiveness to transcendent experiences or restricting the avenues through which the resulting orientation can find expression in public activity. Thus it was a sad fact for Voegelin that the development of personal disorder can be a social or political phenomenon, whereas the engineering of balanced consciousness cannot.

Given this perspective, it is understandable that Voegelin's therapeutic speculation would have gravitated toward the possibilities of personal resistance to a corrupting environment and individualized methods for reorienting others. He described his own work as just such an act of personal resistance and devoted considerable attention to the question of whether rational discussion and debate can prove effective against pneumapathological consciousness.[16] Here again, his scrupulousness in permitting his diagnostic work to dictate his conclusions on the possibility of therapy led to findings that are less than comforting.

Voegelin's diagnostic analysis is premised upon the observation that ideological and pneumapathological closure is a matter not of ignorance or intellectual error but rather of experience and reaction. On the one hand, this implies that the extent of a disorder such as ideological consciousness may be rather less widespread than we might expect from the number and influence of ideologies as identified by Voegelin; it is entirely possible to be hoodwinked by a Marx or a Comte for reason of insufficient experience or study without engaging in a self-conscious revolt against the conditions

---

16. See Voegelin, "On Hegel: A Study in Sorcery," 336–37; *Anamnesis*, 3–4, 9–10; "The Meditative Origin of the Philosophical Knowledge of Order," 43–44.

of existence. But on the other hand, because genuine ideological consciousness within a Second Reality like Marxism or positivism is less a result of the intellectual attractiveness of the doctrine than of its capacity for dulling the tensions of open existence, a rational critique of the particulars of the doctrine is likely to be of no avail in such cases.[17]

Voegelin argued that even after ideologies have long since been "torn to pieces" through scholarly criticism, we can observe that they continue to find adherents.[18] This fact might be difficult to explain for one who understood ideologies simply as defective structures of opinion, but against the backdrop of Voegelin's diagnosis the epigonal afterlife of an ideology such as Marxism is easily understood. Since the passage of two millennia has not extinguished the phenomenon of parousiasm, and since the Marxist faith conforms to a similar pattern in consciousness, it is not surprising that the continual failure of communist revolutions to deliver on their promises has not proven fatal to the appeal of the doctrine.[19] Voegelin's analysis suggests that the provision of a plausible account of the world is only a secondary project within the construction of an ideological Second Reality, and by the same token it would appear that adherence to an ideology is first a mat-

17. Thus, from the 1940s onward, Voegelin ceased to engage in detailed criticism of ideologies, which had been so characteristic of much of his early work. Examples of the earlier form of response are *Die Rassenidee in der Geistesgeschichte von Ray bis Carus* (Berlin, 1933); *Rasse und Staat* (Tübingen, 1933), and "The Growth of the Race Idea," *Review of Politics*, II (1940), 283–317. The chapters on Marx from the abandoned "History" were the last occasions on which Voegelin deigned even to discuss the doctrinal principles of an ideology, and here the shift from the analysis of doctrine to focus on engendering consciousness is already quite apparent. See *From Enlightenment to Revolution*, 240–302 and Chapter 1 above.

18. Voegelin, *Conversations with Eric Voegelin*, 15–19. See also "The Eclipse of Reality," 188–89.

19. Although communism has collapsed and communist parties have been outlawed across Eastern Europe as of this writing in late 1991, Marxism remains a potent political force in many nations. It is also a potent intellectual force worldwide, and the ideology continues to attract converts. Two factors—one circumstantial, one doctrinal—seem to assure the ideology a continued existence. The serious dislocations occasioned by the transition to market economies are likely to prevent its final burial in the East, and the possibility of arguing that Lenin, Stalin, *et al.* botched Marx's recipe for communism by preempting capitalism is likely to sustain its plausibility for some in the West. Given that the ideology has *never* had much going for it in terms of empirical support or theoretical cogency, these factors will probably prove sufficient to prevent the most recent round of real-world disasters from unraveling the ideology's attractiveness as a fantasy of world transformation.

ter of faith—followed by a more or less elaborate project of circum-venting the dissonance between the First and Second Realities.[20]

If ideological consciousness involves a misplaced faith in a mis-placed, immanentized ground of being, is it possible that a re-introduction to genuine faith in a transcendent ground would pro-vide the remedy for which Voegelin was looking? Voegelin's own resistance to ideological disorder—as well as his search for ade-quate representations of order—led him to the study of classical Greek philosophy and Judeo-Christian revelation, but his analysis of the dynamics of existential closure would seem to undercut the possibility of simply directing others toward the same path. The basic problem can be stated simply: exposure to the "healthy" ten-sion of balanced consciousness in the *metaxy* is not likely to re-orient the closed soul, for it was exposure to precisely this tension that first prompted pneumapathological closure. Whether a person has eclipsed one of the poles of participation in reality because of an inability to endure either the corruption of the world or the shadow cast by divinity, a reintroduction to the tension of the *metaxy* will bring but another, perhaps stronger, dose of the same.

The uncertainty from which escape was initially sought will not be alleviated by a spiritual tradition if it is used as an antidote in the authentic form of a symbolization of participation in an essen-tially mysterious reality. This problem might be circumvented by scaling down the spiritual demands of the tradition through the fundamentalist tactic of reducing it to a set of dogmatic proposi-tions, but Voegelin recognized that this expedient is only tempo-rary and can produce the most undesirable of unintended results:

> The symbolism providing an answer to [the basic questions of exis-tence] is of secondary importance to the philosopher. That, however, is not to say that it does not have an important function in protecting the order of existence in both man and society. For the development of an answering construct, even if it should have to be revised in the light of a later, more penetrating analysis of existence, will at least guard for a time against error concerning the truth of existence. But only for a time. For the structure of existence is complicated; it is not known once for

20. Voegelin, "The Eclipse of Reality," 190: "When conflicts with reality compel revisions with some frequency over a period, the activity of projecting can pass from a phase of comparatively naive indulgence to one of a more critical occupation with the standards of projects. For a Second Reality must, on the one hand, satisfy the requirements of the contracted self and, on the other hand, contain enough uneclipsed reality not to be ignored as a crackpot scheme by the contemporaries."

all. If it be forgotten that the answer depends for its truth on the understanding of existence that has motivated it; if it be erected into an idol valid for all time; its effect will be the very opposite of protection. For the sensed, if not clearly known, invalidity of the symbol at a later point in history will be extended by the critics of the symbol to the truth nevertheless contained in it. An obsolete symbol may have the effect of destroying the order of existence it was created to protect.[21]

The symbols of an authentic spiritual tradition are overwhelmingly likely to be misunderstood or rejected out of hand by the subject of a remedial course in religion or philosophy, primarily because pneumapathological consciousness is initiated by a renunciation of the experiences the symbols are intended to convey. It is true that an ideologist or pneumapath will at least have had certain of these experiences, but in the wake of the subsequent revolt against the attendant implications of the experiences, there may be nothing left upon which to rebuild. For example, we saw in the preceding chapter that the experience of contingency had been impressed upon Marx with great forcefulness. He understood that humanity cannot be an autonomous species unless it has created itself, and that all the evidences of practical life contradict this notion. If Marx had remained open to the possibility that the basic conditions of our existence are beyond our control and had simply set out to investigate the extent to which we can contribute to an improvement of the terms of everyday life, it is conceivable that his subsequent work would not have eclipsed the original experience. Yet his work was motivated by a desire not to understand the world but rather to change it, and since fundamental change is impossible unless human contingency is obliterated, Marx was driven not only to depart from his own experience but also to attempt to drive the idea of creation from the minds of the people as well.

One can well imagine the outcome of an effort to reform the Marx of the 1860s by means of a primer on metaphysics or theology. Voegelin had no illusions about the probable result of attempts to use theory as a form of therapy:

> Theory as an explication of certain experiences is intelligible only to those in whom the explication will stir up parallel experiences as the empirical basis for testing the truth of theory. Unless a theoretical exposition activates the corresponding experiences at least to a degree, it

21. Voegelin, "On Debate and Existence," 147.

will create the impression of empty talk or will perhaps be rejected as an irrelevant expression of subjective opinions. A theoretical debate can be conducted only among *spoudaioi* in the Aristotelian sense; theory has no argument against a man who feels, or pretends to feel, unable of re-enacting the experience.[22]

If theoretical debate is only useful in debate among *spoudaioi*, who may benefit as a result but are certainly not the intended subjects of Voegelin's therapeutic project, we must ask whether Voegelin did not come around to the view that as a man with the Platonic temper he had indeed tried the impossible.

As we shall see momentarily, there are indications that this was in fact Voegelin's final view on the therapeutic project. First it will be helpful to suggest why he may have thought that the impossible must be tried. The preceding quotation from 1952 shows that Voegelin knew that debate would be futile, but in 1967 he was to write that it is, nevertheless, a matter of obligation:

> Only if we know, for the purpose of comparison, what the conditions of rational discourse are, shall we find our bearings in the contemporary clash with Second Realities. The best point of departure for the comparative analysis of the problem will be St. Thomas' *Summa Contra Gentiles*. . . . It was written in a period of intellectual turmoil through the contacts with Islam and Aristotelian philosophy, comparable in many respects to our own, with the important difference however that a rational debate with the opponent was still possible or—we should say more cautiously—seemed still possible to Aquinas. . . . It is a situation and an obligation that must be faced in our twentieth century as much as Thomas had to face it in his thirteenth. Hence, if the *sapiens* shuns the situation of debate, especially if he avoids the crucial intellectual issues threatening the beleaguered city, he becomes derelict in his duties to God and man, his attitude is spiritually, morally and politically indefensible.[23]

It might seem that Voegelin painted himself into a corner by arguing that debate is a matter of obligation while also maintaining that it is futile, but he found an interesting (if not wholly satisfying) way out.

Returning for comparison to the situation faced by Aquinas,

22. Voegelin, *The New Science of Politics*, 64–65. For Voegelin's most detailed account of the obstacles that confront the possibility of intellectual debate serving as a method of reorientation see "On Readiness to Rational Discussion," *passim*. See also "Wisdom and the Magic of the Extreme," 260–61.

23. Voegelin, "On Debate and Existence," 144.

Voegelin stated that our present situation is much more difficult for reason of the absence of a common ground upon which a debate might be profitably conducted. Aquinas could hope that the *Summa Contra Gentiles* would fulfill his objectives because the Old Testament was shared with Jews, the New Testament with heretics, and natural reason with pagans and Mohammedans. But in the twentieth century, Voegelin continued, "We must say that we cannot argue by the Old Testament, nor by the New Testament, nor by Reason. Not even by Reason, because rational argument presupposes the community of true existence."[24]

Since ideological consciousness is a self-conscious revolt against the community of true existence, the opponent is beyond rational persuasion and must, Voegelin was later to argue, be regarded not as a partner in debate but rather as an "object of scientific research."[25] Surprisingly enough, however, Voegelin continued to insist that debate is a philosophical duty.[26] What resulted from this apparent paradox is an (admittedly) odd conception of debate:

> We are forced one step further down to cope with the opponent (even the word "debate" is difficult to apply) on the level of existential truth. The speculations of classic and scholastic metaphysics are edifices of reason erected on the experiential basis of existence in truth; they are useless in a meeting with edifices of reason erected on a different experiential basis. Nevertheless, we cannot withdraw into the edifices and let the world go by, for in that case we would be remiss in our duty of "debate." The "debate" has, therefore, to assume the forms of (1) a careful analysis of the noetic structure of existence and (2) an analysis of Second Realities, with regard both to their constructs and the motivating structure of existence in untruth. "Debate" in this form is hardly a matter of reasoning (though it remains one of the Intellect), but rather of the analysis of existence preceding rational constructions; it is medical in character in that it has to diagnose the syndromes of untrue existence and by their noetic structure to initiate, if possible, a healing process.[27]

This passage would seem to suggest that, though Voegelin never renounced his therapeutic intentions, he ultimately came to drop the notion of a distinct therapeutic project in the hope that his diagnosis could itself have a remedial effect.

24. *Ibid.*, 152.
25. Voegelin, *Autobiographical Reflections*, 50.
26. See *The Ecumenic Age*, 184.
27. Voegelin, "On Debate and Existence," 152.

The only indication provided by Voegelin of how a diagnosis could also serve as a therapy is to be found in *Anamnesis*:

> The nihilistic rebellion cannot be overcome on its own level of experiences and symbols, for instance, by means of criticism of ideology, culture, or the times, as attempted by intellectuals who no longer feel easy in their situation. Such attempts can lead only to a confused stirring around in the nothingness of lost reality. The non-noetic thought about order of the kind that rebellion produces offers no point of contact to the noesis. This formulation of the problem seems to show the way to a solution: Whoever has had enough of rebellion against the ground and wishes again to think rationally needs only to turn around and toward that reality against which the symbols of rebellion aggress. It seems that the rebellion itself can become the guideline for the seeker, inasmuch as that against which it rebels is precisely that which he is seeking. The turning away and turning around is indeed the *sine qua non* for finding the way from rebellion to reality; the *periagoge* must in any case be performed.[28]

Unfortunately, this formulation of the problem shows the way to a solution only for the seeker—not the pneumapath. The potential effectiveness of the solution presupposes that its subject is not ensnared within a Second Reality but, on the contrary, has already had enough of the rebellion against the ground. The statement that a remedy will necessarily entail the *periagoge* is true, but as a piece of advice to one who is actively engaged in the revolt it is a bit like advising those with obsessive/compulsive tendencies to stop washing their hands or biting their fingernails. It would seem that the result of Voegelin's search for a form of therapy ended in the observation that for an act of personal revolt to end, the person in question must stop revolting.[29] Once again, this is quite true, but as the conclusion of a great thinker it cannot but disappoint. Nevertheless, part of the measure of the greatness of a thinker is the unwillingness to be goaded by the perception of crisis into finding a solution where none exists.

28. Voegelin, *Anamnesis*, 188.

29. The following exchange appears in "Philosophies of History: An Interview with Eric Voegelin": "Let me ask you a question which you may not wish to answer. Your work has always been brilliantly and objectively descriptive. Would you undertake in any way to make prescriptive suggestions to impede the traumatic deculturalization of our own times?" *Voegelin*: "Well, the prescription is already contained in the description. People have to recover contact with reality, which has been lost in imaginary contacts with imaginary realities." *New Orleans Review*, II (1973), 138. The discussion turns to other subjects immediately after this exchange.

The situation can still not be hopeless, since we know of cases in which individuals have found their way out of ideological Second Realities as well as the other types of disorientation. If a Berdyaev could make his way from Leninism to mysticism, or an Augustine from the extremes of worldliness and otherworldliness to the community between the Cities of God and Man, avenues of reorientation must exist. But the implication of Voegelin's analysis seems to be that only rarely can an individual be led to these avenues; either they appear mysteriously, as if by grace, or are found in the course of a search for more satisfactory representations of one's experience than are provided by Second Realities. We can make the hopeful observation that it is often the most sensitive souls who take flight from the *metaxy*, rather than those who are simply dull to its tensions. Although Voegelin does not make this point, we could venture to say on the basis of his analysis that the soul in revolt may have more in common with prophets and philosophers, at least in terms of spiritual sensitivity and experiential background, than with the general run of humanity. The sensitive but disoriented soul may not, at some point, be able to suppress the experiences of falsity and moral bankrupcy within a Second Reality, which itself exists in a tension with the enduring First Reality.[30] The one true reality inevitably intrudes upon the closed world of an ideological system, and though the tensions imposed by this reality will be no less acute the second time around, there are limits beyond which ideologies fail to provide insulation against the types of experience that can pave the way for a reorientation.[31]

30. For personal accounts of the failure of communist ideology in this sense, see those of Arthur Koestler, Ignazio Silone, Richard Wright, André Gide, Louis Fischer, and Stephen Spender in Richard Crossman, ed., *The God that Failed* (New York, 1949).

31. These events or moments of reflection are of the type Karl Jaspers referred to as "border experiences" or "ultimate situations." The classic example is the apprehension of death, and there is reason to question whether an ideology can provide any guidance whatsoever when this apprehension is presented to consciousness. For instance, the only reference to death of which I am aware in the writings of Marx runs as follows: "Death appears as the harsh victory of the species over the particular individual and seems to contradict their unity; but the particular individual is only a determinate species being and thus mortal." Marx, "Economic and Philosophical Manuscripts of 1844," in *Karl Marx: Selected Writings*, 91. See Karl Jaspers, *Philosophy of Existence* (Philadelphia, 1971), 76–88, and Voegelin, *Science, Politics and Gnosticism*, 109–14.

# 7

## Beyond the Age of Ideology

As we turn to a concluding evaluation of Voegelin's analysis of political disorder, we must ask whether Voegelin was justified in identifying ideological and proto-ideological figures as "spiritually diseased." This actually involves a series of questions: First, has he provided a foundation that is sufficient to elevate the designation of spiritual disease from mere invective to the status of a theoretical classification? Second, should the very use of such a term prompt us to question his tolerance or capacity for empathy? Third, can spiritual disease be identified as an important component within each of the movements that he identified as ideological? And finally, do we have good reason to follow Voegelin in finding an essential sameness between modern and premodern varieties of spiritual disease?

With regard to the first question, Voegelin would certainly have been vulnerable to the charge that he had no foundation from which to diagnose spiritual disease in others had he not provided an elaborately articulated conception of spiritual health. It is one thing to search historical materials for bizarre doctrines or movements and then say that sick people were involved, but quite another to develop and propose critical standards for the designation of manifestations of spiritual health and unhealth. As the foregoing accounts have shown, Voegelin pursued the latter tack in great detail through an extraordinary range of historical settings and, in virtually every case, with explicit analysis of the written evidence that backed a diagnosis of pneumapathological consciousness.

Of course, one who is left unpersuaded by Voegelin's description of healthy consciousness will have little regard for his diagnostic analyses. If there is no transcendent ground of being, there can be no spiritual revolt against such a ground, and Voegelin's concept of psychic imbalance is premised on the validity of his notion of balanced consciousness within the tensions of the *metaxy*. To some extent, therefore, the evaluation of the foundation from which Voegelin diagnosed spiritual disease must be made by the reader, as it would obviously be foolish for me to pronounce on matters of ultimate reality in passing. Suffice it to say that Voegelin was at least thorough enough, by dint of having clearly indicated his own premises on spiritual order, to permit those who are willing to examine his diagnoses to develop an informed evaluation.

A more approachable part of this issue is whether Voegelin's identifications of spiritual disease were theoretical diagnoses or mere attacks against those who ran afoul of his legendary capacity for unflattering characterization. Here we have a common-sense standard at our disposal. Because Voegelin was a writer who minced no words, one has little difficulty in discerning whether a historical figure was or was not held in favor by him. Thus we can ask, were his standards of spiritual health and unhealth applied in an evenhanded and dispassionate manner? An affirmative answer is suggested by the fact that Voegelin followed his self-set standards to very harsh observations on a number of figures for whom he had the greatest respect, including Isaiah, Aristotle, and Paul.[1] This resolute faithfulness to theoretical standards can also be seen in his willingness to emphasize the deformative as well as the formative effects of every differentiation of truth, including the Christian. Conversely, Voegelin did not become so embroiled in his resistance to ideologists and pneumapaths as to be incapable of recognizing merit within their thought or activity.[2] Although his critical remarks can be shockingly (and perhaps needlessly) acrimonious, they rarely bear the markings of a mere attack.

Nevertheless, the very use of the concept of spiritual disease carries a certain volatility in an era when tolerance is a candidate

---

1. On Isaiah see *Israel and Revelation*, 476–501; *The Ecumenic Age*, 25–27; *Autobiographical Reflections*, 68–69. On Aristotle and the "derailment" of philosophy see *Plato and Aristotle*, 276–79, 332–36; *Anamnesis*, 159–66. On "gnostic" tendencies in Paul see *The New Science of Politics*, 126; *The Ecumenic Age*, 239–71; and Walsh, "Voegelin's Response to the Disorder of the Age," 273–75.

2. See Voegelin, "History and Gnosis," 65, 82–83; "The Eclipse of Reality," 189–90; "On Hegel: A Study in Sorcery," 343–44; *From Enlightenment to Revolution*, 299–301.

for the status of the prime academic virtue. Since Voegelin's main diagnostic works appeared at a time when the majority of the members of his discipline were loath even to speak of things as good, his willingness to speak of evil and sickness in politics was sure to draw fire.[3] Not all of the criticism has come from authors who were unsympathetic toward Voegelin's work. Dante Germino, one of the more distinguished of Voegelin's commentators, has written:

> One problem is to distinguish between "error and the person who errs," as John XXIII expressed it. Voegelin frequently seems to suggest that not only the ideas of Hegel, Marx, and the rest of the "Gnostics" are erroneous, but that the thinkers are spiritually diseased as persons. I must confess that I still find it difficult to accept this latter judgment and wonder if it is necessary to condemn these thinkers as whole persons in the way, again, that Voegelin *appears* to argue. [Emphasis in original][4]

Charitable as these remarks are, it may be that Germino's tolerance is misplaced. I would suggest that, to the degree that ideological systematizers have knowingly falsified reality for purposes of enlisting others in a ruinous project of world transformation, it *was* necessary for Voegelin to invoke the concept of spiritual disease; the real problem is that many of those who are subsequently enlisted in one or another way will not have partaken of the experiences that motivated the ideological patriarch and thus would presumably not have fallen prey to the same disorder.[5] To expand upon a point made earlier, it is entirely possible to be swindled by an ideologist or a paraclete for reason of insufficient experience or study, or to be enlisted in a mass movement due to pressures from

3. Cf., e.g., Robert A. Dahl, "The Science of Politics: New and Old," *World Politics*, VII (1955), 479–89; Arthur W. H. Adkins, review of Voegelin's *Plato and Aristotle* and *The World of the Polis, Journal of Hellenic Studies*, LXXXI (1961), 192–93. It might be noted that one of the great costs imposed by a "value-free" methodology is an inability to come to grips with manifestations of evil, however elusive that term may be. There would surely be something dreadfully hollow about an account of concentration camps and gas chambers that was limited to the judgment that they are "dysfunctional."

4. Germino, "Eric Voegelin's Framework for Political Evaluation in His Recently Published Work," 118, n. 29. The tentative tone of the passage is puzzling, since Voegelin used the term *spiritual disease* explicitly and with great frequency.

5. Voegelin made a similar point (though clearly not with the intention of excusing the rank and file) in *From Enlightenment to Revolution*, 242–49.

a corrupt regime or peers or simple boredom, without engaging in a self-conscious revolt against the conditions of existence.

It is the question of whether an individual has *knowingly* falsified reality and engaged in a *self-conscious* revolt that should determine where we draw the line between spiritual disease and lesser disorders. It seems that Voegelin did not always respect this distinction, especially in his later years, and if Voegelin's tolerance is to be questioned, I believe that this is the appropriate ground.[6] Returning to Germino's argument, it would seem that Voegelin has left little room for a distinction between ideologists and their ideas. The premise of his late work (which is characterized by the shift after 1950 from intellectual history to the theory of consciousness) is that ideas are epiphenomenal manifestations of the experiences that set the pattern of an individual soul and its activity. With regard to Hegel and Marx, the thinkers mentioned by Germino, the salient experiences are alienation from the conditions of existence, will to power (to the extent of attempted murders of God), and a hubristic desire to make history culminate in their own efforts. Their ideas are not simply erroneous; on the contrary, they are ingeniously orchestrated according to the inner logic of a spiritual rebellion that seeks popular acceptance. If Voegelin was correct in arguing that both were well aware of what they were doing, it is difficult to understand why criticism should be restricted to the level of ideas.[7]

Nevertheless, Germino's reservations on the question of whether "the rest of the 'Gnostics' " should be regarded as spiritually dis-

6. For example, in the following comment with regard to the inability of his work on the race idea and Kant's work on the idea of evolution to affect ideological conflicts on these topics, Voegelin seems to confuse stupidity with self-conscious closure or the "refusal to apperceive": "One should not think, however, that once this analysis is made, it has any influence on anybody. It does not. Neither did Kant have any influence on anybody in this respect, nor did my analysis of the race idea have any influence in this respect. . . . [T]here is still the same level of stupidity as you find in the 1920s and the same level of stupidity as you find in the time of Kant in the eighteenth century. So nothing happens in practice, even when the problem gets analyzed. One must not expect a rational analysis to make people intelligent all of a sudden. They remain as stupid as they were before." Voegelin, "Autobiographical Statement at Age Eighty-Two," 118.

7. On the intentionality of the Hegelian and Marxian deformations of reality see *Science, Politics and Gnosticism,* 23–28, 34–46; "On Hegel: A Study in Sorcery," *passim; The Ecumenic Age,* 262–66; *Anamnesis,* 3–4. On the general issue of intentionality in pneumapathological consciousness, see esp. "The Eclipse of Reality."

eased (for reason of being partisans of one of the many movements identified as "gnostic" or ideological by Voegelin) seem quite well founded. This point must be made cautiously, given the brevity of Voegelin's treatments of most of these movements, but it must be made nonetheless for this very reason. Of the fourteen ideologies I have listed in Chapter 1 Voegelin has left us with extended analyses only of Hegelianism, Marxism, scientism, positivism, and anarchism, with the last two being restricted to the positivism of Comte and the anarchism of Bakunin. The remainder of these ideologies were either treated peripherally or simply mentioned in passing. Thus we must be cautious and not reject the possibility that Voegelin could have provided grounds for concluding that spiritual disease was indeed an important factor within each of these movements, but we must be still more cautious before arriving at the conclusion that an individual is spiritually diseased on account of being, say, a liberal or an existentialist (and before concluding that liberals and Marxists can be placed on the same plane). Such conclusions would represent, I believe, a misuse of Voegelin's work, though it must be admitted that one who wished to use his work as support for blanket condemnations could plausibly point to passages where Voegelin seems to have done exactly that himself.[8]

In light of the severity of the charge involved in the concept of spiritual disease, it is important to emphasize why the concept must be utilized with the greatest circumspection. Spiritual disease and pneumapathological consciousness refer to an existential state that is distinct from neurophysiological disorders, criminal impulses, or intellectual deficiencies. However, in concrete cases, these variegated phenomena may be very difficult to distinguish. Pneumapathological consciousness can be expressed in criminal behavior or intellectual weaknesses, but mere stupidity or "simple" homicidal mania in an individual could be confused with pneumapathological consciousness if the individual is a participant in an ideological movement. Moreover, when an ideological system becomes the foundation for a widespread intellectual or political movement, it will frequently happen that individuals will encounter the system only in part or in a diluted form and accept it for

8. See Voegelin, *Israel and Revelation*, xii; *Science, Politics and Gnosticism*, 4–5; *From Enlightenment to Revolution*, 69; *Anamnesis*, 3–7, 145–46; "Wisdom and the Magic of the Extreme," 240.

reasons quite different from those that led to its construction. Thus it is essential that diagnoses of spiritual disease be restricted to individual cases, and indeed to those cases where a sufficient body of evidence is available for the spurious factors (which Voegelin himself recognized) to be dismissed and for the self-consciousness of a revolt to be established.[9] On one hand, it is perhaps absurd to demand more of a scholar who was as productive as Voegelin, but on the other hand, it is perhaps incumbent upon one who would speak of spiritual disease to provide clear distinctions on what does and does not constitute such disease, and moreover to refrain from using the term in reference to groups of unnamed individuals.[10] It is probably illegitimate to use the term in reference to any such group, and it is certainly meaningless and counterproductive to speak of a "diseased age."[11]

There may also be reason to fault Voegelin for not having drawn distinctions between the groups and intellectual schools to which he referred as ideological or gnostic movements. One can find Voegelin's arguments for the presence of ideological elements within each of these movements persuasive and yet resist the notion that, say, liberalism and existentialism belong on the same plane with Marxism and fascism.[12] Because ideological elements differ both

9. Voegelin, "Wisdom and the Magic of the Extreme," 236: "I am speaking cautiously of a suspension of consciousness because it is frequently difficult, if not impossible, to determine in the case of an individual activist whether the suspension is an act of intellectual fraud or persuasive self-deception, whether it is a case of plain illiteracy or of the more sophisticated illiteracy imposed by an educational system, whether it is caused by a degree of spiritual and intellectual insensitivity that comes under the head of stupidity, or whether it is due to various combinations of these and other factors such as the desire to attract public attention and make a career." It might be noted that this passage shows that Voegelin was not in the habit of equating pneumapathological consciousness with stupidity, as might be wrongly assumed from the passage quoted in note 6 to this chapter.

10. For examples see the passages cited in note 8 to this chapter.

11. Voegelin's words from "History and Gnosis," 81. See also *The Ecumenic Age*, 266.

12. In the case of a varied tradition such as existentialism, this problem can be aggravated by a lack of analysis at the individual level. For example, Voegelin presumably had no desire to condemn existentialists *per se*, for while he criticized Sartre and Heidegger very sharply, he found much to praise in the works of Jaspers and Camus. On Sartre see "The Eclipse of Reality," 185, 190, and *The Ecumenic Age*, 228. On Heidegger see *Science, Politics and Gnosticism*, 46–49, and "History and Gnosis," 65, 69, 81–83. On Jaspers see "Autobiographical Statement at Age Eighty-

in kind and in relative prominence from movement to movement, it would seem that Voegelin should have provided caveats that would lead readers away from the conclusion that these movements are all of one piece.[13] In light of one hundred and fifty years of what Voegelin called the "dogmatomachy" of inter-ideological conflict, it is true that his analysis of the commonalities characterizing the various movements represented a more important task than that of stressing their differences, but this latter task would have complemented the former and helped to protect it against misunderstandings. For example, though Voegelin wrote that there is a "gnostic" component to be found in liberalism, he also gave indications (in the same article) that liberalism should probably not be considered a gnostic movement in the sense that he usually used the term.[14] In his view liberalism posed less a danger in itself than the danger of creating a spiritual vacuum, through secularism, that could permit the victory of ideologies like Marxism or fascism that can exploit the human penchant for attaching ultimate significance to one's actions.[15] If there is something faintly metastatic about the assumption that "actions undertaken in rational, anticipatory self-interest will lead to harmonious order in society,"[16] it must be remembered that this liberal hope was premised

---

Two," 113, 121. On Camus see *Anamnesis*, 170–72, 189–90, and *Conversations with Eric Voegelin*, 18, 26.

13. The one passage I am aware of in which Voegelin alludes to the possibility of his writings being misused or misunderstood does not shed much light on the question of whether he was either resigned to this fate or was actively seeking to guard against it, though it is interesting nonetheless: "Every analysis . . . can lead to misunderstanding if it falls into hands of people who aren't very bright. Absolutely, the non-brightness of the people who might read you is a fact you have to face. We just have to put up with the fact that there are people who are not sufficiently literate to handle the problems with which we have to deal. I have always had to explain to the students at the beginning of my seminars all my life: there is no such thing as a right to be stupid; there is no such thing as a right to be illiterate; there is no such thing as a right to be incompetent. It is usually taken for granted that you have a right to be all of these things, and will still be regarded as a wonderful person." Voegelin, "Responses at the Panel Discussion of 'The Beginning of the Beginning'" in *The Beginning and the Beyond*, ed. Lawrence, 100.

14. Voegelin, "Liberalism and Its History" (translation of "Der Liberalismus und seine Geschichte," 1960), *Review of Politics*, XXXVII (1974), 512.

15. *Ibid.*, 512, 517–18.

16. *Ibid.*, 515.

upon the sober assumption that most human beings are incapable of giving themselves over to the community without thought for their own narrow interests (and would not acquire this capability even if a harmonious order were to result from liberal social and economic institutions).[17] One would be hard-pressed to find talk of "new men" in the classics of liberalism, and indeed certain liberals were apprehensive about the effects that liberal institutions would have upon the men of their day.[18] Although we should not make too much of this one example, it seems impossible to avoid the conclusion that the prominence of pneumapathological and ideological consciousness varies widely among the set of movements in question, and Voegelin's work is poorer for the lack of distinctions that could do justice to the extent of this variation.

With regard to the question of whether Voegelin was successful in demonstrating continuities at the level of consciousness between modern and premodern forms of spiritual disorientation, we must first note that his thesis could never be "established" to the satisfaction of one who was unwilling to accept his basic theory of experience and symbolization—and not established without difficulty even for those who find the theory valuable.[19] In the last analysis, the confirmation of Voegelin's basic thesis on the historical continuity of pneumapathological consciousness depends on the possibility of establishing the existence of a common layer of experience beneath the various symbolisms developed throughout history for the expression of "existence-in-revolt." This type of interpretation is rather more susceptible to controversy than the less

17. Cf., e.g., John Locke, *Second Treatise of Government* (Indianapolis, 1980), 12–13, 65–66; Alexander Hamilton, John Jay, and James Madison, *The Federalist* (New York, n.d.), papers 6, 10, and 51, pp. 27–33, 53–62, 335–41.

18. Tocqueville's fears regarding the effects of equality of conditions are well known. See *Democracy in America* (New York, 1969), 9–20, 53–57, 189–95, 231–45, 254–61. Less well known are the fears of Adam Smith: "[The workman in industry] generally becomes as stupid and ignorant as it is possible for a human creature to become. . . . [T]he nobler parts of the human character may be, in great measure, obliterated and extinguished in the great body of the people." Quoted in Robert L. Heilbroner, *Marxism: For and Against* (New York, 1980), 130–31.

19. For the most helpful presentations of the theory see Voegelin, "Immortality: Experience and Symbol" and "Equivalences of Experience and Symbolization in History." Two outstanding secondary analyses are Russell Nieli, "From Myth to Philosophy: Eric Voegelin's Theory of Experience and Symbolization" (Ph.D. dissertation, Princeton University, 1979), and Webb, *Eric Voegelin: Philosopher of History*, 52–151.

daunting tasks of placing a text in historical context or arguing for a certain relationship among its parts, but inasmuch as all interpretation ultimately involves the attempt to understand the intentions of the author, Voegelin's interpretive method is not so unusual. Nevertheless, it is the nature of the case that exception can be taken with any interpretation, and when one undertakes to establish an essential unity among as varied a set of texts across as vast a span of time as did Voegelin, strenuous objections are sure to be invited.

Although it would take us too far afield to make the point by way of exhaustive comparisons, I would venture to say that Voegelin's was the most daring and broadly based of the many attempts in this century to analyze the nature of the so-called Age of Ideology. If one compares Voegelin's analysis with the already ambitious attempts of such scholars as J. L. Talmon and Norman Cohn to trace the lineage of ideological movements beyond this Age (into romanticism and medieval millenarianism, respectively), Voegelin's effort to extend the connections to the ancient world and the human condition itself must be seen as an extraordinary undertaking. It would be unfair to expect such an effort to issue in rigorous "demonstrations," which cannot really be expected even from much less grandiose forms of historical and philosophical analysis. This does not mean, however, that we can do no better than to admire Voegelin's boldness and leave others to assess the results of his work.

We can first ask whether Voegelin was able to substantiate the assertion from the first volume of *Order and History* that "the continuum of metastatic movements has never been broken."[20] In retrospect we can say that Voegelin was unable to establish any such continuum at the level of "movements," but that he was able to provide very good reason for believing that ideological consciousness is intimately related to a broader pattern of disorientation that can be observed on the individual level well before the modern period. The problems at the first level have less to do with dissimilarities among the movements that Voegelin investigated than with two other factors: first, the paucity of historical materials (and the thinness or absence of analyses by Voegelin) for many eras and particular movements, and second, the difficulties associated with

20. Voegelin, *Israel and Revelation*, 454. It will be recalled that Voegelin seems to have been using the term *metastatic faith* at this time in much the same generic sense in which he often spoke of gnosticism. See Chapter 3 above.

using the concept of personal spiritual revolt as an explanation of popular movements.

There *is* one important problem of dissimilarity among the movements, namely, the distinction between those movements that sought a transformation of existence through transcendent forces and those that conceived of the transformation as a purely human accomplishment. Although this distinction was blurred in Voegelin's generic usage of the term "gnosticism," that usage was still valid insofar as he was able to show that both types of movements originate from an inability to endure the tensions of existence in the *metaxy*. Since the problem of a blurring can largely be overcome through simple changes in terminology, and since the concept of pneumapathological consciousness can alleviate much of the confusion between historical Gnosticism and psychic "gnosticism," it would seem that more imposing difficulties for the "continuum of movements" thesis are presented by the other two factors.

As was maintained in the conclusion to the preceding chapter, Voegelin's argument for an essential continuity between modern and premodern forms of spiritual revolt cannot be "confirmed" in any very solid way because of a lack of more extended treatments of the Hebrew prophets, the historical Gnostics, the Hermeticists and Alchemists, and the many millennialist sects of the Middle Ages. Although it was also mentioned that Voegelin has inspired a number of studies that can help to fill these gaps, his late work suggests that it should be possible to find evidence of pneumapathological disorientation wherever the process of differentiating a divine Beyond from the immanent realm of existence was begun.[21] This means, in effect, that a full confirmation of his thesis would require an analysis of historical materials not only from Western civilization but also from the Orient and from primitive civilizations throughout the world. In his last years Voegelin began this work through the investigation of ancient Chinese texts and the symbolisms of neo- and paleolithic civilizations in Malta, the Yucatan, France, and England,[22] but it is obvious that a body of

21. Voegelin, "Wisdom and the Magic of the Extreme," 267–68: "Existential consciousness does not have to be noetically differentiated in order to suffer the trials of deformation. In the crisis of the Egyptian Old Empire, in the third millennium B.C., a rich literature of deformative rebellion and of resistance to deformation conducts the existential debate in the language of the cosmological myth."

22. For analysis of Chinese texts see Voegelin, *The Ecumenic Age*, 272–99,

evidence sufficient to "demonstrate" Voegelin's thesis will not be available within the foreseeable future—if ever. Thus it is more sensible to approach Voegelin's diagnostic work as a set of hypotheses to be considered where they prove helpful in understanding a particular case rather than as a completed theory to be proven or disproven.

In general, these hypotheses will probably tend to prove more helpful in investigations of individual cases as opposed to movements. Because the pneumapathological consciousness of a spiritual rebel is no more a group phenomenon than is the transcendent experience of a mystic, there must always be a presumption against explaining events such as wars, revolutions, or even intellectual trends in the terms of Voegelin's diagnosis (even though the pneumapath can, like the mystic, affect the consciousness of others). It is difficult to see how the conditions that must be met for a valid diagnosis of spiritual disease could ever be satisfied in an investigation of such events, and thus it would also be difficult to support Voegelin's early finding of an unbroken chain of "metastatic" movements.[23]

This said, we can nevertheless propose the conclusion that Voegelin's diagnostic studies stand as a contribution of singular importance for understanding the nature of ideological thought. To have penetrated beneath the intellectual history of ideologies to the inner workings of the ideological mind was one of his greatest achievements, and by developing an analysis of ideological consciousness that can encounter it on the deepest levels of human experience, Voegelin may have provided the first truly philosophical approach to the phenomenon of ideology. He has made it possible to account for the specifically modern aspects of ideologies (by identifying their undercurrent of scientistic reaction against the opaque symbols of a doctrinalized Christianity) while also accounting for their perennial elements of alienation, closure, chiliasm, and hubristic will to power. Voegelin has taken us beyond the conception of our era as a novel "Age of Ideology" through his restora-

---

306–13. For accounts of his work on neo- and paleolithic symbolisms see *Conversations with Eric Voegelin*, 85–94, and "Autobiographical Statement at Age Eighty-Two," 122–31.

23. Indeed, the first link in the proposed chain is suspect, since Voegelin's concept of metastatic faith was developed from an analysis of only one event involving one prophet, and as such does not stem from an analysis of a movement at all.

tive application of the classical concepts of *morbus animi, aspernatio rationis, libido dominandi, hybris, pleonexia, polypragmosyne,* and antidivine and antihuman self-assertiveness. In addition, by showing that ideological consciousness originates from the same experiences of tension that can give rise to an orientation toward transcendence, Voegelin was able to provide a precise and sophisticated explanation of those similarities between ideology and religion that have led a generation of analysts to conceive of ideology as a "quasi-religious" mode of thought.[24] One of the principal merits of this explanation is that it permits an understanding of the resemblance between ideological and religious patterns of disorientation without implying that religion is itself a form of disorientation. Voegelin showed that a differentiated religious tradition does not provide a "solution" for the tensions imposed by the human condition but, rather, a heightened sensitivity to tension that may lead either to balanced consciousness or to millenarian escapism, closure within doctrine, and violent intolerance of competing doctrines; thus, he was able to provide a wealth of original insights into the similarity of ideological and religious fanaticism while simultaneously maintaining a clear distinction between an authentically religious consciousness and a fanaticism of either variety.

If Voegelin did not leave us with a remedy for the fanaticism that can arise from pneumapathological consciousness, he did at least enable us to understand the nature and history of psychic disorder by reference to a parallel history of spiritual order. We have seen that Voegelin's work began as a response to the civilizational crisis of modernity, and that he characterized philosophy as "an act of resistance illuminated by conceptual understanding."[25] The success of such a struggle can never be complete or permanent, since the wellsprings of disorder flow from the human condition itself, but one can still speak of successes in a philosopher's act of resistance:

> Philosophy is not a doctrine of right order, but the light of wisdom that falls on the struggle; and help is not a piece of information about truth,

24. *E.g.,* Löwith, *Meaning in History;* Raymond Aron, *The Opium of the Intellectuals* (New York, 1962); Eric Hoffer, *The True Believer: Thoughts on the Nature of Mass Movements* (New York, 1963); Henri de Lubac, *The Drama of Atheist Humanism* (Cleveland, 1963); Leszek Kolakowski, *Main Currents of Marxism: Its Origin, Growth and Dissolution* (New York, 1981), III, 525–26.

25. Voegelin, *Plato and Aristotle,* 68.

but the arduous effort to locate the forces of evil and identify their nature. For half the battle is won when the soul can recognize the shape of the enemy and, consequently, knows that the way it must follow leads in the opposite direction.[26]

26. *Ibid.*, 62–63.

# Bibliography

Note: This Bibliography is divided into three parts: The first is a chronological listing of the works of Eric Voegelin. The second lists, alphabetically by author, works by others about Voegelin. These first two sections are the most comprehensive listings of their kind to date. The third part lists the most important other works consulted in the course of writing this book.

## Works by Eric Voegelin

1922    "Die gesellschaftliche Bestimmtheit soziologischer Erkenntnis." *Zeitschrift für Volkswirtschaft und Sozialpolitik*, n.s., II, 331–48.

1923    Review of *Logik und Rechtswissenschaft*, by F. Kaufmann. *Zeitschrift für Öffentliches Recht*, III, 707–708.

1924    "Reine Rechtslehre und Staatslehre." *Zeitschrift für Öffentliches Recht*, IV, 80–131.

       "Die Zeit in der Wirtschaft." *Archiv für Sozialwissenschaft und Sozialpolitik*, LIII, 186–211.

1925    "Über Max Weber." *Deutsche Vierteljahrsschrift für Literaturwissenschaft und Geistesgeschichte*, III, 177–93.

1926    "Die Verfassungsmässigkeit des 18. Amendments zur United States Constitution." *Zeitschrift für Öffentliches Recht*, V, 445–64.

       "Wirtschafts- und Klassengegensatz in Amerika." *Unterrichtsbriefe des Instituts für angewandte Soziologie*, V, 6–11.

1927    "Kelsen's Pure Theory of Law." *Political Science Quarterly*, XLII, 268–76.

       "La Follette und die Wisconsin-Idee." *Zeitschrift für Politik*, XVII, 309–21.

       "Zur Lehre von der Staatsform." *Zeitschrift für Öffentliches Recht*, VI, 572–608.

1928    "Die ergänzende Bill zum Federal Reserve Act." *Nationalwirtschaft*, II, 225–29.

"Die ergänzende Bill zum Federal Reserve Act und die Dollarsta-
bilization." *Mitteilungen des Verbandes österreicher Banken und Bankiers*, X, 252–59.

"Konjunkturforschung und Stabilisation des Kapitalismus." *Mitteilungen des Verbandes österreichischer Banken und Bankiers*, IX,
252–59.

"Der Sinn der Erklärung der Menschen- und Bürgerrechte von
1789." *Zeitschrift für Öffentliches Rechts*, VIII, 82–120. Über die
Form des amerikanischen Geistes. Tübingen: J. C. B. Mohr.

"Zwei Grundbegriffe der Humeschen Gesellschaftslehre." *Archiv
für angewandte Soziologie*, I, 11–16.

1929     "Die Souveränitätstheorie Dickinsons und die Reine Rechtslehre."
*Zeitschrift für Öffentliches Recht*, VIII, 413–34.

"Die Transaktion." *Archiv für angewandte Soziologie*, I, 14–21.

1930     "Die amerikanische Theorie vom Eigentum." *Archiv für angewandte
Soziologie*, II, 165–72.

"Die amerikanische Theorie vom ordenlichen Rechtsverfahren und
vom der Freiheit." *Archiv für angewandte Soziologie*, III, 40–57.

"Die Einheit des Rechts und das soziale Sinngebilde Staat." *Internationale Zeitschrift für Theorie des Rechts*, I, 58–59.

"Max Weber." *Kölner Vierteljahreshefte für Soziologie*, IX, 1–16.

"Die österreichische Verfassungsreform von 1929." *Zeitschrift für
Politik*, XIX, 585–615.

1931     "Das Sollen im System Kants." In *Gesellschaft, Staat und Recht*, edited by Alfred Verdrosz. Vienna: Springer.

"Die Verfassungslehre von Carl Schmitt / Versuch einer konstruk-
tiven Analyse ihrer staats-theoretischen Prinzipien." *Zeitschrift
für Öffentliches Recht*, XI, 80–109.

1932     "Nachwort." In *Die Kunst des Denkens*, edited by Ernst Dimnet.
Freiburg: Herder.

Review of *Die Grundlagen des Öffentliches Rechts*, by K. Herman.
*Zeitschrift für Öffentliches Recht*, XII, 630–31.

1933     Die Rassenidee in der Geistesgeschichte von Ray bis Carus. Berlin:
Junker & Duennhaupt.

*Rasse und Staat*. Tübingen: J. C. B. Mohr.

Review of *Gemeinschaft und Staat*, by F. W. Jerusalem. *Zeitschrift für
Öffentliches Recht*, XIII, 764.

1934     Review of *Nationality and Government, with Other War Time Essays*
and *The Prospects of Democracy and Other Essays*, by A. E. Zim-
mern. *Zeitschrift für Öffentliches Recht*, XIV, 269.

Review of *Politische und soziologische Staatslehre*, by M. Rumpf. *Zeitschrift für Öffentliches Recht*, XIV, 268–69.

Review of *Das Rechtsgefühl in Justiz und Politik*, by A. E. Hoche.
*Zeitschrift für Öffentliches Recht*, XIV, 270–71.

Review of *Der sinnhafte Aufbau der sozialen Welt*, by Alfred Schutz. In *Zeitschrift für Öffentliches Recht*, XIV, 668–72.

Review of *Verfassungsrecht und soziale Struktur*, by D. Schindler. *Zeitschrift für Öffentliches Recht*, XIV, 256–57.

1935    "Rasse und Staat." In *Psychologie des Gemeinschaftslebens*, edited by Otto Klemm. Jena: Fischer.

"Le Regime Administratif. Advantages et Inconvenients, zusammen mit Adolf Merkl." *Mémoires de l'Academie Internationale de Droit Comparé*, II, 126–49.

1936    *Der Autoritäre Staat*. Vienna: Springer.

"Josef Redlich." *Jur. Blätter*, LXV, 485–86.

"Volksbildung, Wissenschaft und Politik." *Monatsschrift für Kultur und Politik*, I, 594–603.

1937    "Changes in the Ideas on Government and Constitution in Austria Since 1918." *Austrian Memorandum*, No. 3. Paris: International Studies Conference on Peaceful Change.

Review of *Carl Schmitts Theorie des "Politischen,"* by H. Krupka. *Zeitschrift für Öffentliches Recht*, XVII, 665.

Review of *Faschismus und Nationalsozialismus*, by Berger. *Zeitschrift für Öffentliches Recht*, XVII, 671–72.

Review of *Rechtssoziologie*, by B. Horvath. *Zeitschrift für Öffentliches Recht*, XVII, 667–71.

"Das Timurbild der Humanisten / Eine Studie zur politischen Mythenbildung." *Zeitschrift für Öffentliches Recht*, XVII, 545–92.

1938    *Die Politischen Religionen*. Vienna: Bermann-Fischer.

1939    Review of *The Ruling Class*, by G. Mosca. *Journal of Politics*, I, 434–36.

1940    "Extended Strategy: A New Technique of Dynamic Relations." *Journal of Politics*, II, 189–200.

"The Growth of the Race Idea." *Review of Politics*, II, 283–317.

1941    "Might and Right." (Review of *Law, the State, and the International Community*, by J. B. Scott.) *Review of Politics*, III, 122–23.

"The Mongol Orders of Submission to European Powers, 1245–1255." *Byzantion*, XV, 378–413.

"Some Problems of German Hegemony." *Journal of Politics*, III, 154–68.

"Two Recent Contributions to the Science of Law." (Review of *Introduction to the Sociology of Law*, by N. S. Timasheff, and *Jurisprudence: The Philosophy and Method of the Law*, by E. Bodenheimer.) *Review of Politics*, III, 399–404.

1942    Review of *The Structure of the Nazi Economy* by M. Y. Sweezy, and *The Dual State: A Contribution to the Theory of Dictatorship*, by E. Frankel. *Journal of Politics*, IV, 269–72.

"The Theory of Legal Science: A Review." *Louisiana Law Review*, IV, 554–72.

1944   "Nietzsche, the Crisis, and the War." *Journal of Politics*, VI, 177–212.

"Political Theory and the Pattern of General History." *American Political Science Review*, XXXVIII, 746–54.

Review of *The Decline of Liberalism as an Ideology*, by John H. Hallowell. *Journal of Politics*, VI, 107–109.

"Siger de Brabant." *Philosophy and Phenomenological Research*, IV, 507–26.

1945   Review of *Contemporary Italy: Its Intellectual and Moral Origins*, by C. C. Sforza. *Journal of Politics*, VII, 94–97.

1946   "Bakunin's Confession." *Journal of Politics*, VIII, 24–43.

Review of *The Lessons of Germany*, by G. Eisler *et al. American Political Science Review*, XL, 385–86.

Review of *Soviet Politics: At Home and Abroad*, by F. L. Schuman. *Journal of Politics*, VIII, 212–20.

1947   "Plato's Egyptian Myth." *Journal of Politics*, IX, 307–24.

Review of *The Myth of the State*, by Ernst Cassirer. *Journal of Politics*, IX, 445–47.

Review of *Post-War Governments of Europe*, by D. Fellman. *American Political Science Review*, XLI, 595–96.

Review of *Soviet Legal Theory: Its Social Background and Development*, by R. Schlessinger. *Journal of Politics*, IX, 129–31.

"Zu Sanders 'Allgemeiner Staatslehre.'" *Österreichische Zeitschrift für Öffentliches Recht*, n.s., I, 106–35.

1948   "The Origins of Scientism." *Social Research*, IV, 462–94.

"Political Theory and the Pattern of General History." In *Research in Political Science*, edited by Ernest S. Griffith. Chapel Hill: University of North Carolina Press.

Review of *Homo Ludens: Versuch einer Bestimmung des Spielelements in der Kultur*, by J. Huizinga. *Journal of Politics*, X, 179–87.

1949   "The Philosophy of Existence: Plato's *Gorgias*." *Review of Politics*, XI, 477–98.

Review of *The New Science*, by Giovanni Battista Vico, translated by G. Bergin and M. A. Fisch. *Catholic Historical Review*, XXXV, 75–76.

Review of *On Tyranny: An Interpretation of Xenophon's Hiero*, by Leo Strauss. *Review of Politics*, XI, 241–44.

Review of *Western Political Thought: A Historical Introduction from the Origins to Rousseau*, by J. Bowle. *Review of Politics*, XI, 262–63.

1950   "The Formation of the Marxian Revolutionary Idea." *Review of Politics*, XII, 275–302.

1951   "Machiavelli's Prince: Background and Formation." *Review of Politics*, XIII, 142–68.

1952    "Gnostische Politik." *Merkur*, IV, 301–17.

"Goethe's Utopia." In *Goethe After Two Centuries*, edited by Carl Hammer. Baton Rouge: Louisiana State University Press.

"More's *Utopia*." *Österreichische Zeitschrift für Öffentliches Recht*, n.s., III, 451–68.

*The New Science of Politics: An Introduction*. Chicago: University of Chicago Press.

1953    "The Oxford Political Philosophers." *Philosophical Quarterly*, III, 97–114.

Review of *Geschichtswissenschaft*, by F. Wagner. *American Political Science Review*, XLVII, 261–62.

Review of *The Origins of Totalitarianism*, by Hannah Arendt. With "A Reply" by Arendt and a "Concluding Remark" by Voegelin. *Review of Politics*, XV, 68–85.

"The World of Homer." *Review of Politics*, XV, 491–523.

1954    Review of *Plato's Modern Enemies and the Theory of Natural Law*, by John Wild. *American Political Science Review*, XLVIII, 859–62.

1955    Review of *Politique et Philosophie chez Thomas Hobbes*, by R. Polin. *American Political Science Review*, XLIX, 597–98.

1956    *Israel and Revelation*. Baton Rouge: Louisiana State University Press. Vol. I of *Order and History*. 5 vols.

"Necessary Moral Bases for Communication in a Democracy." In *Problems of Communication in a Pluralistic Society*. Milwaukee: Marquette University Press.

1957    *Plato and Aristotle*. Baton Rouge: Louisiana State University Press. Vol. III of *Order and History*. 5 vols.

*The World of the Polis*. Baton Rouge: Louisiana State University Press. Vol. II of *Order and History*. 5 vols.

1958    "Der Prophet Elias." *Hochland*, I, 325–39.

1959    "Demokratie im neuen Europa." *Gesellschaft—Staat—Erziehung*, IV, 293–300.

"Diskussionsbereitschaft." In *Erziehung zur Freiheit*, edited by Albert Hunold. Erlenbach-Zürich: Rentsch.

*Die Neue Wissenschaft der Politik / Eine Einführung*. Translation of *The New Science of Politics: An Introduction* (1952), with a foreword to the German edition. Munich: Pustet.

*Wissenschaft, Politik, und Gnosis*. Munich: Koesel.

1960    "El concepto de la 'buena sociedad.'" *Cuadrenos del Congreso por la Libertad de la Cultura*, Supplement 40, pp. 25–28.

"Historiogenesis." *Philosophisches Jahrbuch*, LXVIII, 419–46. Reprinted in *Philosophia Viva: Festschrift für Alois Dempf*, edited by Max Müller and Michael Schmaus. Freiburg/Munich: Albert, 1960. Reprinted in *Anamnesis: Zur Theorie der Geschichte und Poli-*

*tik* (1966). Translated and expanded in *The Ecumenic Age* (1974).

"Der Liberalismus und seine Geschichte." In *Christentum und Liberalismus: Studien und Bericht der katholischen Akademie in Bayern*, XIII, edited by Karl Forster. Munich: Zink.

"Religionersatz / Die gnostischen Massenbewegunen unserer Zeit." *Wort und Wahrheit*, XV, 5–18.

"La Société industrielle à la recherche de la raison." In *Colloques de Rheinfelden*, edited by Raymond Aron and George Kennan. Paris: Calmann-Levy.

"Verantwortung und Freiheit in Wirtschaft und Demokratie." *Die Aussprache*, X, 207–13.

1961    "Die industrielle Gesellschaft auf der Suche nach der Vernunft." Translation of "La Société industrielle à la recherche de la raison" (1960). In *Die industrielle Gesellschaft und die drei Welten*. Zurich: EVZ-Verlag.

"Les Perspectives d'Avenir de la civilisation occidentale." In *L'Historie et ses Interprétations: Entretiens autour de Arnold Toynbee*, edited by Raymond Aron. The Hague: Mouton.

"On Readiness to Rational Discussion." Translation of "Diskussionsbereitschaft" (1959). In *Freedom and Serfdom*, edited by Albert Hunold. Dordrecht: D. Reidel.

"Toynbee's History as a Search for Truth." In *The Intent of Toynbee's History*, edited by Edward T. Gargan. Chicago: Loyola University Press.

1962    "World Empire and the Unity of Mankind." *International Affairs*, XXXVIII, 170–88.

1963    "Hacia Una Nueva Ciencia del Orden Social." *Atlantida: Revista del pensamiento actual*, I, 121–37.

"Industrial Society in Search of Reason." Translation of "La Société industrielle à la recherche de la raison" (1960). In *World Technology and Human Destiny*, edited by Raymond Aron. Ann Arbor: University of Michigan Press.

"Das Rechte von Natur." *Österreichische Zeitschrift für Öffentliches Recht*, n.s., XIII, 38–51. Reprinted in *Anamnesis: Zur Theorie der Geschichte und Politik* (1966). English translation in *Anamnesis* (1978).

1964    "Demokratie und Industriegesellschaft." In *Die Unternehmerische Verantwortung in Unserer Gesellschaftsordnung*. Walter-Raymond Stiftung, IV. Cologne: West-deutscher Verlag.

"Ewiges Sein in der Zeit." In *Zeit und Geschichte: Dankesgabe an Rudolf Bultmann zum 80. Geburtstag*, edited by Erich Dinkler. Tübingen: J. C. B. Mohr. Reprinted in *Die Philosophie und die Frage nach dem Fortschritt*, edited by Helmut Kuhn and Franz Wiedmann. Munich: Pustet. Reprinted in *Anamnesis: Zur Theorie der*

*Geschichte und Politik* (1966). English translation in *Anamnesis* (1978).

"Der Mensch in Gesellschaft und Geschichte." *Österreichische Zeitschrift für Öffentliches Rechts*, n.s., XIV, 1–13.

1965    "Was ist Natur." *Historica*, I, 1–18. Reprinted in *Anamnesis: Zur Theorie der Geschichte und Politik* (1966).

1966    *Anamnesis: Zur Theorie der Geschichte und Politik*. Munich: Piper.

"Die deutsche Universität und die Ordnung der deutschen Gesellschaft." In *Die Deutsche Universität im Dritten Reich*, edited by L. Kotter. Munich: Piper. Reprinted as "Universität und Öffentlichkeit: Zur Pneumopathologie der deutschen Gesellschaft." *Wort und Wahrheit*, XXI, 497–518.

1967    "Immortality: Experience and Symbol." *Harvard Theological Review*, LX, 235–79.

"On Debate and Existence." *Intercollegiate Review*, III, 143–52.

1968    "Configurations in History." In *The Concept of Order*, edited by Paul Kuntz. Seattle: University of Washington Press.

"Helvetius." With Peter Leuschner. In *Aufklärung und Materialismus im Frankreich des 18. Jahrhunderts*, edited by Arno Baruzzi. Munich: List Verlag.

*La nuova Scienza politica*. Translation of *The New Science of Politics: An Introduction* (1952), with an Introduction by A. Del Noce. Turin: Borla.

*Science, Politics and Gnosticism*. Translation of *Wissenschaft, Politik, und Gnosis* (1959), with a Foreword to the American edition. Chicago: Henry Regnery.

"Zur Geschichte des Politischen Denkens." In *Zwischen Revolution und Restoration: Politisches Denkens in England in 17. Jahrhundert*. Munich: List.

1969    "History and Gnosis." In *The Old Testament and Christian Faith*, edited by Bernard Anderson. New York: Herder and Herder.

1970    "The Eclipse of Reality." In *Phenomenology and Social Reality*, edited by Maurice Natanson. The Hague: Martinus Nijhoff.

"Equivalences of Experience and Symbolization in History." In *Eternità e Storia, I valori permanenti nel divenire storico*. Florence: Valecchi.

1971    "The Gospel and Culture." In *Jesus and Man's Hope*, edited by D. Miller and D. G. Hadidian. Pittsburgh: Pittsburgh Theological Seminary Press.

"Henry James's 'The Turn of the Screw.' " With a Prefatory Note by Robert Heilman, a letter from Robert Heilman, and a Postscript: "On Paradise and Revolution." *Southern Review*, n.s., VII, 3–48.

"On Hegel: A Study in Sorcery." *Studium Generale*, XXIV, 335–68.

1972    *Anamnesis: Theoria della Storia e della Politica.* Translation of *Anamnesis: Zur Theorie der Geschichte und Politik* (1966). Milan: Giuffre.

1973    "On Classical Studies." *Modern Age*, XVII, 2–8.
        "Philosophies of History: An Interview with Eric Voegelin." *New Orleans Review*, II, 135–39.

1974    *The Ecumenic Age.* Baton Rouge: Louisiana State University Press. Vol. IV of *Order and History.* 5 vols.
        "Liberalism and Its History." Translation of "Der Liberalismus und seine Geschichte" (1960). *Review of Politics*, XXXVII, 504–20.

1975    *From Enlightenment to Revolution.* Edited by John H. Hallowell. Durham, N.C.: Duke University Press.
        "Response to Professor Altizer's 'A New History and a New but Ancient God?'" *Journal of the American Academy of Religion*, XLIII, 765–72. Reprinted in *Eric Voegelin's Thought: A Critical Appraisal*, edited by Ellis Sandoz. Durham, N.C.: Duke University Press, 1982.

1978    *Anamnesis.* Partial translation of *Anamnesis: Zur Theorie der Geschichte und Politik* (1966), with a new Chapter 1, "Remembrance of Things Past." Notre Dame, Ind.: University of Notre Dame Press.

1980    *Conversations with Eric Voegelin.* Transcript of four lectures and discussions held in Montreal in 1965, 1967, 1970, and 1976, edited by Eric O'Connor, S.J. Montreal: Thomas More Institute.

1981    "Der meditative Ursprung philosophischen Ordnungswissens." *Zeitschrift für Politik*, XXVIII, 130–37.
        "On Christianity" and "On Gnosticism." (Two letters to Alfred Schutz, 1953.) In *The Philosophy of Order: Essays on History, Consciousness, and Politics*, edited by Peter J. Opitz and Gregor Sebba. Stuttgart: Klett-Cotta.
        "Wisdom and the Magic of the Extreme: A Meditation." *Southern Review*, n.s., XVII, 235–87.
        "The American Experience." *Modern Age*, XXVI, 332–33.
        "Epilogue." In *Eric Voegelin's Thought: A Critical Appraisal*, edited by Ellis Sandoz. Durham, N.C.: Duke University Press.

1984    "Autobiographical Statement at Age Eighty-Two." In *The Beginning and the Beyond: Papers from the Gadamer and Voegelin Conferences*, edited by Frederick Lawrence. Supplementary Issue of *Lonergan Workshop*, IV. Chico, Calif.: Scholar's Press.
        "Consciousness and Order." Translation of "Vorwort" to *Anamnesis: Zur Theorie der Geschichte und Politik* (1966). In *The Beginning and the Beyond: Papers from the Gadamer and Voegelin Conferences*, edited by Frederick Lawrence. Supplementary Issue of *Lonergan Workshop*, IV. Chico, Calif.: Scholar's Press.

"The Meditative Origin of the Philosophical Knowledge of Order." Translation of "Der meditative Ursprung philosophischen Ordnungswissens" (1981). In *The Beginning and the Beyond: Papers from the Gadamer and Voegelin Conferences,* edited by Frederick Lawrence. Supplementary Issue of *Lonergan Workshop,* IV. Chico, Calif.: Scholar's Press.

1985    "Equivalences of Experience and Symbolization in History." (Reprint of 1970 essay with author's corrections.) *Philosophical Studies* (Dublin), XXVIII, 88–103.

"The German University and the Order of German Society: A Reconsideration of the Nazi Era." Translation of "Die deutsche Universität und die Ordnung der deutschen Gesellschaft" (1966). *Intercollegiate Review,* XX, 7–27.

"Quod Deus dicitur." *Journal of the American Academy of Religion,* LIII, 569–84.

1986    *Political Religions.* Translation of *Die politischen Religionen* (1938). Lewiston, N.Y.: Edwin Mellen Press.

1987    *In Search of Order.* Baton Rouge: Louisiana State University Press. Vol. V of *Order and History.* 5 vols.

1989    *Autobiographical Reflections.* Edited by Ellis Sandoz. Baton Rouge: Louisiana State University Press.

1990    *"What Is History?" and Other Late Unpublished Writings.* Edited by Thomas A. Hollweck and Paul Caringella. Vol. XXVIII of *The Collected Works of Eric Voegelin.* 34 vols. projected. Baton Rouge: Louisiana State University Press.

1991    *"The Nature of the Law" and Related Legal Writings.* Edited by Robert Anthony Pascal, James Lee Babin, and John William Corrington. Vol. XXVII of *The Collected Works of Eric Voegelin,* 34 vols. projected. Baton Rouge: Louisiana State University Press.

## Works on Eric Voegelin

Adkins, Arthur W. H. Review of *The World of the Polis* and *Plato and Aristotle. Journal of Helenic Studies,* LXXXI (1961), 192–93.

Adler, F. Review of *Der Autoritäre Staat. Praeger Juristische Zeitschrift,* XI (1936), 745.

Albright, W. F. Review of *Israel and Revelation. Theological Studies,* XXII (1961), 270–79. Reprinted in Albright, *History, Archaeology, and Christian Humanism.* London: Black, 1965.

Altizer, Thomas J. J. "A New History and a New but Ancient God." *Journal of the American Academy of Religion,* XLIII (1975), 757–64. With a response by Eric Voegelin, 765–72. Reprinted in *Eric Voegelin's Thought: A Critical Appraisal*, edited by Ellis Sandoz. Durham, N.C.: Duke University Press, 1982.

———. Review of *Anamnesis*. *Journal of Religion*, LIX (1979), 375–76.

Amberger, H. Review of *Die Rassenidee in der Geistesgeschichte von Ray bis Carus*. *Die Sonne*, XIII (1936), 371.

Ammerman, Robert. Review of *Order and History*, Volumes I–III. *Philosophy and Phenomenological Research*, XIX (1958), 539–40.

Anastoplo, George. "On How Eric Voegelin Has Read Plato and Aristotle." *Independent Journal of Philosophy*, V/VI (1988), 85–91.

Anderson, Bernhard W. "Politics and the Transcendent." *Political Science Reviewer*, I (1971), 1–29. Revised and expanded in *Eric Voegelin's Search for Order in History*, edited by Stephen A. McKnight. Rev. ed. Lanham, Md.: University Press of America, 1987.

Anderson, William. Review of *The New Science of Politics*. *Journal of Politics*, XV (1953), 563–68.

Archard, R. M. Review of *Israel and Revelation*. *Theologische Zeitschrift*, XIV (1958), 138–39.

Atkins, Anselm. "Eric Voegelin and the Decline of Tragedy." *Drama Survey*, V (1966), 280–85.

Aufricht, Hans. "A Restatement of Political Theory: A Note on Eric Voegelin's *The New Science of Politics*. *Western Political Quarterly*, VI (1953), 448–68. Reprinted in *Eric Voegelin's Search for Order in History*, edited by Stephen A. McKnight. Rev. ed. Lanham, Md.: University Press of America, 1987.

Baruzzi, A. "Reflections on the World and History in the Tradition of Eric Voegelin." *Filozof Istraz* (Yugoslavia), XXVII (1988), 1199–1202.

———. Review of *Order and History*, Volumes I–III. *Thought*, XXXIII (1958), 273–78.

Berry, Thomas. Review of *The World of the Polis*. *Sign*, V (1958), 66–67.

Beum, Robert. "Modernity and the Left: An Equivalence." *Georgia Review*, XXVII (1973), 309–20.

Bloom, Allan. Review of *Wissenschaft, Politik, und Gnosis*. *American Political Science Review*, LIV (1960), 226–27.

Bradford, M. E. "A Generation of the Intellectual Right: At the Head of the Column." *Modern Age*, XXVI (1982), 292–96.

———. "A New Science of Politics." *Social Research*, XX (1953), 230–35.

Bradley, Gerard V. "Church Autonomy in the Constitutional Order: The End of Church and State." *Louisiana Law Review*, XLIX (1989), 1057–87.

Brecht, Arnold. Review of *The New Science of Politics*. *Annals of the American Academy of Political and Social Sciences*, CCCVII (1953), 215–16.

Brehier, E. Review of *Rasse und Staat*. *La Revue critique d'historie et de Littérature*, n.s., C (1939), 367–68.

Brinkmann, C. Review of *Über die Form des amerikanischen Geistes*. *Historische Zeitschrift*, CXL (1929), 109–11.

Brohmer, Review of *Die Rassenidee in der Geistesgeschichte von Ray bis Carus.* *Zeitschrift für deutsche Bildung,* XI (1935), 330.

Brooks, Cleanth. "Walker Percy and Modern Gnosticism." *Southern Review,* n.s., XII (1977), 677–87. Revised version in *The Art of Walker Percy: Stratagems for Being,* edited by Panthea R. Broughton. Baton Rouge: Louisiana State University Press, 1977.

Brown, Trusdell S. Review of *Order and History,* Volumes I–III. *Annals of the American Academy of Political and Social Sciences,* CCCXIV (1958), 168–74, 187–88.

Byrne, Patrick H. "The Significance of Voegelin's Work for the Philosophy of Science." In *The Beginning and the Beyond: Papers from the Gadamer and Voegelin Conferences,* edited by Frederick Lawrence. Supplementary Issue of *Lonergan Workshop,* IV. Chico, Calif.: Scholar's Press, 1984.

Caringella, Paul. "Eric Voegelin's View of History as a Drama of Transfiguration." *International Philosophical Quarterly,* XXXIII (1990), 7–22.

Carmody, Denise L., and John Tully Carmody. "Voegelin and the Restoration of Order: A Meditation." *Horizons,* XIV (1987), 82–96.

Cavanaugh, Gerald. Review of *From Enlightenment to Revolution.* *American Historical Review,* LXXXI (1976), 359.

Cherniss, H. Review of *Plato and Aristotle.* *Lustrum,* V (1960), 445.

Chroust, A. H. Review of *The World of the Polis.* *Thomist,* XXI (1958), 381–91.

Coggin, Bruce W. "Eric Voegelin's Early Career: The Life and Thought of the Philosopher Up to Publication of *Political Religions.*" *The World & I,* I (1986), 696–703.

———. "Sir John Fortescue on Organic Politics." *Modern Age,* XXIII (1979), 266–71.

Cooper, Barry. "A Fragment from Eric Voegelin's History of Western Political Thought." *Political Science Reviewer,* VII (1977), 23–52.

———. "An Introduction to Voegelin's Account of Western Civil Theologies." In *Voegelin and the Theologian: Ten Studies in Interpretation,* edited by John Kirby and William M. Thompson. Lewiston, N.Y.: Edwin Mellen Press, 1983.

———. *The Political Theory of Eric Voegelin.* Toronto Studies in Theology, XXVII. Lewiston, N.Y.: Edwin Mellen Press, 1986.

———. "Voegelin's Concept of Historiogenesis." *Historical Reflections/ Réflexions historiques,* IV (1978), 231–51.

Corrington, John William. "*Order and History*: The Breaking of the Program." *Denver Quarterly,* X (1975), 115–22.

———. "A Rebirth of Philosophical Thought." (Review of *The Voegelinian Revolution: A Biographical Introduction,* by Ellis Sandoz, and *Eric Voegelin's Thought: A Critical Appraisal,* edited by Ellis Sandoz.) *Southern Review,* n.s., XX (1984), 738–42.

Corsale, Massimo. Review of *Science, Politics and Gnosticism.* *Revista internazionale de Filosofia del dritto,* XLVIII (1971), 195–96.

D'Agostino, A. Review of *Anamnesis. Revista internazionale di Filosofia del Dritto*, L (1973), 576–77.

Dahl, Robert A. "The Science of Politics: New and Old." *World Politics*, VII (1955), 479–89.

Dallmayr, Fred. "Voegelin's Search for Order." In Dallmayr, *Margins of Political Discourse*. Albany: State University of New York Press, 1989.

De Fraine, J. Review of *Israel and Revelation. Biidraien* (Maastricht). (1957), 78.

Dempf, Alois. Review of *Anamnesis. Philosophisches Jahrbuch*, LXXIV (1967), 405–406.

Dempf, Alois, Hannah Arendt, and Friedrich Engel-Janosi, eds. *Politische Ordnung und menschliche Existenz: Festgabe für Eric Voegelin zum 60. Geburtstag*. Munich: C. H. Beck, 1962.

Denton, Robert C. Review of *Israel and Revelation. American Theological Review*, XLVI (1965), 231.

Dillon, Michael. "Symbolization and the Search for Order." *Intercollegiate Review*, XI (1976), 103–11.

DiNapoli, Thomas J., and Ernest Easterly III. "The Break in Voegelin's Program." *Political Science Reviewer*, VII (1977), 1–21.

———. "The Nightmare Years." *The World & I*, I (1986), 687–90.

Douglass, Bruce. "The Gospel and Political Order: Eric Voegelin on the Political Role of Christianity." *Journal of Politics*, XXXVIII (1976), 25–45.

———. Review of *The Ecumenic Age. Christian Century*, III (1976), 155–56.

Dugern, B. Review of *Der Autoritäre Staat. Historische Zeitschrift*, CLVII (1937), 152.

Dupre, Louis. "A Conservative Anarchist: Eric Voegelin 1901–1985." *Clio: A Journal of Literature, History, and the Philosophy of History*, XIV (1985), 423–31.

East, John. "Eric Voegelin and American Conservative Thought." *Modern Age*, XXII (1978), 114–32.

Ehrenberg, Victor. Review of *The World of the Polis. Historische Zeitschrift*, CLXXI (1959), 364–73.

Ehrlich, E. L. Review of *Israel and Revelation. Zeitschrift für Religions und Geistesgeschichte*, X (1958), 295–96.

Engel-Janosi, Friedrich. Review of *Order and History*, Volumes I–III. *Wort und Wahrheit*, XIII (1958), 538–44.

Fisch, Harold. Review of *Israel and Revelation. Journal of Jewish Studies*, IX (1958), 203–204.

Fischer, Edgar Jay. Review of *Israel and Revelation. Annals of the American Academy of Political and Social Sciences*, CCCX (1957), 233.

Fohren, Georg. "Israels Staatsordnung im Rahmen des Alten Orients." *Zeitschrift für Öffentliches Recht*, n.s., VIII (1957), 129–48.

Franklin, J. A. Review of *The New Science of Politics. Political Science Quarterly*, LXVIII (1953), 157–58.

Franz, Michael. "Supplemental Bibliography." In *Eric Voegelin's Search for*

*Order in History*, edited by Stephen A. McKnight. Rev. ed. Lanham, Md.: University Press of America, 1987.

Freeman, J. Leiper. Review of *From Enlightenment to Revolution*. *Journal of Politics*, XXXVIII (1976), 190–93.

Freund, J. Review of *Anamnesis*. *Revue de Metaphysique et de Morale*, LXXIII (1968), 386–87.

Fueyo, J. F. "Eric Voegelin y su Reconstruccion de la Ciencia Politica." *Revista de Estudios Politicos*, LXXIX (1955), 67–116.

Galgan, G. L. Review of *Anamnesis*. *Library Journal*, CIII (1978), 1064.

Gargan, Edward. "The Ultimate Service of History." (Review of *Order and History*, Volumes I–III.) *Critic*, XVI (1958), 7–8, 62–63.

Gebhardt, Jurgen. "Epilogue." In *In Search of Order*, by Eric Voegelin. Baton Rouge: Louisiana State University Press, 1987.

———. "Eric Voegelin: Leben und Werk." *Politische Vierteljahresschrift*, XXVI (1985), 313–17.

Gehman, H. S. "A Theology of History." *Interpretation*, XII (1958), 318–21.

Gerloff, W. "Eric Voegelin's *Anamnesis*." *Southern Review*, n.s., VIII (1971), 68–88.

———. Review of *Über die Form des amerikanischen Geistes*. *Vergangenheit und Gegenwart*, LIV (1931), 452–54.

Germino, Dante. "Eric Voegelin: The In-Between of Human Life." In *Contemporary Political Philosophers*, edited by Anthony de Crespigny and Kenneth R. Minogue. New York: Dodd, Mead, 1975.

———. "Eric Voegelin's Contribution to Contemporary Political Theory." *Review of Politics*, XXVI (1964), 378–402.

———. "Eric Voegelin's Framework for Political Evaluation in His Recently Published Work." *American Political Science Review*, LXXII (1978), 110–321. Reprinted in *Eric Voegelin's Thought: A Critical Appraisal*, edited by Ellis Sandoz. Durham, N.C.: Duke University Press, 1982.

———. *Political Philosophy and the Open Society*. Baton Rouge: Louisiana State University Press, 1982.

———. Review of *The Ecumenic Age*. *Journal of Politics*, XXXVII (1975), 847–48.

———. Review of *From Enlightenment to Revolution*. *National Review*, XXVII (1975), 1185–86.

———. "Two Conceptions of Political Philosophy." In *The Post-Behavioral Era*, edited by G. W. Carey and G. S. Graham, Jr. New York: McKay, 1972.

———. "Voegelin, Christianity, and Political Theory: *The New Science of Politics* Reconsidered." *Revista internazionale di filosofia del dritto*, LXII (1985), 40–64.

Gerwith, Alan. Review of *The New Science of Politics*. *Ethics*, LXIII (1953), 142–44.

Geyer, E. Review of *Rasse und Staat*. *Mitteilungen der Anthropologischen Gesellschaft*, LXIV (1934), 339.

Glaser, L. Review of *Die Rassenidee in der Geistesgeschichte von Ray bis Carus*. *Schönere Zukunft*, IX (1933), 801.

Gottfried, Paul E. "On the European Roots of Modern American Conservatism." *Thought*, LV (1980), 196–206.

———. *The Search for Historical Meaning: Hegel and the Postwar American Right*. De Kalb: Northern Illinois University Press, 1986.

Greenberg, Moshe. Review of *Israel and Revelation*. *American Political Science Review*, LI (1957), 1101–1103.

Gueguen, John A. "Voegelin's *From Enlightenment to Revolution*: A Review Article." *Thomist*, XLII (1978), 123–34.

Guerke, N. Review of *Rasse und Staat*. *Deutsche Literatur-Zeitung*, IV (1933), 2196–98.

———. Review of *Rasse und Staat*. *Verwaltungs-Blatt*, LIV (1933), 781–85.

Hadas, Moses. Review of *Order and History*, Volumes I–III. *Journal of the History of Ideas*, XIX (1958), 442–44.

Hallowell, John. "Editor's Preface." In *From Enlightenment to Revolution*, by Eric Voegelin. Durham, N.C.: Duke University Press, 1975.

———. "Existence in Tension: Man in Search of His Humanity." *Political Science Reviewer*, II (1972), 162–84. Reprinted in *Eric Voegelin's Search for Order in History*, edited by Stephen A. McKnight. Rev. ed. Lanham, Md.: University Press of America, 1987.

Harrigan, Anthony. "The Changing Pattern of Voegelin's Conception of History and Consciousness." *Southern Review*, n.s., VII (1971), 49–67. Reprinted in *Eric Voegelin's Search for Order in History*, edited by Stephen A. McKnight. Rev. ed. Lanham, Md.: University Press of America, 1987.

———. "Political Gnosticism." *Christian Century*, LXX (1953), 386.

Havard, William. "The Disenchantment of the Intellectuals." In *Politische Ordnung und menschliche Existenz: Festgabe für Eric Voegelin zum 60. Geburtstag*, edited by Alois Dempf, Hannah Arendt, and Friedrich Engel-Janosi. Munich: C. H. Beck, 1962.

———. "The Method and Results of Philosophical Anthropology in America." *Archiv für Rechts- und Sozialphilosophie*, LVII (1961), 395–415.

———. "Notes on Voegelin's Contributions to Political Theory." *Polity*, X (1977), 33–64. Revised and expanded version in *Eric Voegelin's Thought: A Critical Appraisal*, edited by Ellis Sandoz. Durham, N.C.: Duke University Press, 1982.

———. Review of *The Ecumenic Age*. *American Historical Review*, LXXXI (1976), 557–58.

———. "Voegelin's Diagnosis of the Western Crisis." *Denver Quarterly*, X (1975), 127–34.

Heilke, Thomas W. *Voegelin on the Idea of Race: An Analysis of Modern European Racism*. Baton Rouge: Louisiana State University Press, 1990.

Hermann, Klaus J. Review of *Anamnesis*. *Canadian Journal of Political Science*, III (1970), 492–94.

Hesch, M. Review of *Die Rassenidee in der Geistesgeschichte von Ray bis Carus. Vergangenheit und Gegenwart*, XXV (1935), 627.

Hollweck, Thomas. "Gedanken zur Arbeitsmethode Eric Voegelins." *Philosophisches Jahrbuch*, LXXXVIII (1981), 136–52.

Hook, Sidney. Review of *Israel and Revelation*. *Society for Old Testament Study Booklist* (1957), 57.

Horn, R. L. Review of *Israel and Revelation*. *Union Theological Seminary Quarterly Review*, XII (1957), 65–67.

Hughes, E. C. Review of *Rasse und Staat*. *American Journal of Sociology*, XL (1934), 337–78.

Hughes, Glenn. "Eric Voegelin's View of History as a Drama of Transfiguration." *International Philosophical Quarterly*, XXX (1990), 449–64.

Hummel, H. Review of *Israel and Revelation*. *Concordia Theological Monthly*, XXIX (1958), 53–54.

James, E. O. Review of *Israel and Revelation*. *Hibbert Journal*, LV (1957), 408–10.

Kerferd, G. B. Review of *The World of the Polis* and *Plato and Aristotle*. *Classical Review*, IX (1959), 251–52.

Keulman, Kenneth. *The Balance of Consciousness: Eric Voegelin's Political Theory*. University Park, Pa.: Pennsylvania State University Press, 1991.

———. "The Noetic Structure of the Psyche in the Theory of Consciousness in Eric Voegelin." Ph.D. dissertation, St. Michael's College, Institute of Christian Thought, University of Toronto, 1979.

Kirby, John. "The Divine and the Human in Voegelin's 'What is Political Reality.'" Ph.D. dissertation, St. Michael's College, Institute of Christian Thought, University of Toronto, 1980.

———. Review of *The Ecumenic Age* and *From Enlightenment to Revolution*. *Canadian Journal of Political Science*, IX (1976), 363–64.

———. "Symbolism and Dogmatism: Voegelin's Distinction." *Ecumenist*, XIII (1975), 26–31.

Kirby, John, and William M. Thompson, eds. *Voegelin and the Theologian: Ten Studies in Interpretation*. Lewiston, N.Y.: Edwin Mellen Press, 1983.

Kirk, Russell. "Behind the Veil of History." *Yale Review*, XLVI (1957), 466–76.

———. "Eric Voegelin's Normative Labor." In Kirk, *Enemies of the Permanent Things: Observations of Abnormality in Literature and Politics*. New Rochelle, N.Y.: Arlington House, 1969.

———. "In Search of Eric Voegelin." *New Oxford Review* (June, 1978), 19–20.

Kohn, Hans. "Politics and Ethics." *Nation*, CLXXVI (1953), 57.

Kolnai, M. Review of *Der Autoritäre Staat*. *Der österreichische Volkswirt*, XXIX (1936), 51.

Kramm, Lothar. "Gaining the Open Horizon: Eric Voegelin's Search for Order." *History of Political Thought*, VII (1986), 511–26.

———. "Das Problem einer Philosophischen Historiographie: Zum Werk von Eric Voegelin." *Zeitschrift für Politik*. XXVIII (1981), 116–29.

Kuhn, Helmut. Review of *Plato and Aristotle*. *Historische Zeitschrift*, CXCI (1960), 360–64.

Laver, S. "On 'The Meditative Origin of the Philosophical Consciousness of Order.'" In *The Beginning and the Beyond: Papers from the Gadamer and Voegelin Conferences*, edited by Frederick Lawrence. Supplementary Issue of *Lonergan Workshop*, IV. Chico, Calif.: Scholar's Press, 1984.

———. Review of *The World of the Polis* and *Plato and Aristotle*. *Journal of Jewish Studies*, IX (1958), 107–108.

Lawrence, Frederick, ed. "Theology's Situation: Questions to Eric Voegelin." In *The Beginning and the Beyond: Papers from the Gadamer and Voegelin Conferences*, edited by Frederick Lawrence. Supplementary Issue of *Lonergan Workshop*, IV. Chico, Calif.: Scholar's Press (1984).

Lebzelter, V. Review of *Die Rassenidee in der Geistesgeschichte von Ray bis Carus*. *Blätter für deutsche Philosophie*, VIII (1934), 192–93.

Legaz, L. Review of *Der Autoritäre Staat*. *Universidad* (Saragossa), XIV (1937), 594.

Lenz, A. Review of *Der Autoritäre Staat*. *Zeitschrift für Öeffentliches Recht*, XVII (1937), 258.

Levy, David J. "Eric Voegelin and the Spirit of the Age." *The World & I* (April, 1988), 453–58.

———. "The Life of Order and the Order of Life: Eric Voegelin on Modernity and the Problem of Philosophical Anthropology." *Man and World*, XXIV (1991), 241–65.

———. *Political Order: Philosophical Anthropology, Modernity, and the Challenge of Ideology*. Baton Rouge: Louisiana State University Press, 1987.

———. "Voegelin as Philosopher." *Modern Age*, XXIV (1980), 47–54.

Lucey, William L. Review of *The New Science of Politics*. *Social Order*, III (1953), 95–96.

Lutkens, C. Review of *Über die Form des amerikanischen Geistes*. *Archiv für Sozialwissenschaft und Sozialpolitik*, LXII (1929), 615.

Lutterbeck, G. A. Review of *Rasse und Staat*. *Stimme der Zeit*, CXXIX (1935), 68.

McCarrol, Joseph. "Man in Search of Divine Order in History." *Philosophical Studies* (Dublin), XXVIII (1981), 15–44.

———. "Some Growth Areas in Voegelin's Analysis." *Philosophical Studies* (Dublin), XXXI (1986–87), 280–300.

McDonald, L. C. "Voegelin and the Positivists: A New Science of Politics?" *Midwest Journal of Political Science*, I (1957), 233–51.

McGuire, Martin R. P. Review of *Order and History*, Volumes I–III. *Catholic Historical Review*, XLVIII (1962), 410–12.

McKnight, Stephen A. "Cassirer, Toynbee, and Voegelin on the Intelligible Unity of History." Ph.D. dissertation, Emory University, 1972.

———. *The Modern Age and the Recovery of Ancient Wisdom: A Reconsideration of Historical Consciousness, 1450–1650*. Columbia: University of Missouri Press, 1991.

———. "Recent Developments in Voegelin's Philosophy of History." *Sociological Analysis*, XXXVI (1975), 357–65.

———. "The Renaissance Magus and the Modern Messiah." *Religious Studies Review*, V (1979), 81–88.

———. *Sacralizing the Secular: The Renaissance Origins of Modernity*. Baton Rouge: Louisiana State University Press, 1989.

———. "Understanding Modernity: A Reappraisal of the Gnostic Element." *Intercollegiate Review*, XIV (1979), 107–17.

———. "Voegelin on the Modern Intellectual and Political Crises." *Sociological Analysis*, XXXVII (1976), 265–71.

———, ed. *Eric Voegelin's Search for Order in History*. Baton Rouge: Louisiana State University Press, 1978. Rev. ed. Lanham, Md.: University Press of America, 1987.

Marks, J. H. Review of *Israel and Revelation*. *Theology Today*, XV (1958), 266–69.

Mason, John Brown. Review of *Der Autoritäre Staat*. *American Sociological Review*, II (1937), 479–80.

Mauchline, J. Review of *The World of the Polis* and *Plato and Aristotle*. *Journal of Semitic Studies*, V (1960), 84–85.

Mayer, J. Review of *The New Science of Politics*. *Dublin Review*, CCXXIX (1955), 114–15.

Mead, Walter B. "Christian Ambiguity and Social Disorder." *Interpretation*, III (1973), 221–42.

———. "Restructuring Reality: Signs of the Times." *Review of Politics*, XXXIV (1972), 342–66.

Metz, Karl Heinz. "Unordnung und Geschichte: Historiographische Randbemerkungen zum Werk Eric Voegelins." *Saeculum*, XXXIV (1983), 105–25.

Meyendorf, A. Review of *Der Autoritäre Staat*. *Political Science Quarterly*, LIII (1937), 478–79.

Midgley, E. B. F. *The Ideology of Max Weber: A Thomist Critique*. Totowa, N.J.: Barnes and Noble, 1983.

Miller, Eugene. "Positivism, Historicism, and Political Inquiry." *American Political Science Review*, LXVI (1972), 816.

Molnar, Thomas. "Eric Voegelin: A Portrait, an Appreciation." *Modern Age*, XXV (1981), 381–87.

———. Review of *Science, Politics and Gnosticism*. *Modern Age*, XIV (1970), 334–37.

———. "Voegelin as Historian." *Modern Age*, XIX (1975), 427–29.

Montgomery, Marion. "Eric Voegelin and the End of Our Questioning." *Modern Age*, XXIII (1979), 233–45.

———. "Eric Voegelin as Prophetic Philosopher." *Southern Review*, n.s., XXIV (1988), 115–33.

————. "Flannery O'Connor, Eric Voegelin, and the Question that Lies Between Them." *Modern Age*, XXII (1978), 133–43.

————. *The Men I Have Chosen for Fathers: Literary and Philosophical Passages.* Columbia: University of Missouri Press, 1990.

————. "The Poet and the Disquieting Shadow of Being: Flannery O'Connor's Voegelinian Dimension." *Intercollegiate Review*, XIII (1977), 3–14.

Morgan, Miles. Review of *From Enlightenment to Revolution*. *Journal of Politics*, XXXVIII (1976), 191.

Moulakis, Athanasios. "Political Reality and History in the Work of Eric Voegelin." In *The Promise of History*, edited by Athanasios Moulakis. Berlin: De Gruyter, n.d.

Muhlmann, W. Review of *Rasse und Staat*. *Archiv für Rassen und Gesellschaftsbiologie*, XXVII (1934), 431–33.

Muller, H. J. "Shuddering Before the Mystery." *New Republic*, CXXV (1956), 19–20.

Muller, Steven. Review of *Politische Ordnung und menschliche Existenz: Festgabe für Eric Voegelin zum 60. Geburtstag*, edited by Alois Dempf, Hannah Arendt, and Friedrich Engel-Janosi. *American Political Science Review*, LVI (1963), 967–68.

Nieli, Russell. "Eric Voegelin: Gnosticism, Mysticism, and Modern Radical Politics." *Southern Review*, n.s., XXIII, 332–48.

————. "From Myth to Philosophy: Eric Voegelin's Theory of Experience and Symbolization." Ph.D. dissertation, Princeton University, 1979.

Niemeyer, Gerhart. "Conservatism and the New Political Theory." *Modern Age*, XXIII (1979), 115–22.

————. "The Depth and Height of Political Order." *Review of Politics*, XXI (1958), 588–96.

————. "Eric Voegelin, 1952." *Modern Age*, XXVI (1982), 262–66.

————. "Eric Voegelin's Achievement." *Modern Age*, IX (1965), 132–40.

————. "Eric Voegelin's Philosophy and the Drama of Mankind." *Modern Age*, XX (1976), 28–39.

————. "The Fulness of the Quest: Eric Voegelin's Final Volume." In *Eric Voegelin's Search for Order in History*, edited by Stephen A. McKnight. Rev. ed. Lanham, Md.: University Press of America, 1987

————. "God and Man, World and Society: The Last Work of Eric Voegelin." *Review of Politics*, LI (1989), 107–23.

————. "Greatness in Political Science: Eric Voegelin (1901–1985)." *Modern Age*, XXIX (1985), 104–109.

————. "The Order of Consciousness." *Review of Politics*, XXX (1968), 251–56.

————. "The Order of History and the History of Order." *Review of Politics*, XIX (1957), 403–409.

————. "The Philosophy of Religion and History." *Modern Age*, XXVII (1983), 83–85.

Nisbet, Robert. "Eric Voegelin's Vision." *Public Interest,* VII (1983), 110–17.
Noble, David W. "Conservatism in the USA." *Journal of Contemporary History* (Great Britain), XIII (1978), 635–52.
North, R. S. S. Review of *Israel and Revelation. Bibliotheca Orientalis,* XVIII (1961), 85–87.
Oates, W. J. Review of *Plato and Aristotle. Classical Journal,* LVI (1960), 90–92.
Opitz, Peter J. "Autorenportrait: Eric Voegelin." *Criticon Konservative Zeitschrift,* XIX (1973), 200–204.
Opitz, Peter J., and Gregor Sebba, eds. *The Philosophy of Order: Essays on History, Consciousness, and Politics.* Stuttgart: Klett-Cotta, 1981.
Palvi, M. Review of *Über die Form des amerikanischen Geistes. Archiv für Rechts- und Wirtschaftsphilosophie,* XXII (1929), 645–47.
Pangle, Thomas. Review of *From Enlightenment to Revolution. Political Theory,* IV (1976), 105–108.
Panichas, George A. "*The New York Times* and Eric Voegelin." *Modern Age,* XXIX (1985), 98–103.
Parry, Stanley. "The Restoration of Tradition." *Modern Age,* V (1961), 125–38.
Pauken, Mary Ann. "On Eagles' Wings: Eric Voegelin's Onto-Theological Conception of History." Ph.D. dissertation, University of Texas, 1986.
Perkins, Pheme. "Gnosis and the Life of the Spirit: The Price of Pneumatic Order." In *Voegelin and the Theologian: Ten Studies in Interpretation,* edited by John Kirby and William M. Thompson. Lewiston, N.Y.: Edwin Mellen Press, 1983.
Perkmann, A. Review of *Der Autoritäre Staat. Monatsschrift für Kultur und Politik* (November, 1936), 1041.
Peters, Ted. "Voegelin for the Theologian." *Dialog,* XXVIII (1989), 210–22.
Pistoia, Franco. Review of *Science, Politics and Gnosticism. Giornale di Metafisica,* XXVI (1971), 538–39.
Pitamic, L. Review of *Über die Form des amerikanischen Geistes. Österreichische Zeitschrift für Öffentliches Recht,* VIII (1929), 637–39.
Plessner, N. Review of *Rasse und Staat. Zeitschrift für Öffentliches Recht,* XIV (1934), 407.
Porteous, N. W. Review of *Order and History,* Volumes I–III. *English Historical Review,* LXX (1960), 288–90.
Porter, J. M. "A Philosophy of History as a Philosophy of Consciousness." *Denver Quarterly,* X (1975), 96–104.
———. "Eric Voegelin's Philosophy of History and Consciousness." *Marxist Perspectives,* III (1980), 152–69.
Pritchard, J. B. Review of *Israel and Revelation. American Historical Review,* LXIII (1958), 640–44.
Purcell, Brendan. "Solzhenitsyn's Struggle for Personal, Social, and Historic Anamnesis." *Philosophical Studies* (Dublin), XXVIII (1981), 62–87.

Rabl, O. Review of *Der Autoritäre Staat. Historische Vierteljahrsschrift*, XXXI (1937), 397–406.

Rasch, E. Review of *Rasse und Staat. Koelnische Zeitung*, June 18, 1933.

Renthe-Fink, L. Review of *Die Rassenidee in der Geistesgeschichte von Ray bis Carus. Berliner Boersenzeit*, March 25, 1933.

Rhodes, James M. *The Hitler Movement: A Modern Millenarian Revolution.* Stanford: Hoover Institution Press, 1980.

———. "Philosophy, Revelation, and Political Theory: Leo Strauss and Eric Voegelin." *Journal of Politics*, XLIX (1987), 1036–60.

———. "Voegelin and Christian Faith." *Center Journal*, II (1983), 55–105.

Richard, G. Review of *Rasse und Staat. Nouvelle revue de Hongrie*, XLII (1935), 73–75.

Rivero, F. H. Review of *Science, Politics and Gnosticism. Revista Venozolana de Filosofia*, I (1973), 135–38.

Robinson, C. A. Review of *Order and History*, Volumes I–III. *American Historical Review*, LXIII (1958), 939–41.

Rosen, Stanley. "Order and History." *Review of Metaphysics*, XII (1958), 257–76.

Rosenfelder, K. Review of *Die Rassenidee in der Geistesgeschichte von Ray bis Carus. Nordische Stimmen* (Erfurt), V (1939), 109.

Roucek, J. S. Review of *The New Science of Politics. American Sociological Review*, XIX (1954), 494–95.

Rowley, H. H. Review of *Israel and Revelation. Journal of Biblical Literature*, LXXVI (1957), 157–58.

Russell, Greg. "Eric Voegelin on the Truth of the In-Between Life: A Meditation on Existential Unrest." *Interpretation*, XVI (1989), 415–25.

Sander, F. Review of *Der Autoritäre Staat. Praeger Juristische Zeitschrift*, XVII (1937), 278.

Sandoz, Ellis. "Eric Voegelin and the Nature of Philosophy." *Modern Age*, XIII (1969), 152–68.

———. "The Foundations of Voegelin's Political Theory." *Political Science Reviewer*, I (1971), 30–73.

———. "In Memoriam: Eric Voegelin." *Southern Review*, n.s., XXI (1985), 372–75.

———. Introduction to *In Search of Order*, by Eric Voegelin. Baton Rouge: Louisiana State University Press, 1987.

———. "The Philosophical Science of Politics Beyond Behavioralism." In *The Post-Behavioral Era*, edited by G. W. Carey and G. S. Graham, Jr. New York: McKay, 1972.

———. Review of *From Enlightenment to Revolution. Western Political Quarterly*, XXVIII (1975), 744–45.

———. Review of *Order and History*, Volumes I–III. *Social Research*, XXVIII (1961), 229–34.

———. Review of *Science, Politics and Gnosticism. National Review*, XXI (1969), 32–33.

————. "The Science and Demonology of Politics." *Intercollegiate Review,*
V (1968), 117–23.

————. *The Voegelinian Revolution: A Biographical Introduction.* Baton Rouge:
Louisiana State University Press, 1981.

————. "Voegelin Read Anew: Political Philosophy in the Age of Ideology." *Modern Age,* XVII (1973), 257–63.

————. "Voegelin's Idea of Historical Form." *Cross Currents,* XII (1962),
41–63.

————. *Eric Voegelin's Significance for the Modern Mind.* Baton Rouge: Louisiana State University Press, 1991.

————, ed. *Eric Voegelin's Thought: A Critical Appraisal.* Durham, N.C.:
Duke University Press, 1982.

Schall, James V. "On the Relation Between Political Philosophy and Science." *Gregorianum,* LXIX (1988), 205–23.

————. *The Politics of Heaven and Hell: Christian Themes from Classical, Medieval, and Modern Political Philosophy.* Lanham, Md.: University Press of
America, 1984.

Schoeps, H. J. Review of *Israel and Revelation. Historische Zeitschrift,*
CLXXIV (1957), 606–607.

Schonemann, F. Review of *Über die Form des amerikanischen Gesites. Literatur
Zeitung,* VI (1929), 1258.

Schram, Glen. "Eric Voegelin, Christian Faith, and the American University." *Dialog,* XVI (1977), 130–35.

Scullard, H. H. Review of *Order and History,* Volumes I–III. *History,* XLIV
(1959), 33–34.

Sebba, Gregor. "Eric Voegelin: From Enlightenment to Universal Humanity." *Southern Review,* n.s., XI (1975), 918–25.

————. "Order and Disorders of the Soul: Eric Voegelin's Philosophy of
History." *Southern Review,* n.s., III (1967), 282–310.

————. "Prelude and Variations on the Theme of Eric Voegelin." *Southern
Review,* n.s., XIII (1977), 646–76. Revised and expanded in *Eric Voegelin's Thought: A Critical Appraisal,* edited by Ellis Sandoz. Durham, N.C.:
Duke University Press, 1982.

————. "The Present State of Political Theory." *Polity,* I (1968), 259–70.

Shankman, Steven. "Reason and Revelation in the Pre-Enlightenment:
Eric Voegelin's Analysis and the Case of Swift." *Religion and Literature,*
XVI (1984), 1–24.

Shinn, Roger L. "Another 'Leap of Being.'" *Christian Century,* LCCV
(1958), 1053–54.

————. Review of *The World of the Polis. Saturday Review,* March 27, 1958,
p. 27.

————. "Societies and Symbols." *Christian Century,* LCCIV (1957), 894.

Sisk, John P. "On Intoxication." *Commentary,* LIII (1972), 59–61.

Smith, Page. "Spengler, Toynbee, and Voegelin." In Smith, *The Historian
and History.* New York: Knopf, 1964.

Stanlis, Peter. Review of *Order and History*. Volumes I–III. *Modern Age*, III (1958), 189–96.

Sturm, Douglas. "Politics and Divinity: Three Approaches in American Political Thought." *Thought*, LII (1977), 333–65.

Taubes, Jacob, ed. *Gnosis und Politik*. Vol. II of *Religionstheorie und politische Theologie*. Munich: Wilhelm Fink/Ferdinand Schoeningh, 1984.

Thomas, Ivo. Review of *The Ecumenic Age*. *American Journal of Jurisprudence*, XX (1975), 168–69.

Trimpi, Wesley. "Reason and the Classical Premises of Literary Decorum." *Independent Journal of Philosophy*, V/VI (1988), 103–11.

Ungerer, M. Review of *Die Rassenidee in der Geistesgeschichte von Ray bis Carus*. *Kantstudien*, XXXIX (1934), 371–73.

Vander Goot, Henry. "Eric Voegelin: An Inquiry into the Philosophy of Order." *Politikon*, V (1978).

———. "Mere History? An Appreciation and Evaluation of Political Religions." *The World & I*, I (1986), 691–95.

Wainright, Eric H. "The Zetema of Eric Voegelin: Symbol and Experience in Political Reality." Ph.D. dissertation, University of South Africa, 1978.

Walgrave, J. Review of *Israel and Revelation*. *Tildschrift voor Philosophie*, XX (1958), 358–63.

Walsh, David. "Voegelin's Response to the Disorder of the Age." *Review of Politics*, XLVI (1984), 266–87.

Wand, Bernard. Review of *The New Science of Politics*. *Philosophical Review*, LXII (1953), 608–609.

Weatherby, Harold L. "Myth, Fact, and History." *Modern Age*, XXII (1978), 144–50.

Webb, Eugene. *Eric Voegelin: Philosopher of History*. Seattle: University of Washington Press, 1981.

———. "Eric Voegelin's Theory of Revelation." *Thomist*, XLII (1978), 95–122. Reprinted in *Eric Voegelin's Thought: A Critical Appraisal*, edited by Ellis Sandoz. Durham, N.C.: Duke University Press, 1982.

———. "In Memoriam: Politics and the Problem of a Philosophical Rhetoric in the Thought of Eric Voegelin." *Journal of Politics*, XLVIII (1986), 260–73.

———. *Philosophers of Consciousness: Polanyi, Lonergan, Voegelin, Ricoeur, Girard, Kierkegaard*. Seattle: University of Washington Press, 1988.

Weil, R. Review of *Order and History*, Volumes I–III. *Revue des Etudes grecques*, LXXIII (1960), 47–48.

Weiss, Raymond L. "Voegelin's Biblical Hermeneutics." *Independent Journal of Philosophy*, V/VI (1988), 81–84.

Widulsky, Peter. Review of *From Enlightenment to Revolution*. *Aitia*, III (1976), 25–29.

Wilhelmsen, Frederick D. "Eric Voegelin and the Christian Tradition." In

Wilhelmsen, *Christianity and Political Philosophy*. Athens, Ga.: University of Georgia Press, 1978.

———. Review of *The Ecumenic Age*. *Triumph* (January, 1975), 32–35.

———. Review of *Israel and Revelation*. *Modern Age*, III (1958), 182–89.

Will, Edouard. Review of *The World of the Polis* and *Plato and Aristotle*. *Revue de Philologie*, 3rd ser., XXXIII (1959), 97–98.

Williams, R. H. Review of *Die politischen Religionen*. *American Sociological Review*, VI (1941), 402–404.

Wilson, F. G. Review of *The New Science of Politics*. *American Political Science Review*, LXVII (1953), 442–43.

Wirth, Louis. Review of *Über die Form des amerikanischen Geistes*. *American Journal of Sociology*, XXXVI (1931), 681.

Wiser, James L. "Eric Voegelin: A Study in the Revival of Political Science." *Polity*, XLVI (1985), 295–312.

———. "Eric Voegelin and the Eclipse of Philosophy." *Denver Quarterly*, X (1975), 108–14.

———. "From Cultural Analysis to Philosophical Anthropology: An Examination of Voegelin's Concept of Gnosticism." *Review of Politics*, XLII (1980), 92–104.

———. "Philosophy and Human Order." *Political Science Reviewer*, II (1972), 137–61.

———. "Philosophy as Inquiry and Persuasion." In *Eric Voegelin's Search for Order in History*, edited by Stephen A. McKnight. Rev. ed. Lanham, Md.: University Press of America, 1987.

———. "Political Science and the Appeal to Common Sense." In *The Good Man in Society: Active Contemplation*, edited by John A. Gueguen, Michael Henry, and James Rhodes. Lanham, Md.: University Press of America, 1989.

———. Review of *From Enlightenment to Revolution*. *Thought*, LII (1977), 214–15.

Wright, Martin. Review of *The New Science of Politics*. *International Affairs*, XXXI (1955), 336–37.

Zylstra, Bernard. "Voegelin on Unbelief and Revolution." *Antirevolutionarie Staatkunde*, XLVI (1976), 155–65.

## Additional Works Consulted

Aeschylus. *Prometheus Bound*. In *Prometheus, with a Translation of Aeschylus' "Prometheus Bound,"* by E. A. Havelock. Seattle: University of Washington Press, 1968.

Aiken, Henry David. *The Age of Ideology: The Nineteenth Century Philosophers*. Boston: Houghton Mifflin, 1957.

Arendt, Hannah. *Between Past and Future: Eight Exercises in Political Thought*. Harmondsworth, U.K.: Penguin, 1977.

————. *The Origins of Totalitarianism.* San Diego: Harcourt Brace Jovanovich, 1973.

Aristophanes. *The Complete Plays of Aristophanes.* Toronto: Bantam, 1962.

Aristotle. *The Basic Works of Aristotle.* New York: Random House, 1941.

Aron, Raymond. *The Opium of the Intellectuals.* New York: Norton, 1962.

Augustine. *City of God.* Translated by Henry Bettenson. Harmondsworth, U.K.: Penguin, 1984.

————. *The Political Writings of St. Augustine.* South Bend, Ind.: Gateway, 1962.

————. *St. Augustine on the Psalms.* Translated by Scholastica Hebgin and Felicitas Corrigan. 2 vols. Westminster, Md.: Neuman Press, 1960.

Bacon, Francis. *The Great Instauration.* Arlington Heights, Ill.: Harlan Davidson, 1980.

Barth, Hans. *Truth and Ideology.* Berkeley: University of California Press, 1976.

Becker, Carl L. *The Heavenly City of the Eighteenth-Century Philosophers.* New Haven: Yale University Press, 1932.

Bell, Daniel. *The End of Ideology: On the Exhaustion of Political Ideas in the Fifties.* New York: Free Press, 1960.

Bennett, W. Lance. *Public Opinion in American Politics.* New York: Harcourt Brace Jovanovich, 1980.

Bergson, Henri. *The Two Sources of Morality and Religion.* Notre Dame: University of Notre Dame Press, 1977.

Bishirjian, Richard. *The Development of Political Theory: A Critical Analysis.* Dallas: Society for the Study of Traditional Culture, 1978.

Bracher, Karl Dietrich. *The Age of Ideologies: A History of Political Thought in the Twentieth Century.* New York: St. Martin's, 1985.

Camus, Albert. *The Rebel: An Essay on Man in Revolt.* New York: Vintage, 1956.

Charles, R. H. *Eschatology: The Doctrine of a Future Life in Israel, Judaism, and Christianity.* New York: Schocken, 1963.

Charlesworth, James H. *Apocalyptic Literature and Testaments.* Vol. I of Charlesworth, *The Old Testament Pseudepigrapha.* Garden City: Doubleday, 1983.

Cohn, Norman. *The Pursuit of the Millennium.* Rev. ed. New York: Oxford University Press, 1970.

Comte, August. *The Positive Philosophy.* New York: AMS Press, 1974.

Crossman, Richard, ed. *The God that Failed.* New York: Harper and Brothers, 1949.

Cushman, Robert E. *Therapeia: Plato's Conception of Philosophy.* Chapel Hill: University of North Carolina Press, 1958.

Danielou, Jean. *The Theology of Jewish Christianity.* Chicago: Henry Regnery, 1964.

Dempf, Alois. *Sacrum Imperium.* Darmstadt: Wissenschaftliche Buchgesellschaft, 1962.

Descartes, René. *Discourse on Method and Meditations*. Translated by Lawrence J. Lafleur. Indianapolis: Bobbs-Merrill, 1960.

Dobbs, Darrell. "Reckless Rationalism and Heroic Reverence in Homer's *Odyssey*." *American Political Science Review*, LXXXI (1987), 491–508.

Dolbeare, Kenneth M., and Linda J. Medcalf. *American Ideologies Today*. London: Croom Helm, 1988.

Eliade, Mircea. *The Forge and the Crucible*. New York: Harper and Brothers, 1962.

Engels, Friedrich. *The Peasant War in Germany*. Moscow: Progress Publishers, 1972.

Eusebeus. *The History of the Church from Christ to Constantine*. Translated by G. A. Williamson. Harmondsworth, U.K.: Penguin, 1965.

Feuer, Lewis S. *Ideology and the Ideologists*. New York: Harper and Row, 1975.

Feuerbach, Ludwig. *Principles of the Philosophy of the Future*. Indianapolis: Hackett, 1986.

French, Peter. *John Dee: The World of an Elizabethan Magus*. London: Routledge and Kegan Paul, 1972.

Fromm, Erich. *Escape from Freedom*. New York: Avon, 1965.

Gay, Peter. *The Enlightenment: An Interpretation*. 2 vols. New York: Norton, 1966, 1969.

Germino, Dante. *Beyond Ideology: The Revival of Political Theory*. New York: Harper & Row, 1967.

Gueguen, John A., Michael Henry, and James Rhodes, eds. *The Good Man in Society: Active Contemplation*. Lanham, Md.: University Press of America, 1989.

Gunnell, John G. *Political Theory: Tradition and Interpretation*. Cambridge, Mass.: Winthrop, 1979.

Gurian, Waldemar. *Bolshevism: An Introduction to Soviet Communism*. Notre Dame, Ind.: University of Notre Dame Press, 1952.

Halle, Louis J. *The Ideological Imagination*. Chicago: Quadrangle Books, 1972.

Hamilton, Alexander, John Jay, and James Madison. *The Federalist*. New York: Modern Library, n.d.

Heilbroner, Robert L. *Marxism: For and Against*. New York: Norton, 1980.

Herodotus. *The Histories*. Harmondsworth, U.K.: Penguin, 1954.

Hobbes, Thomas. *Leviathan*. Harmondsworth, U.K.: Penguin, 1968.

Hoffer, Eric. *The True Believer: Thoughts on the Nature of Mass Movements*. New York: Time, Inc., 1963.

Horsley, Richard A., with John S. Hanson. *Bandits, Prophets, and Messiahs: Popular Movements in the Time of Jesus*. New York: Harper and Row, 1988.

James, Elizabeth M. *Political Theory: An Introduction to Interpretation*. Chicago: Rand McNally, 1976.

James, William. *The Varieties of Religious Experience*. Harmondsworth, U.K.: Penguin, 1982.

Jaspers, Karl. *Man in the Modern Age*. Garden City, N.Y.: Doubleday, 1957.

———. *The Origin and Goal of History*. London: Routledge and Kegan Paul, 1953.

———. *Philosophy of Existence*. Philadelphia: University of Pennsylvania Press, 1971.

Jonas, Hans. *The Gnostic Religion*. Boston: Beacon, 1972.

Kissin, S. F. *Farewell to Revolution: Marxist Philosophy and the Modern World*. New York: St. Martin's Press, 1978.

Kolakowski, Leszek. *Main Currents of Marxism: Its Origin, Growth, and Dissolution*. 3 vols. Oxford: Oxford University Press, 1981.

Kramnick, Isaac, and Frederick M. Watkins, eds. *The Age of Ideology: Political Thought, 1750 to the Present*. Englewood Cliffs, N.J.: Prentice-Hall, 1979.

Lacoque, Andre. *The Book of Daniel*. Translated by David Pellauer. Atlanta: John Knox Press, 1979.

Lactantius. *Lactantius: The Minor Works*. Washington, D.C.: Catholic University of America Press, 1965.

Layton, Bentley, trans. *The Gnostic Scriptures*. Garden City, N.Y.: Doubleday, 1987.

Leff, Gordon. *Heresy in the Later Middle Ages*. New York: Columbia University Press, 1967.

Lichtheim, George. *"The Concept of Ideology" and Other Essays*. New York: Vintage, 1967.

Locke, John. *Second Treatise of Government*. Indianapolis: Hackett, 1980.

Löwith, Karl. *From Hegel to Nietzsche: The Revolution in Nineteenth-Century Thought*. Garden City, N.Y.: Anchor, 1967.

———. *Meaning in History: The Theological Implications of the Philosophy of History*. Chicago: University of Chicago Press, 1949.

Lubac, Henri de. *The Drama of Atheist Humanism*. Cleveland: World Publishing, 1963.

McGinn, Bernard, ed. *Apocalyptic Spirituality: Treatises and Letters of Lactantius, Adso of Montier-en-Der, Joachim of Fiore, the Franciscan Spirituals, Savonarola*. New York: Paulist Press, 1979.

———. *Visions of the End: Apocalyptic Traditions in the Middle Ages*. New York: Columbia University Press, 1979.

McGuire, J. E. "Neoplatonism and Active Principles." In *Hermeticism and the Scientific Revolution*. Los Angeles: Clark Memorial Library, 1977.

McLellan, David. *Ideology*. Minneapolis: University of Minnesota Press, 1986.

Manheim, Karl. *Ideology and Utopia*. New York: Harvest, 1936.

Marx, Karl. *A Contribution to the Critique of Political Economy*. Moscow: Progress Publishers, 1970.

———. *Early Writings*. Edited by T. B. Bottomore. New York: McGraw Hill, 1963.

————. *Karl Marx: Selected Writings.* Edited by David McLellan. Oxford: Oxford University Press, 1977.

Marx, Karl, and Friedrich Engels. *The German Ideology.* Moscow: Progress Publishers, 1976.

————. *On Communist Society.* Moscow: Progress, 1978.

————. *On Religion.* Moscow: Progress, 1975.

Metzger, Bruce M. *An Introduction to the Apocrypha.* New York: Oxford University Press, 1957.

Molnar, Thomas. *Utopia: The Perennial Heresy.* New York: Sheed and Ward, 1967.

Montgomery, Marion. *The Reflective Journey Toward Order: Essays on Dante, Wordsworth, Eliot, and Others.* Athens, Ga.: University of Georgia Press, 1973.

Morgenthau, Hans J. *Politics Among Nations: The Struggle for Power and Peace.* 4th ed. New York: Alfred A. Knopf, 1967.

Murray, Michael. *Modern Philosophy of History: Its Origin and Destination.* The Hague: Martinus Nijhoff, 1970.

Nasr, Seyyed, Hamid Dabashi, and Seyyed Vali Reza Nasr, eds. *Expectation of the Millennium: Shi'ism in History.* Albany: State University of New York Press, 1989.

Nickelsburg, George W. E. *Jewish Literature Between the Bible and the Mishnah.* Philadelphia: Fortress Press, 1981.

Niemeyer, Gerhart. *Between Nothingness and Paradise.* Baton Rouge: Louisiana State University Press, 1971.

Nietzsche, Friedrich. *The Portable Nietzsche.* Edited by Walter Kaufmann. Harmondsworth, U.K.: Penguin, 1976.

————. *The Will to Power.* Edited by Walter Kaufmann. New York: Vintage, 1968.

Parekh, Bhikhu. *Marx's Theory of Ideology.* London: Croom Helm, 1982.

Plamenatz, John. *Ideology.* London: Macmillan, 1970.

Plato. *The Collected Dialogues of Plato.* Edited by Edith Hamilton and Huntington Cairns. Princeton: Princeton University Press, 1961.

————. *The Laws of Plato.* Translated by Thomas L. Pangle. New York: Basic Books, 1980.

————. *The Republic of Plato.* Translated by Allan Bloom. New York: Basic Books, 1968.

Ricoeur, Paul. *Lectures on Ideology and Utopia.* Edited by George H. Taylor. New York: Columbia University Press, 1986.

————. *The Symbolism of Evil.* Boston: Beacon, 1969.

Robinson, James M., ed. *The Nag Hammadi Library in English.* San Francisco: Harper and Row, 1977.

Rosen, Stanley. *The Ancients and the Moderns.* New Haven: Yale University Press, 1989.

Rossi, Paolo. *Francis Bacon: From Magic to Science.* Chicago: University of Chicago Press, 1968.

Rowland, Christopher. *The Open Heaven: A Study of Apocalyptic in Judaism and Early Christianity*. New York: Crossroad, 1982.

Russell, D. S. *The Method and Message of Jewish Apocalyptic*. Philadelphia: Westminster, 1964.

Sandoz, Ellis. *Political Apocalypse: A Study of Dostoevsky's Grand Inquisitor*. Baton Rouge: Louisiana State University Press, 1971.

Schweitzer, Albert. *The Quest for the Historical Jesus*. Translated by W. Montgomery. New York: Macmillan, 1968.

Snell, Bruno. *The Discovery of the Mind: The Greek Origins of European Thought*. New York: Harper & Brothers, 1960.

Solzhenitsyn, Aleksandr I. *The Gulag Archipelago, 1918–1956: An Experiment in Literary Investigation*. New York: Harper & Row, 1979.

Stone, Michael Edward. *Scriptures, Sects, and Visions*. Philadelphia: Fortress Press, 1980.

Talmon, J. L. *The Origins of Totalitarian Democracy*. New York: Praeger, 1960.

———. *Political Messianism: The Romantic Phase*. New York: Praeger, 1960.

———. *Romanticism and Revolt: Europe, 1815–1848*. New York: Harcourt, Brace & World, 1967.

Thrupp, Sylvia L., ed. *Millennial Dreams in Action: Essays in Comparative Study*. The Hague: Mouton, 1962.

Thucydides. *History of the Peloponnesian War*. Harmondsworth, U.K.: Penguin, 1954.

Tillinghast, Pardon E., ed. *Approaches to History: Selections in the Philosophy of History from the Greeks to Hegel*. Englewood Cliffs, N.J.: Prentice-Hall, 1963.

Tocqueville, Alexis de. *Democracy in America*. Garden City, N.Y.: Anchor, 1969.

Toynbee, Arnold. *An Historian's Approach to Religion*. London: Oxford University Press, 1956.

Tucker, Robert C. *Philosophy and Myth in Karl Marx*. 2d ed. Cambridge: Cambridge University Press, 1972.

Tuveson, Ernest Lee. *The Avatars of Thrice Great Hermes: An Approach to Romanticism*. Lewisburg, Pa.: Bucknell University Press, 1981.

———. *Millennium and Utopia: A Study in the Background of the Idea of Progress*. Berkeley: University of California Press, 1949.

Waite, Robert G. *The Psychopathic God: Adolf Hitler*. New York: Mentor, 1977.

Wakefield, Walter L., and Austin Evans. *Heresies of the High Middle Ages*. New York: Columbia University Press, 1969.

Walsh, David. *The Mysticism of Interworldly Fulfillment: A Study of Jacob Boehme*. Gainesville: University Presses of Florida, 1983.

———. "Revising the Renaissance: New Light on the Origins of Modern Political Thought." *Political Science Reviewer*, XI (1981), 27–52.

Walzer, Michael. *Exodus and Revolution*. New York: Basic Books, 1985.

Weiss, Johannes. *Jesus' Proclamation of the Kingdom of God*. Edited and Translated by Richard H. Hiers and David L. Holland. Philadelphia: Fortress Press, 1971.

Wessell, Leonard P., Jr. *Karl Marx, Romantic Irony, and the Proletariat*. Baton Rouge: Louisiana State University Press, 1979.

————. *Prometheus Bound: The Mythic Structure of Karl Marx's Scientific Thinking*. Baton Rouge: Louisiana State University Press, 1984.

Westman, Robert S. "Magical Reform and Astronomical Reform: The Yates Thesis Revisited." In *Hermeticism and the Scientific Revolution*. Los Angeles: Clark Memorial Library, 1977.

Wild, John. *Plato's Modern Enemies and the Theory of Natural Law*. Chicago: University of Chicago Press, 1953.

————. *Plato's Theory of Man: An Introduction to the Realistic Philosophy of Culture*. New York: Octagon, 1964.

Wiser, James L. "The Force of Reason: On Reading Plato's *Gorgias*." In *The Ethical Dimension of Political Life: Essays in Honor of John H. Hallowell*, edited by Francis Canavan. Durham, N.C.: Duke University Press, 1983.

————. "Philosophy as Political Action: A Reading of the *Gorgias*." *American Journal of Political Science*, XIX (1975), 313–22.

Yates, Frances A. *Giordano Bruno and the Hermetic Tradition*. Chicago: University of Chicago Press, 1964.

# Index